THE WITCHER®

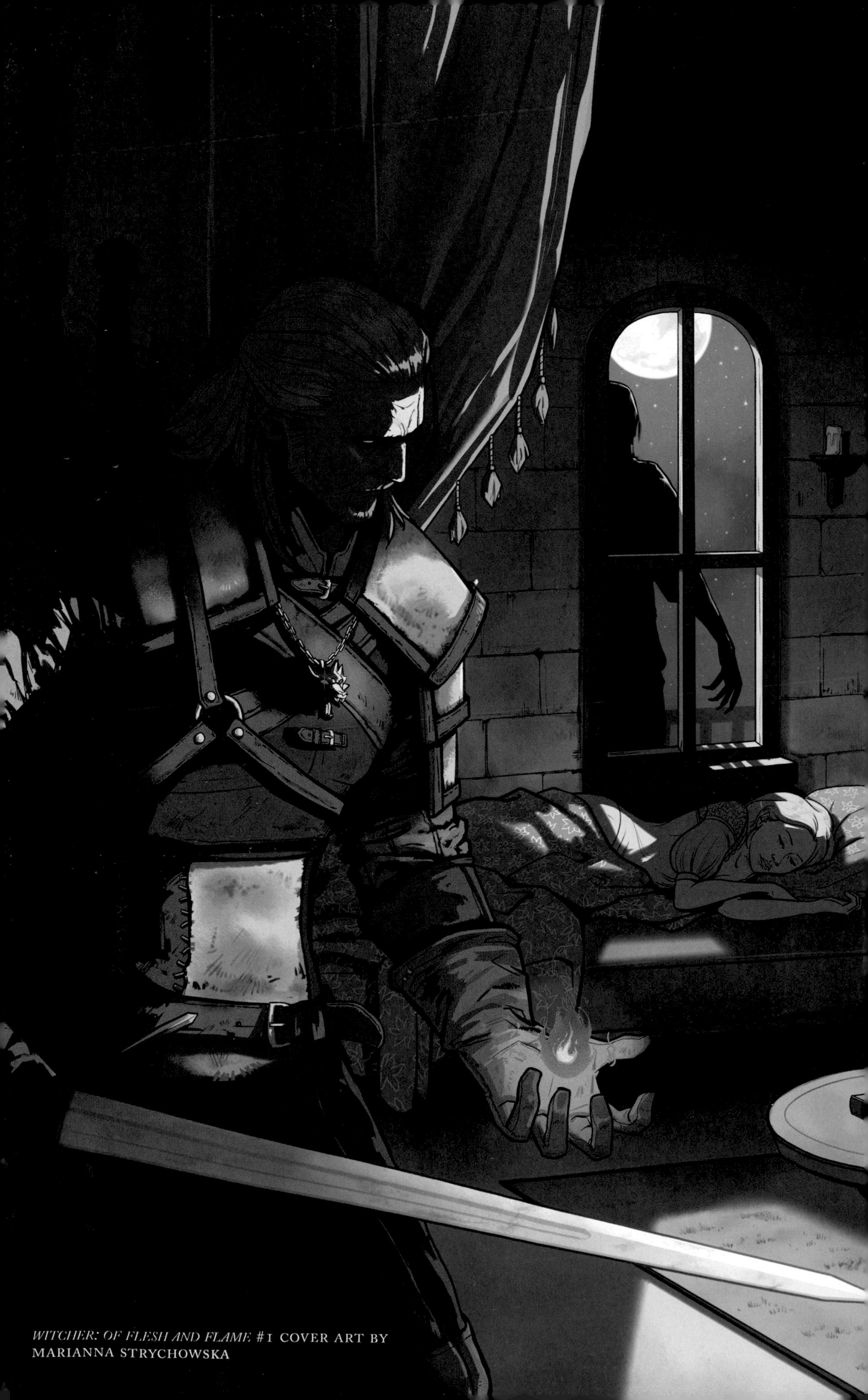

WITCHER: OF FLESH AND FLAME #1 COVER ART BY
MARIANNA STRYCHOWSKA

THE WITCHER®

OF FLESH AND FLAME

STORY
Aleksandra Motyka

ART
Marianna Strychowska

❖

COLORS
Lauren Affe

LETTERS
Steve Dutro

COVER ART
Marianna Strychowska

DARK HORSE BOOKS

PUBLISHER . . . . Mike Richardson
EDITOR . . . . Megan Walker
ASSISTANT EDITOR . . . . Joshua Engledow
DESIGNER . . . . Skyler Weissenfluh
DIGITAL ART TECHNICIAN . . . . Allyson Haller
CD PROJEKT RED EDITORIAL . . . . . . Rafał Jaki

Special thanks to CD Projekt Red, including: **Michał Nowakowski**, *VP of Business Development* • **Adam Badowski**, *Head of Studio* • **Marcin Blacha**, *Story Director*

The Witcher *game is based on a novel of Andrzej Sapkowski.*

THE WITCHER VOLUME 4: OF FLESH AND FLAME

This volume collects issues #1 through #4 of the Dark Horse Comics series *The Witcher: Of Flesh and Flame.*

Published by
Dark Horse Books
A division of
Dark Horse Comics LLC
10956 SE Main Street
Milwaukie, OR 97222

DarkHorse.com
TheWitcher.com
Facebook.com/DarkHorseComics
Twitter.com/DarkHorseComics

First edition: July 2019
ISBN 978-1-50671-109-6

10 9 8 7 6 5 4 3 2 1
Printed in China

Library of Congress Cataloging-in-Publication Data

Names: Motyka, Aleksandra, author. | Strychowska, Marianna, artist. | Affe,
  Lauren, colourist. | Dutro, Steve, letterer. | Sapkowski, Andrzej.
  Wiedźmin.
Title: Of flesh and flame / story, Aleksandra Motyka ; art, Marianna
  Strychowska ; colors, Lauren Affe ; letters, Steve Dutro ; cover, Marianna
  Strychowska.
Description: First edition. | Milwaukie, OR : Dark Horse Books, July 2019. |
  Series: The Witcher ; Volume 4 | "This volume collects issues #1 through
  #4 of the Dark Horse Comics series The Witcher: Of Flesh and Flame." |
  "The Witcher game is based on a novel of Andrzej Sapkowski."
Identifiers: LCCN 2018061318 | ISBN 9781506711096
Subjects: LCSH: Comic books, strips, etc.
Classification: LCC PN6728.W5887 M68 2019 | DDC 741.5/973--dc23
LC record available at https://lccn.loc.gov/2018061318

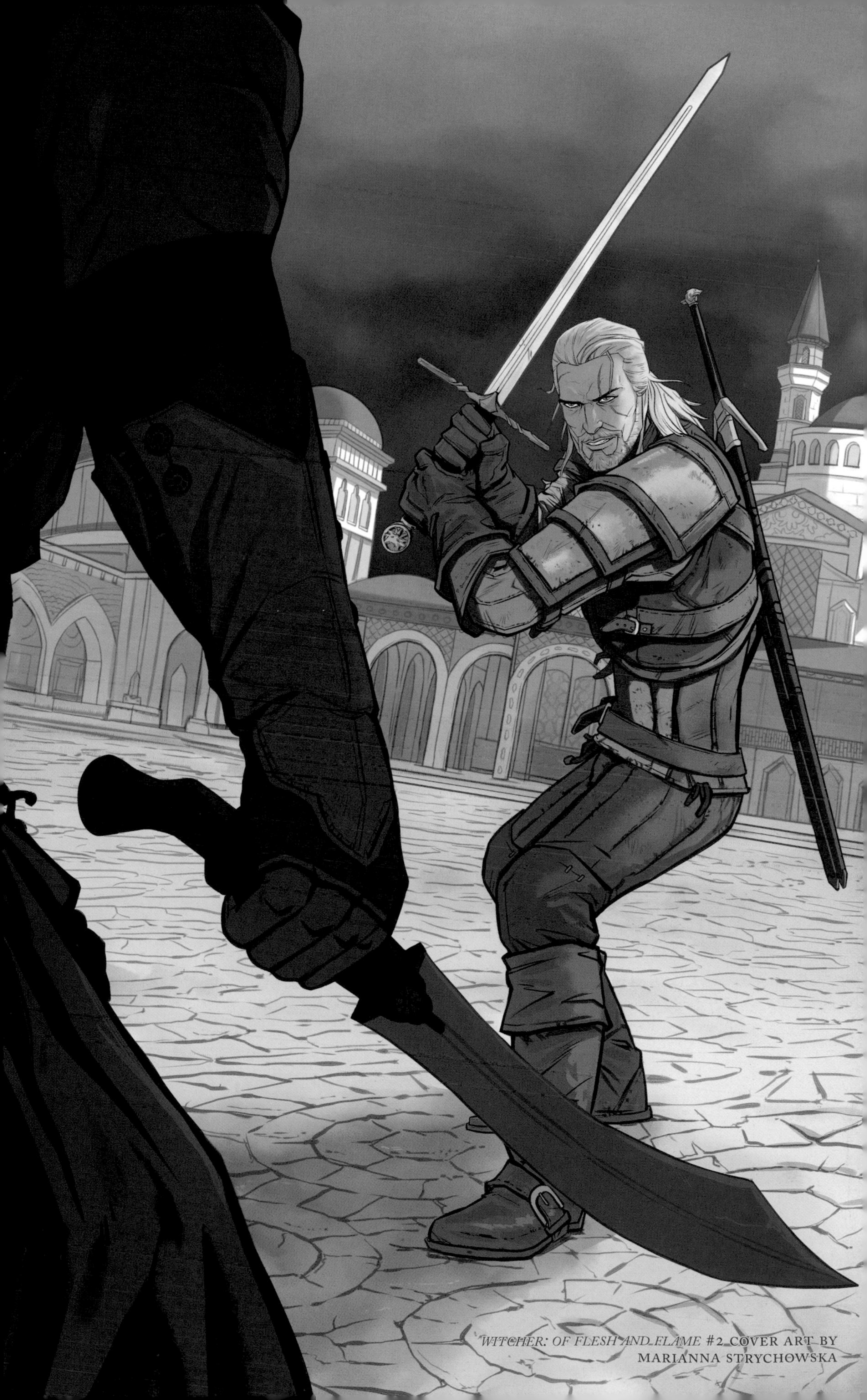

WITCHER: OF FLESH AND FLAME #2 COVER ART BY
MARIANNA STRYCHOWSKA

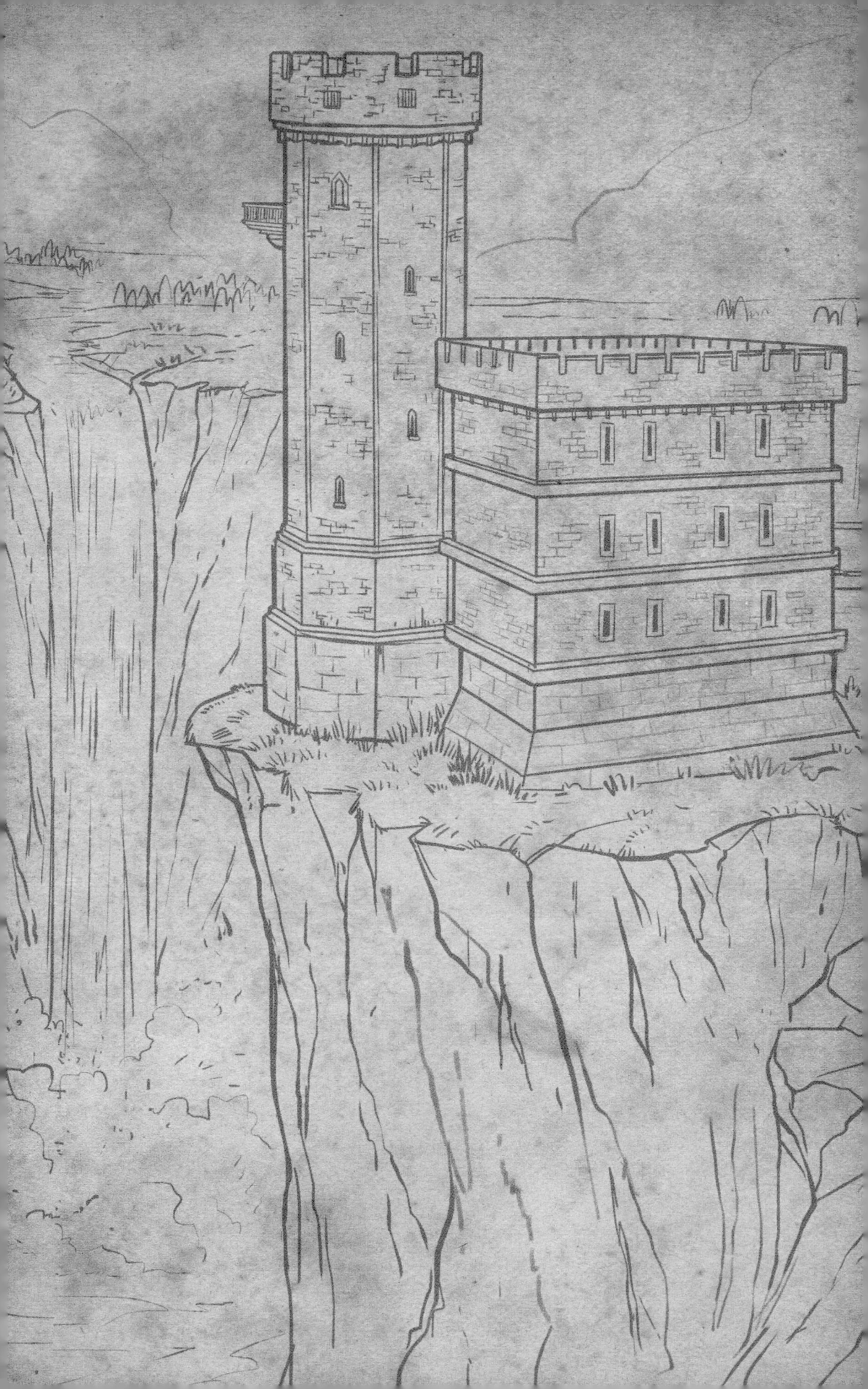

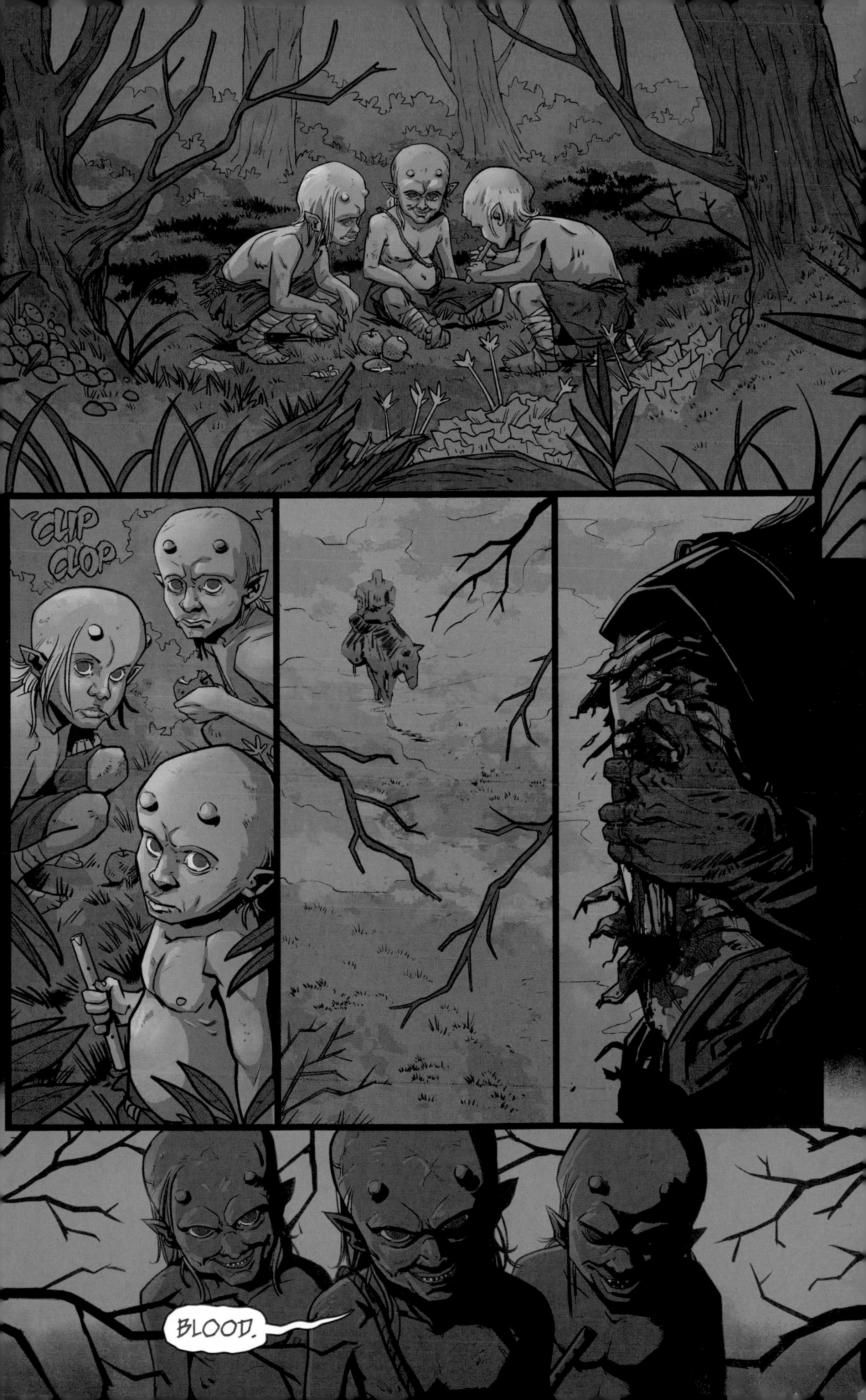
CLIP CLOP
BLOOD.

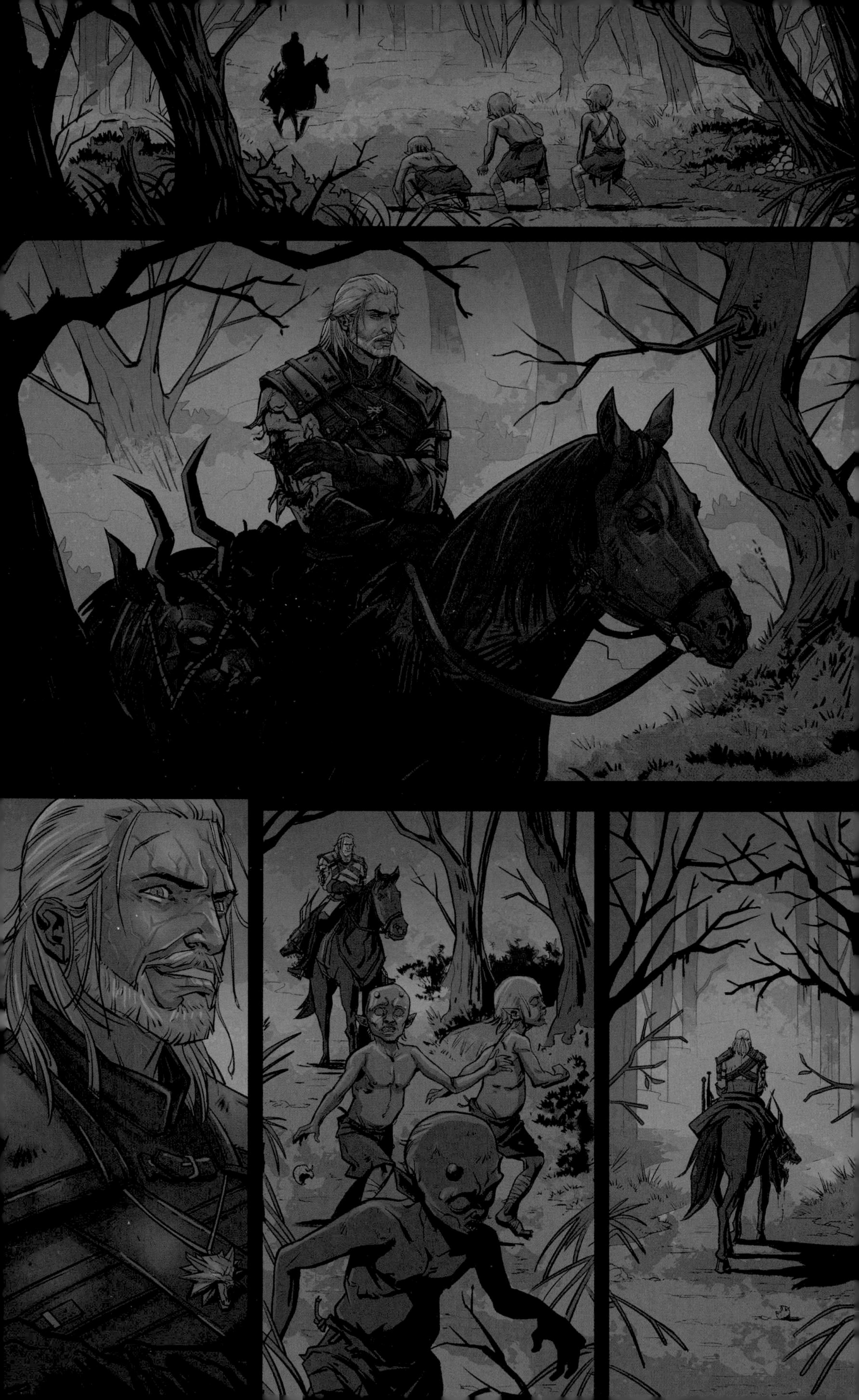

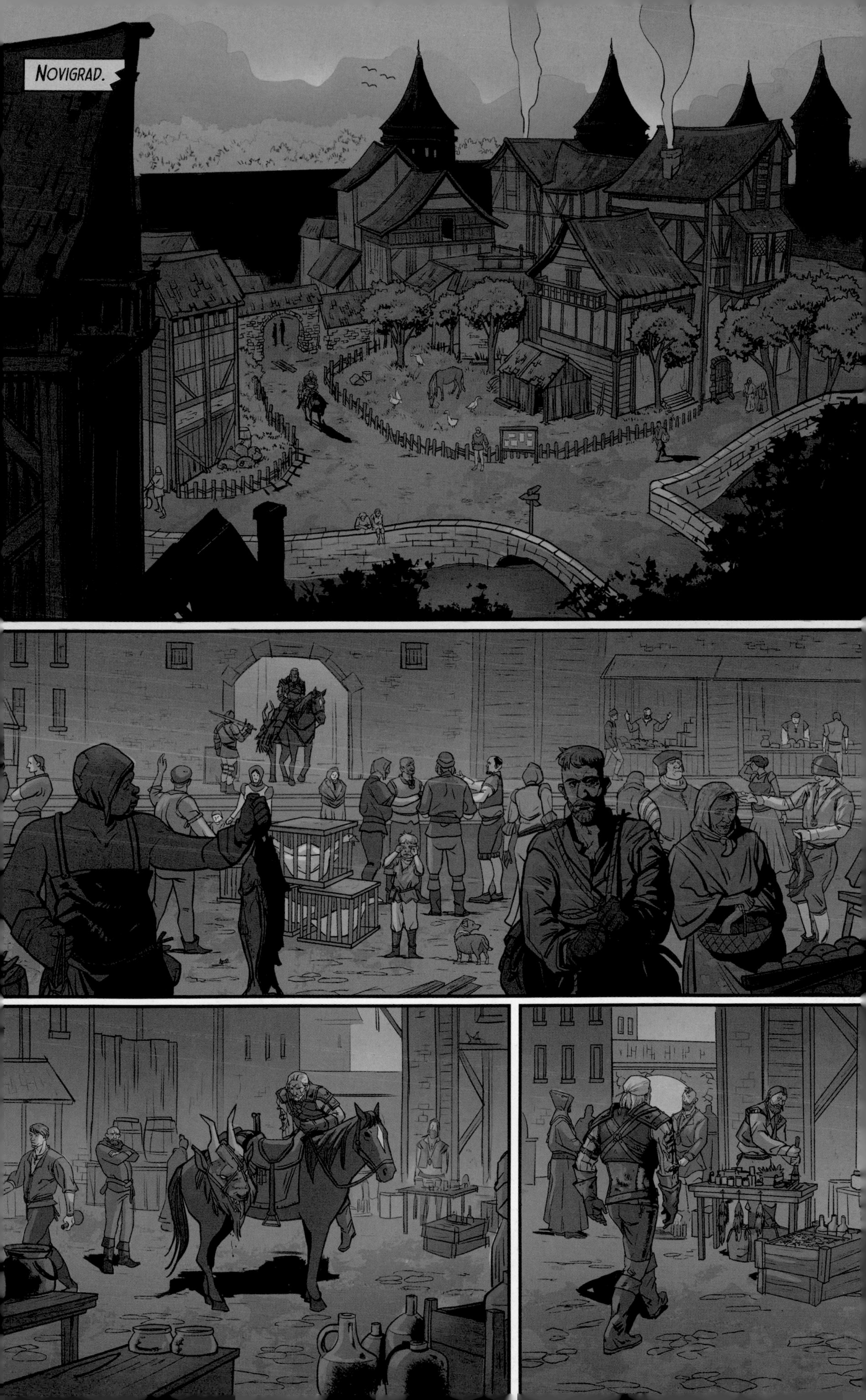
NOVIGRAD.

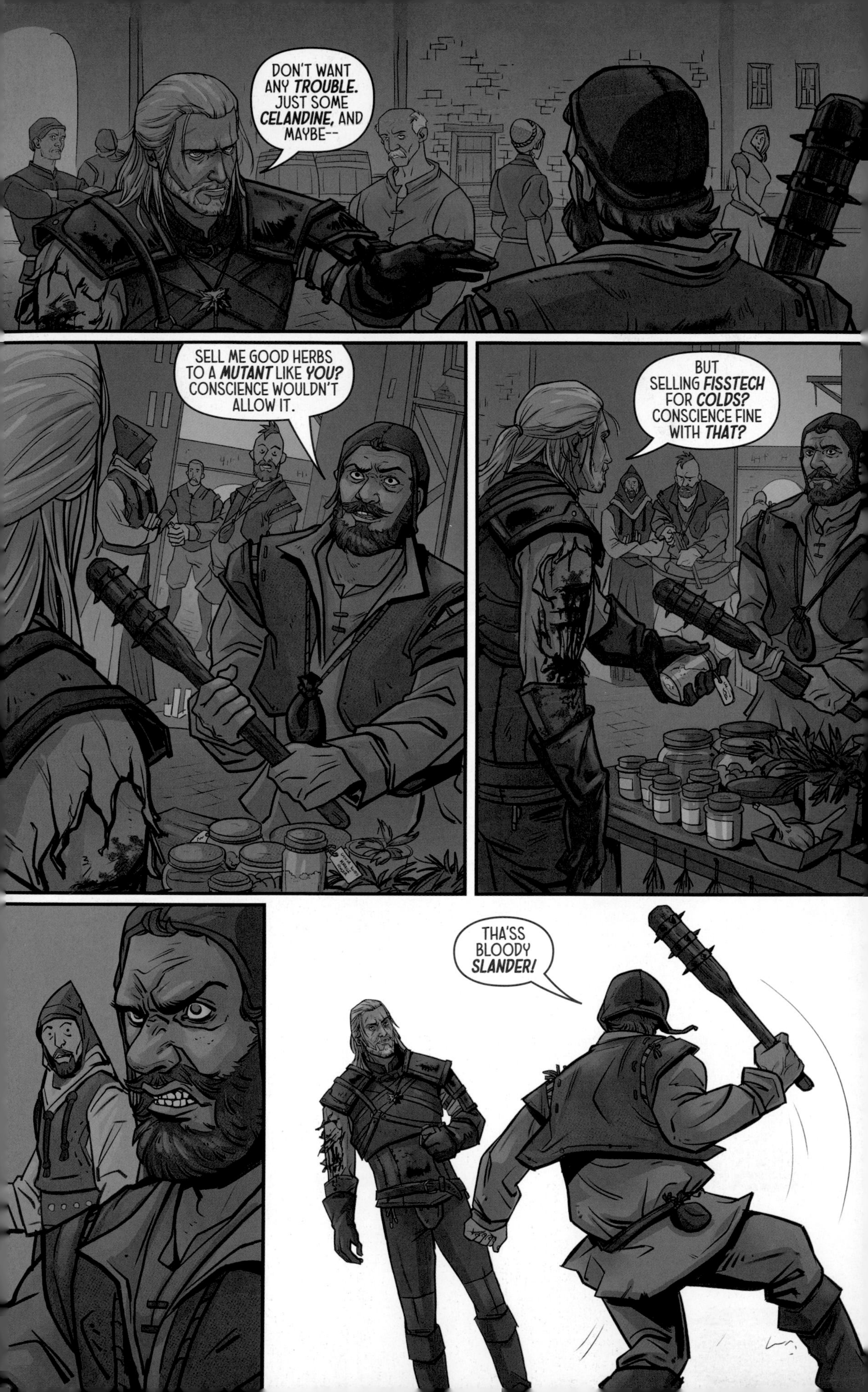
DON'T WANT ANY TROUBLE. JUST SOME CELANDINE, AND MAYBE--
SELL ME GOOD HERBS TO A MUTANT LIKE YOU? CONSCIENCE WOULDN'T ALLOW IT.
BUT SELLING FISSTECH FOR COLDS? CONSCIENCE FINE WITH THAT?
THA'SS BLOODY SLANDER!

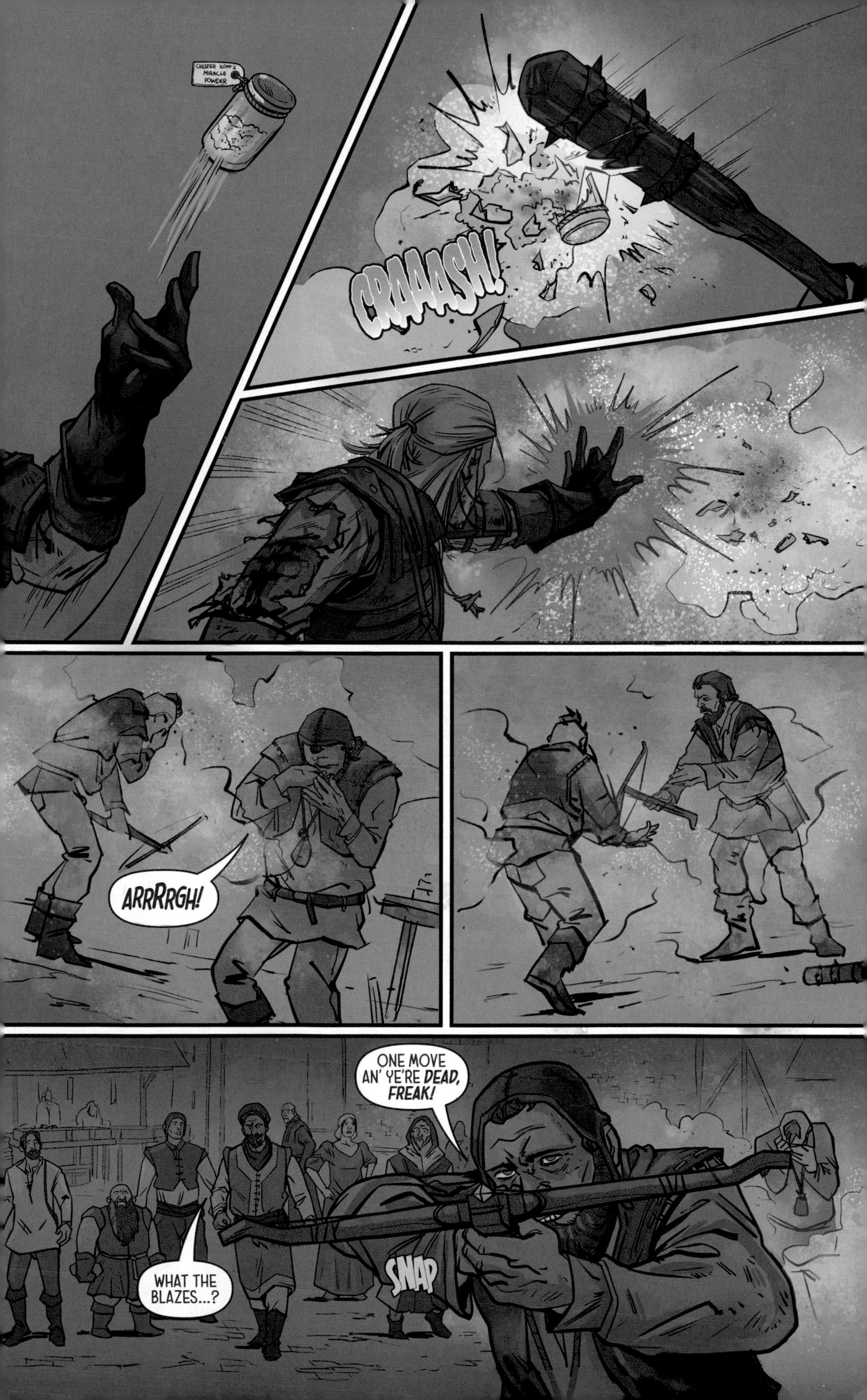
CHESTER KOFF'S MIRACLE POWDER
CRAAASH!
ARRRRGH!
ONE MOVE AN' YE'RE *DEAD, FREAK!*
WHAT THE BLAZES...?
SNAP

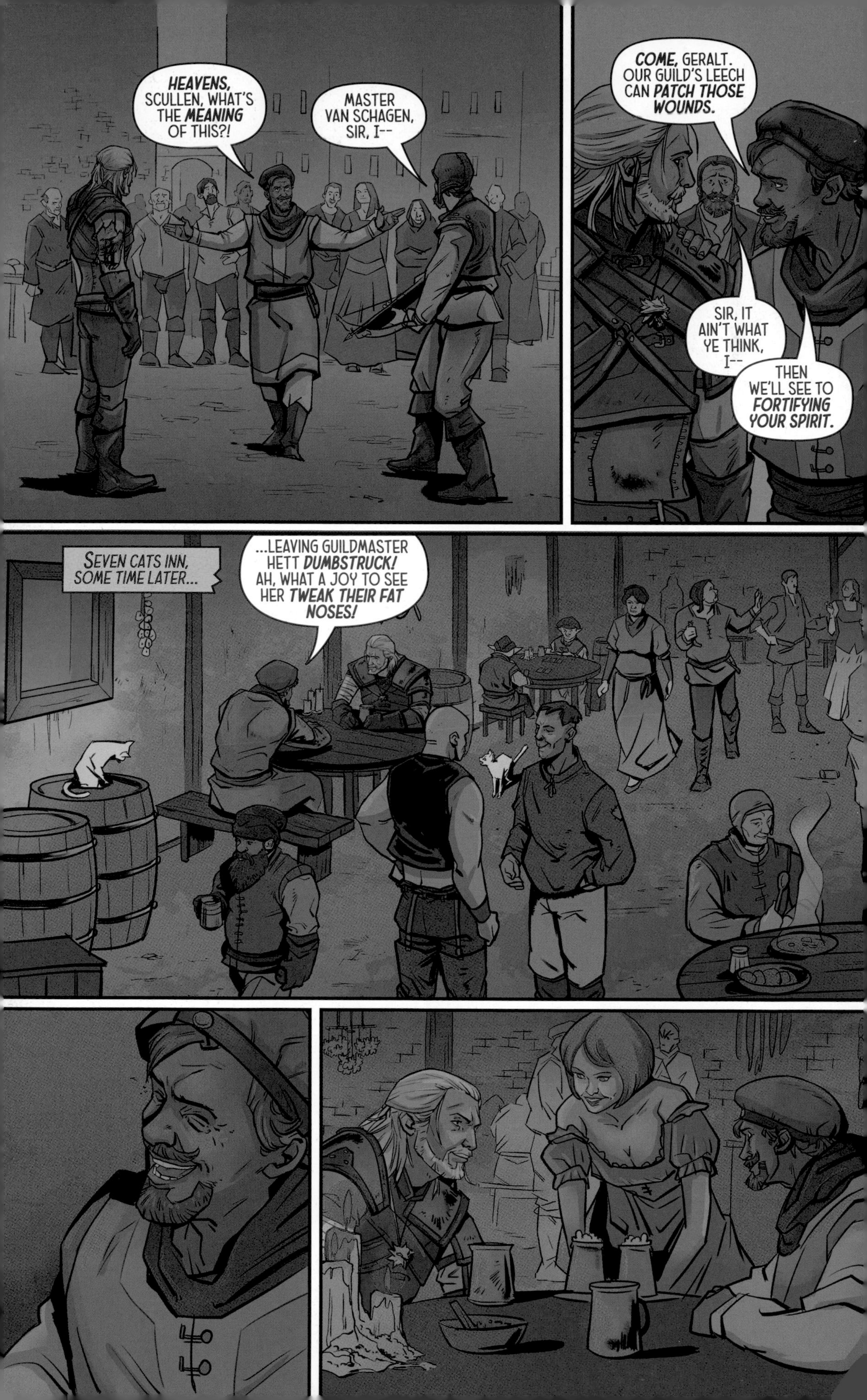
HEAVENS, SCULLEN, WHAT'S THE MEANING OF THIS?!
MASTER VAN SCHAGEN, SIR, I--
COME, GERALT. OUR GUILD'S LEECH CAN PATCH THOSE WOUNDS.
SIR, IT AIN'T WHAT YE THINK, I--
THEN WE'LL SEE TO FORTIFYING YOUR SPIRIT.
SEVEN CATS INN, SOME TIME LATER...
...LEAVING GUILDMASTER HETT DUMBSTRUCK! AH, WHAT A JOY TO SEE HER TWEAK THEIR FAT NOSES!

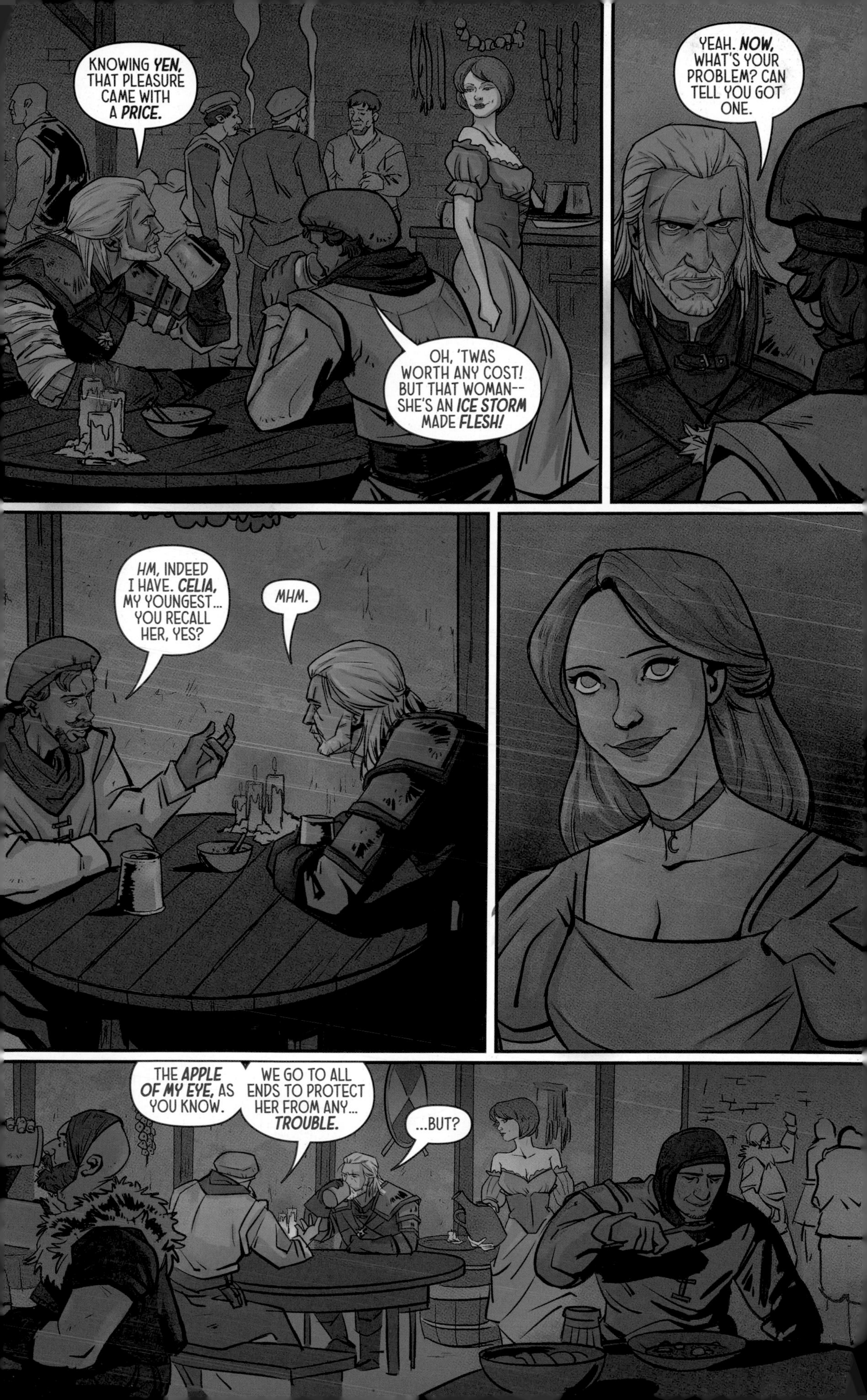

KNOWING **YEN,** THAT PLEASURE CAME WITH A **PRICE.**
OH, 'TWAS WORTH ANY COST! BUT THAT WOMAN-- SHE'S AN ***ICE STORM*** MADE ***FLESH!***
YEAH. ***NOW,*** WHAT'S YOUR PROBLEM? CAN TELL YOU GOT ONE.
HM, INDEED I HAVE. ***CELIA,*** MY YOUNGEST... YOU RECALL HER, YES?
MHM.
THE ***APPLE OF MY EYE,*** AS YOU KNOW.
WE GO TO ALL ENDS TO PROTECT HER FROM ANY... ***TROUBLE.***
...BUT?

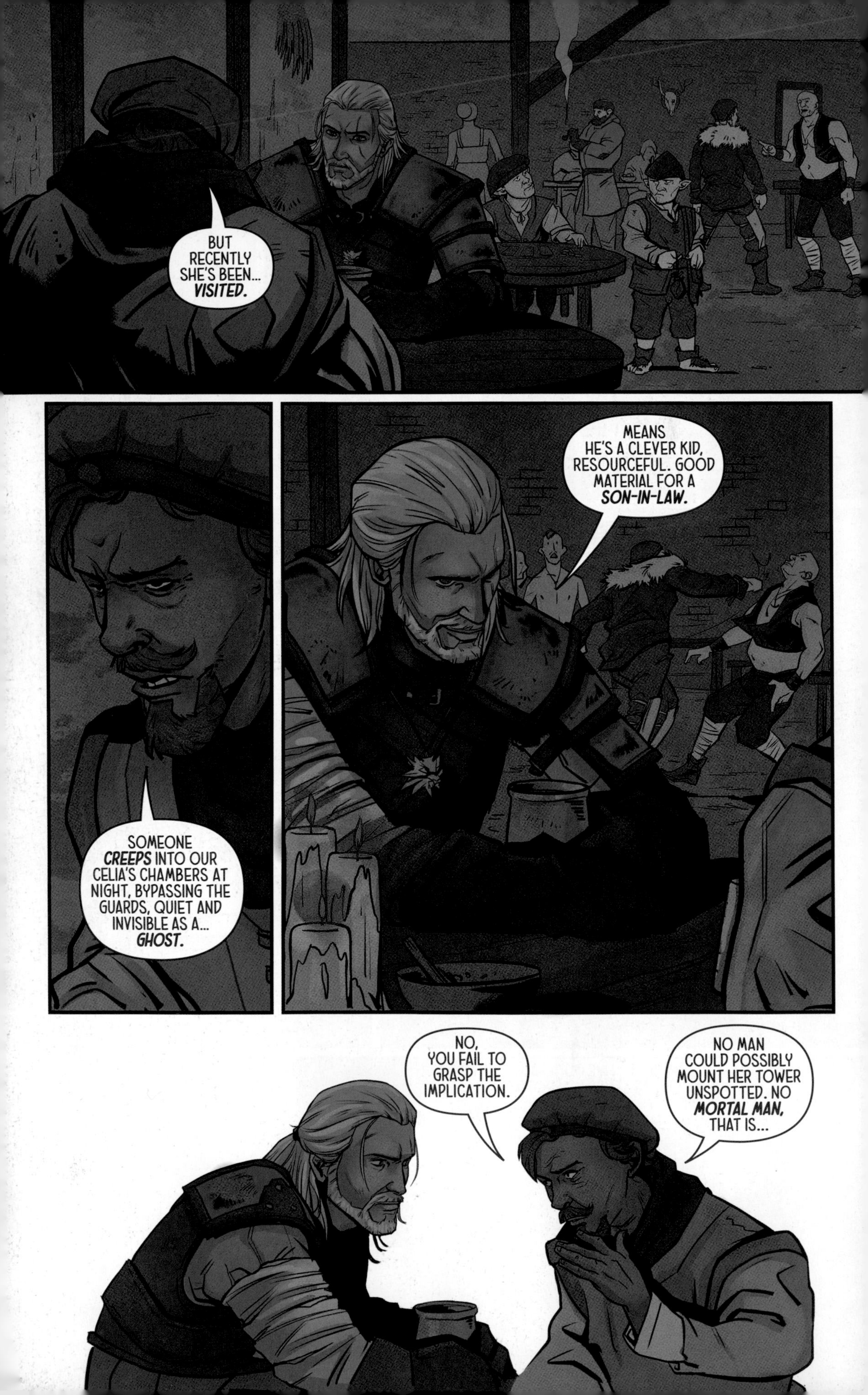
BUT RECENTLY SHE'S BEEN... VISITED.
SOMEONE CREEPS INTO OUR CELIA'S CHAMBERS AT NIGHT, BYPASSING THE GUARDS, QUIET AND INVISIBLE AS A... GHOST.
MEANS HE'S A CLEVER KID, RESOURCEFUL. GOOD MATERIAL FOR A SON-IN-LAW.
NO, YOU FAIL TO GRASP THE IMPLICATION.
NO MAN COULD POSSIBLY MOUNT HER TOWER UNSPOTTED. NO MORTAL MAN, THAT IS...

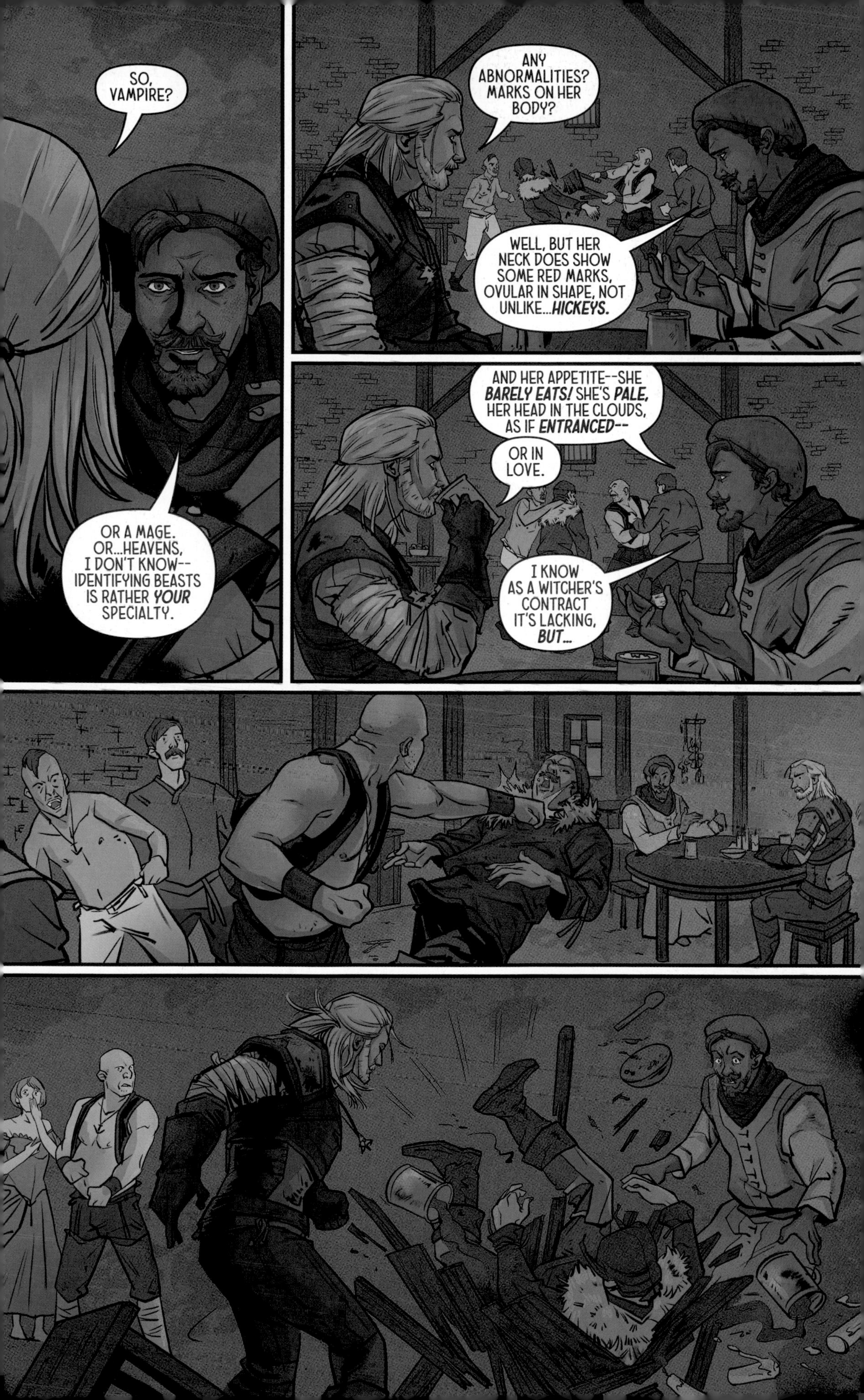
SO, VAMPIRE?
OR A MAGE. OR...HEAVENS, I DON'T KNOW-- IDENTIFYING BEASTS IS RATHER YOUR SPECIALTY.
ANY ABNORMALITIES? MARKS ON HER BODY?
WELL, BUT HER NECK DOES SHOW SOME RED MARKS, OVULAR IN SHAPE, NOT UNLIKE...HICKEYS.
AND HER APPETITE--SHE BARELY EATS! SHE'S PALE, HER HEAD IN THE CLOUDS, AS IF ENTRANCED--
OR IN LOVE.
I KNOW AS A WITCHER'S CONTRACT IT'S LACKING, BUT...

IT'S FINE. I'LL LOOK INTO IT.

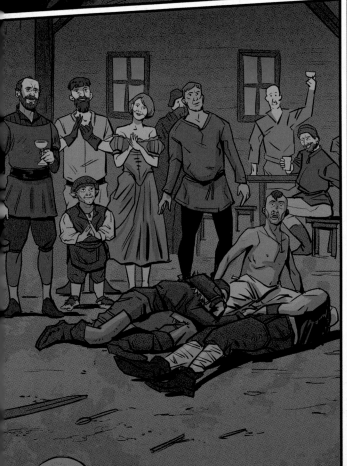

I THANK YOU.

COULD YOU COME AT ONCE? *TONIGHT?*

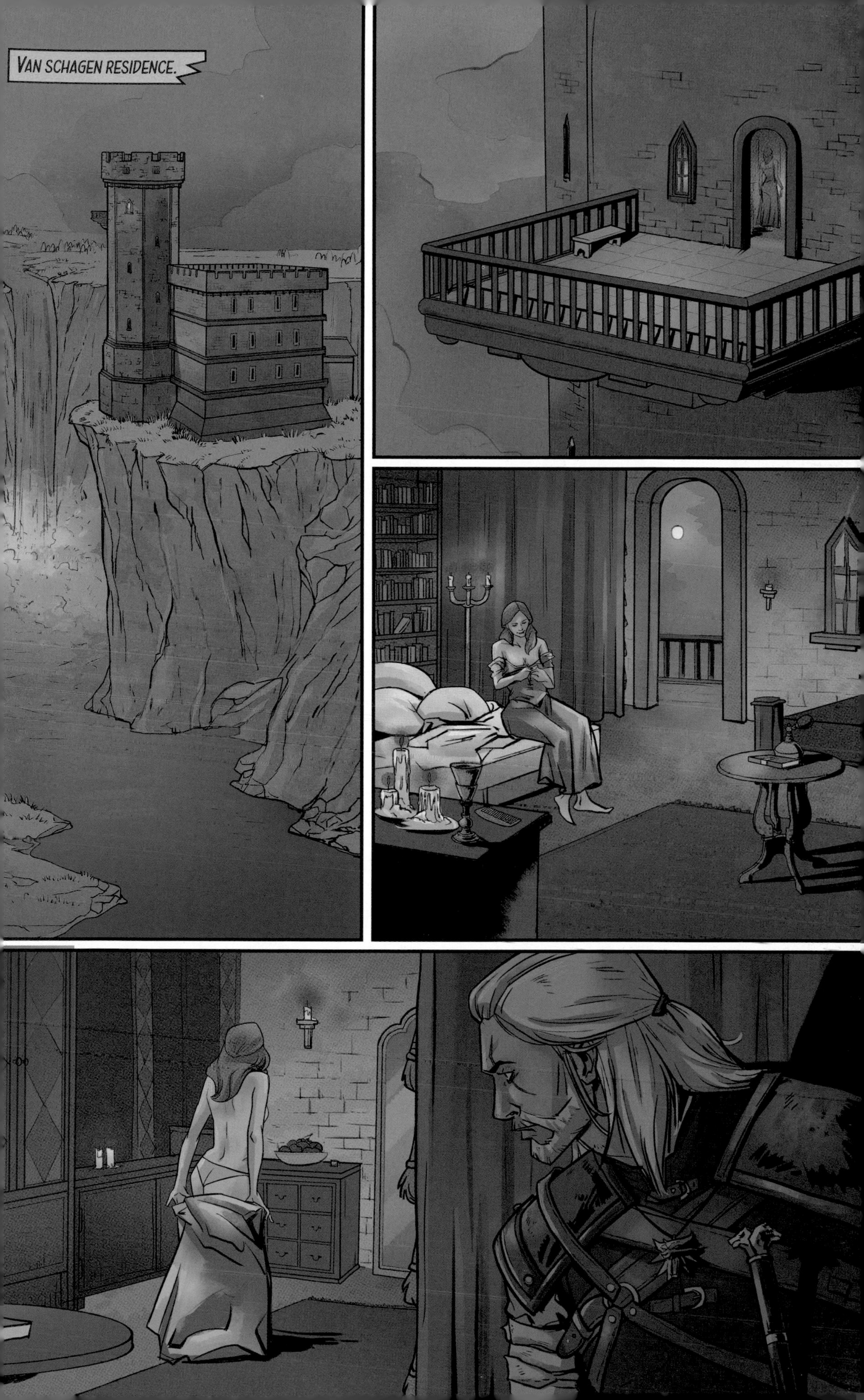
VAN SCHAGEN RESIDENCE.

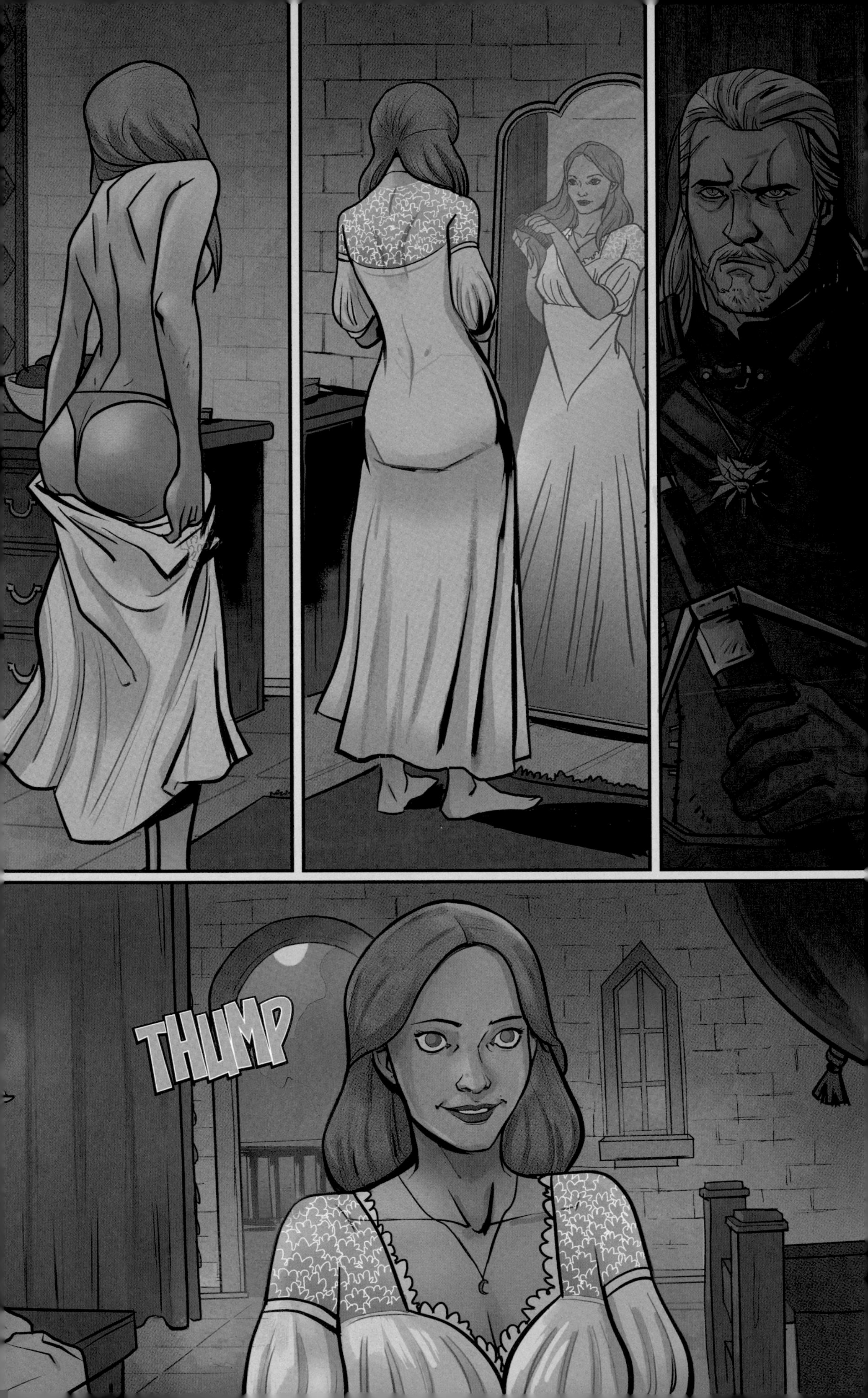
THUMP

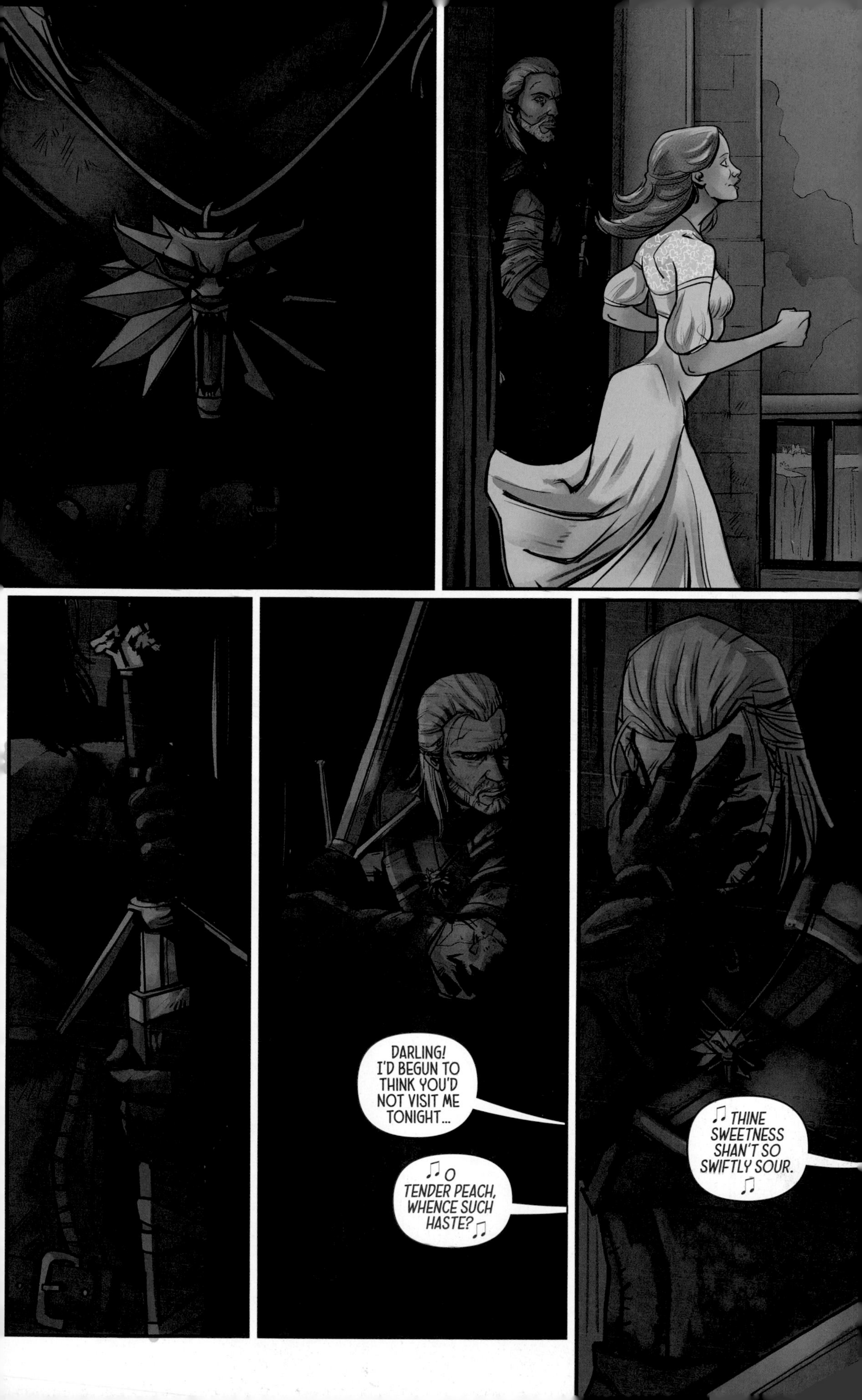
DARLING! I'D BEGUN TO THINK YOU'D NOT VISIT ME TONIGHT...
♫ O TENDER PEACH, WHENCE SUCH HASTE? ♫
♫ THINE SWEETNESS SHAN'T SO SWIFTLY SOUR. ♫

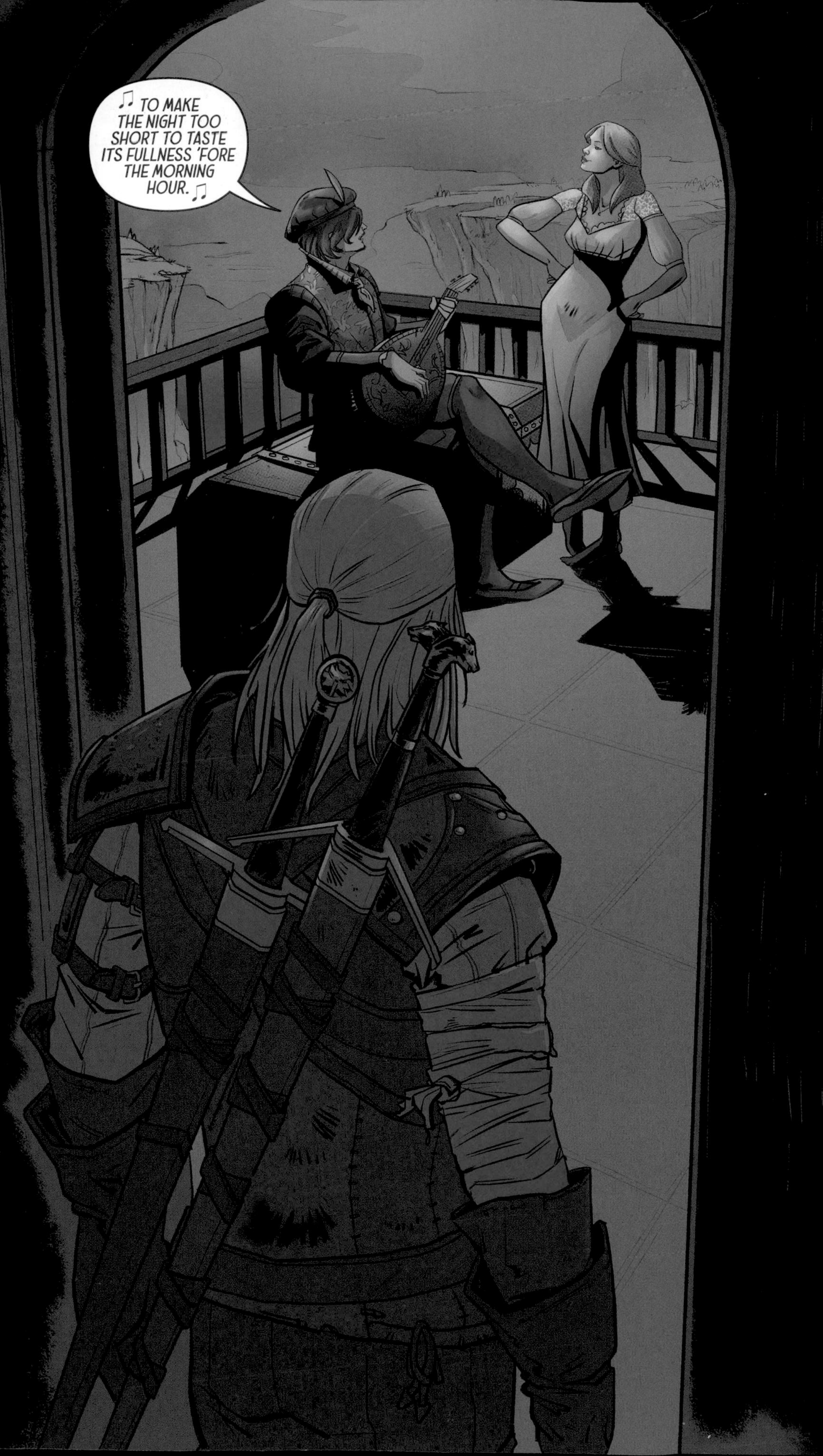
♫ TO MAKE THE NIGHT TOO SHORT TO TASTE ITS FULLNESS 'FORE THE MORNING HOUR. ♫

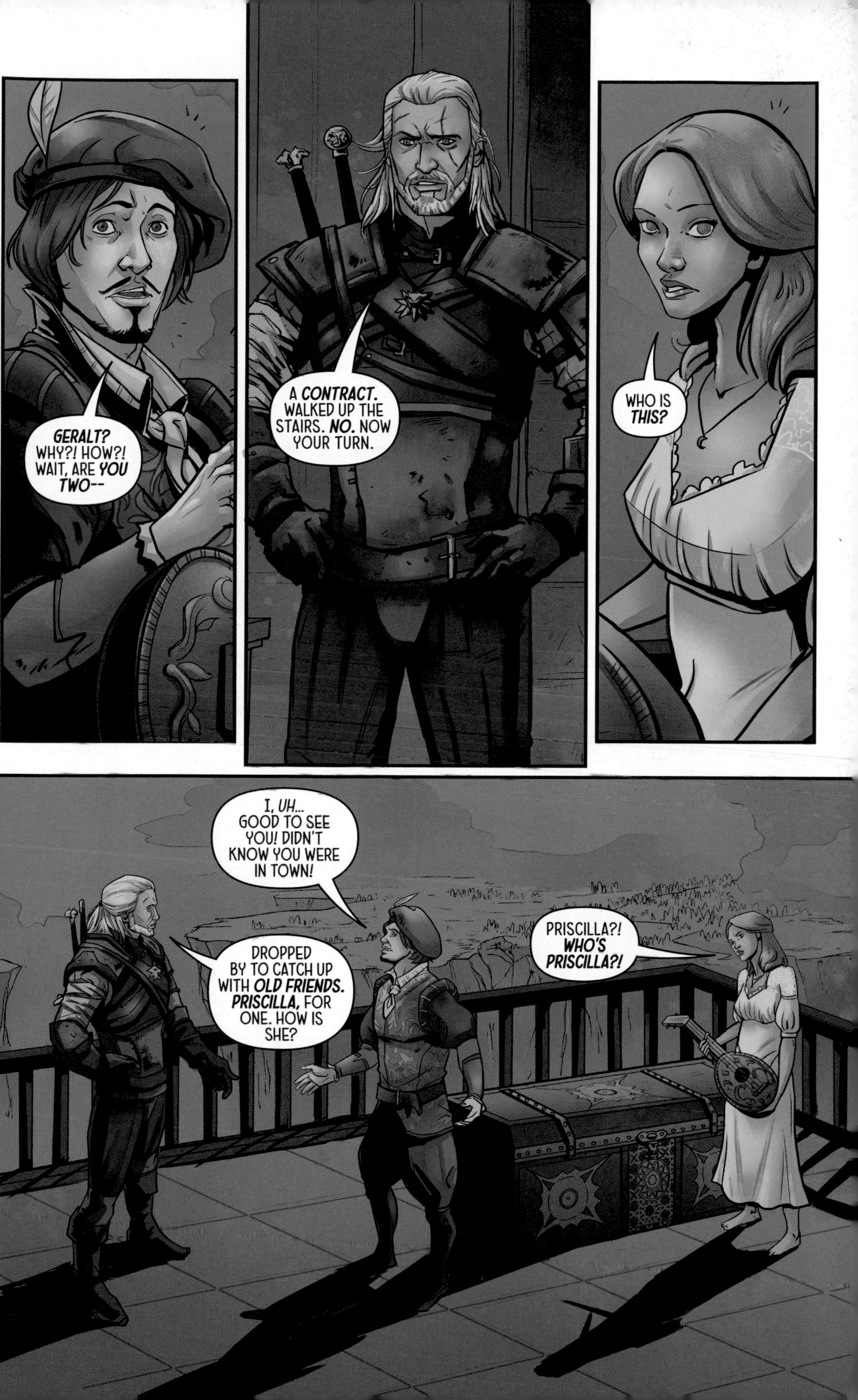
GERALT? WHY?! HOW?! WAIT, ARE YOU TWO--
A CONTRACT. WALKED UP THE STAIRS. NO. NOW YOUR TURN.
WHO IS THIS?
I, UH... GOOD TO SEE YOU! DIDN'T KNOW YOU WERE IN TOWN!
DROPPED BY TO CATCH UP WITH OLD FRIENDS. PRISCILLA, FOR ONE. HOW IS SHE?
PRISCILLA?! WHO'S PRISCILLA?!

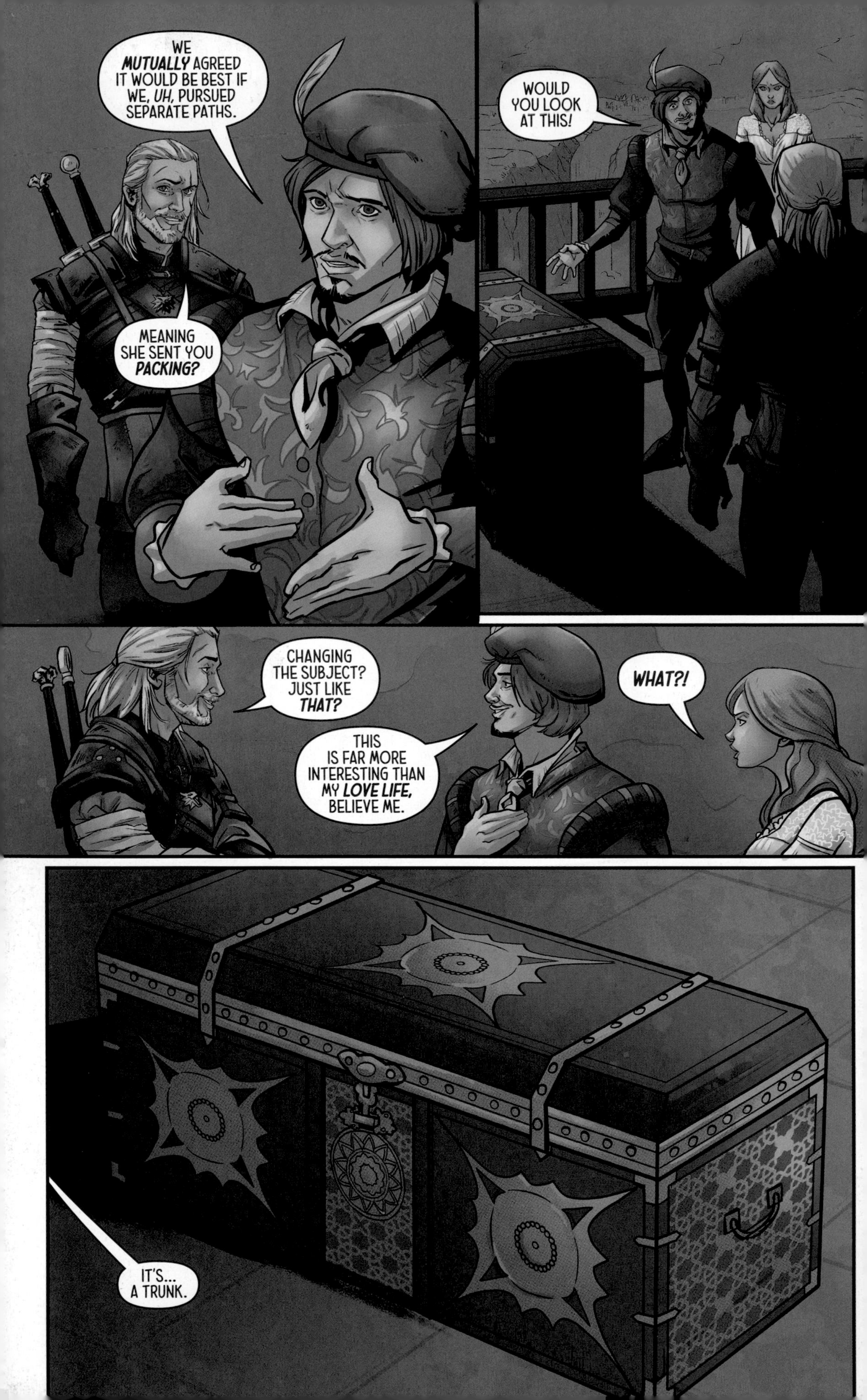
WE *MUTUALLY* AGREED IT WOULD BE BEST IF WE, *UH*, PURSUED SEPARATE PATHS.
MEANING SHE SENT YOU *PACKING?*
WOULD YOU LOOK AT THIS!
CHANGING THE SUBJECT? JUST LIKE *THAT?*
THIS IS FAR MORE INTERESTING THAN MY *LOVE LIFE,* BELIEVE ME.
WHAT?!
IT'S... A TRUNK.

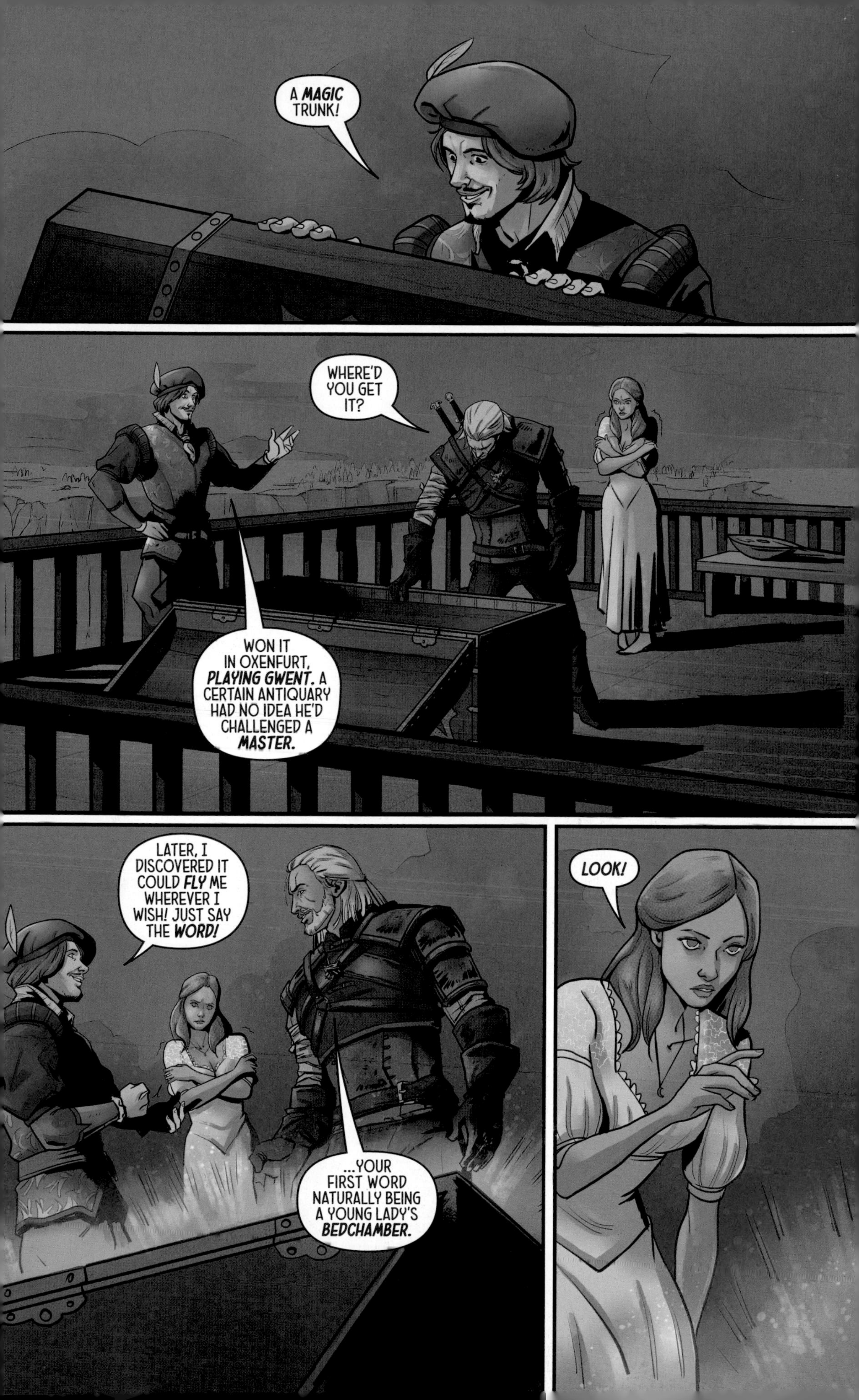
A MAGIC TRUNK!
WHERE'D YOU GET IT?
WON IT IN OXENFURT, PLAYING GWENT. A CERTAIN ANTIQUARY HAD NO IDEA HE'D CHALLENGED A MASTER.
LATER, I DISCOVERED IT COULD FLY ME WHEREVER I WISH! JUST SAY THE WORD!
...YOUR FIRST WORD NATURALLY BEING A YOUNG LADY'S BEDCHAMBER.
LOOK!

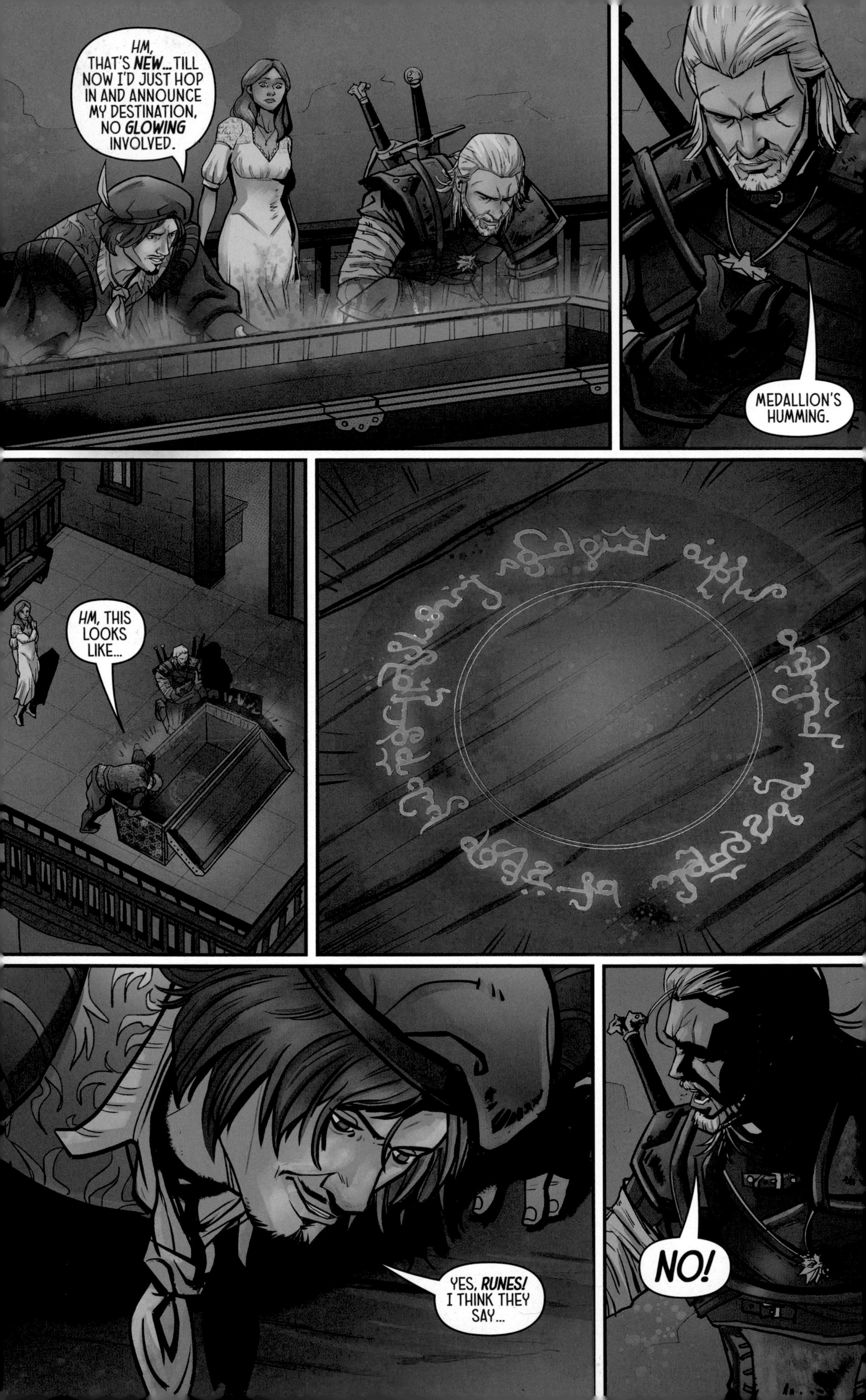
HM, THAT'S NEW... TILL NOW I'D JUST HOP IN AND ANNOUNCE MY DESTINATION, NO GLOWING INVOLVED.
MEDALLION'S HUMMING.
HM, THIS LOOKS LIKE...
YES, RUNES! I THINK THEY SAY...
NO!

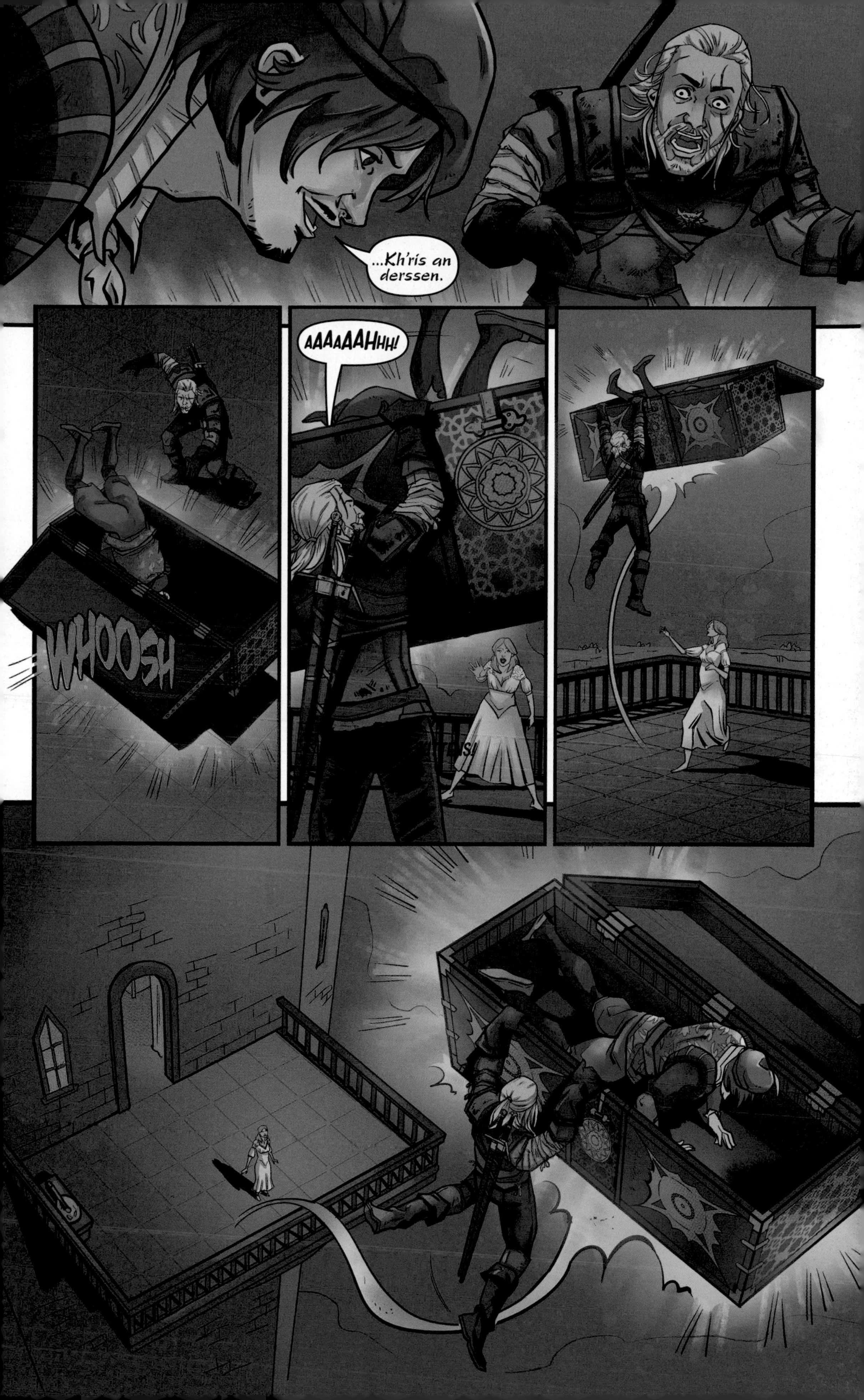
...Kh'ris an derssen.
WHOOSH
AAAAAAHHH!

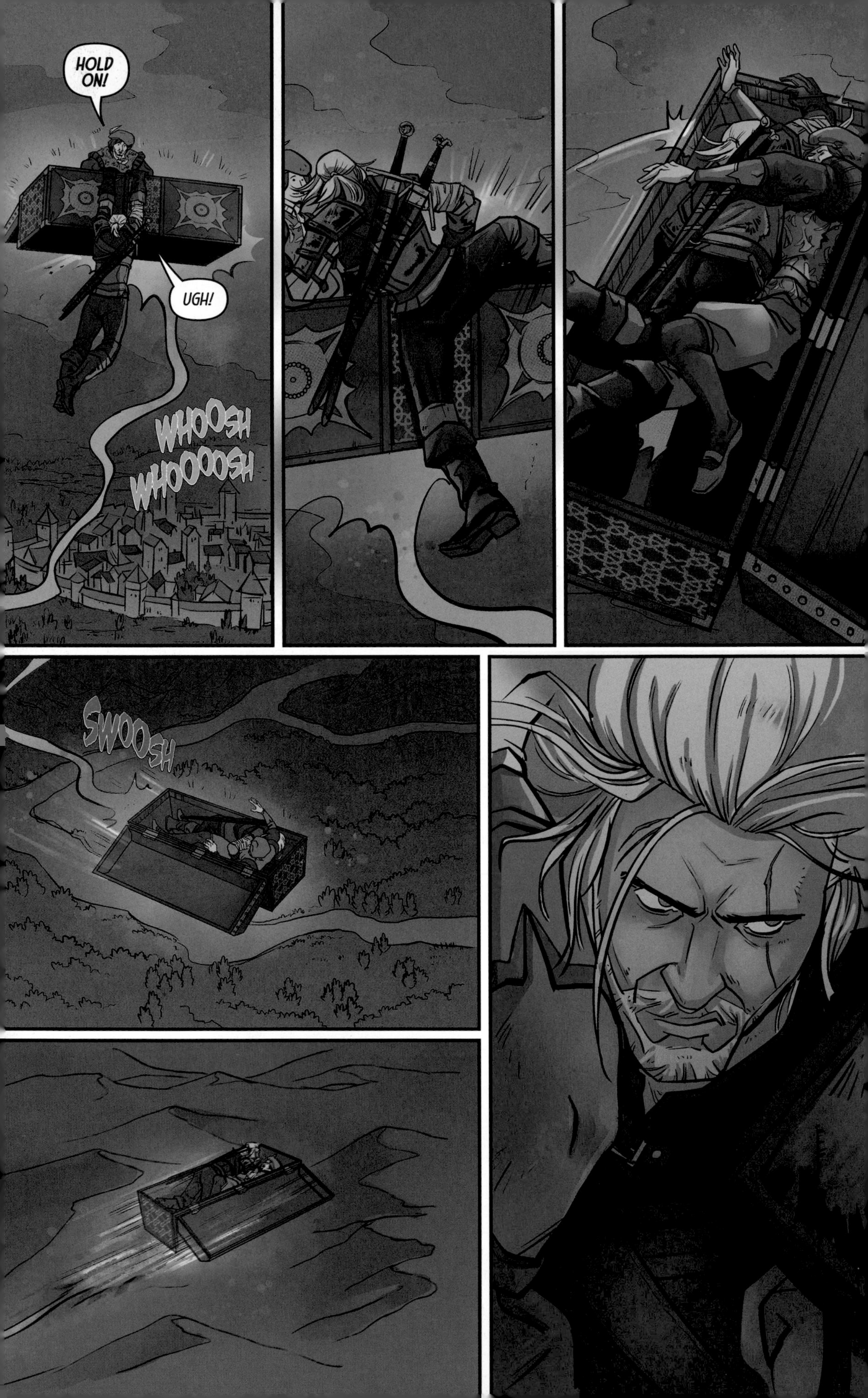
HOLD ON!
UGH!
WHOOSH
WHOOOOSH
SWOOSH

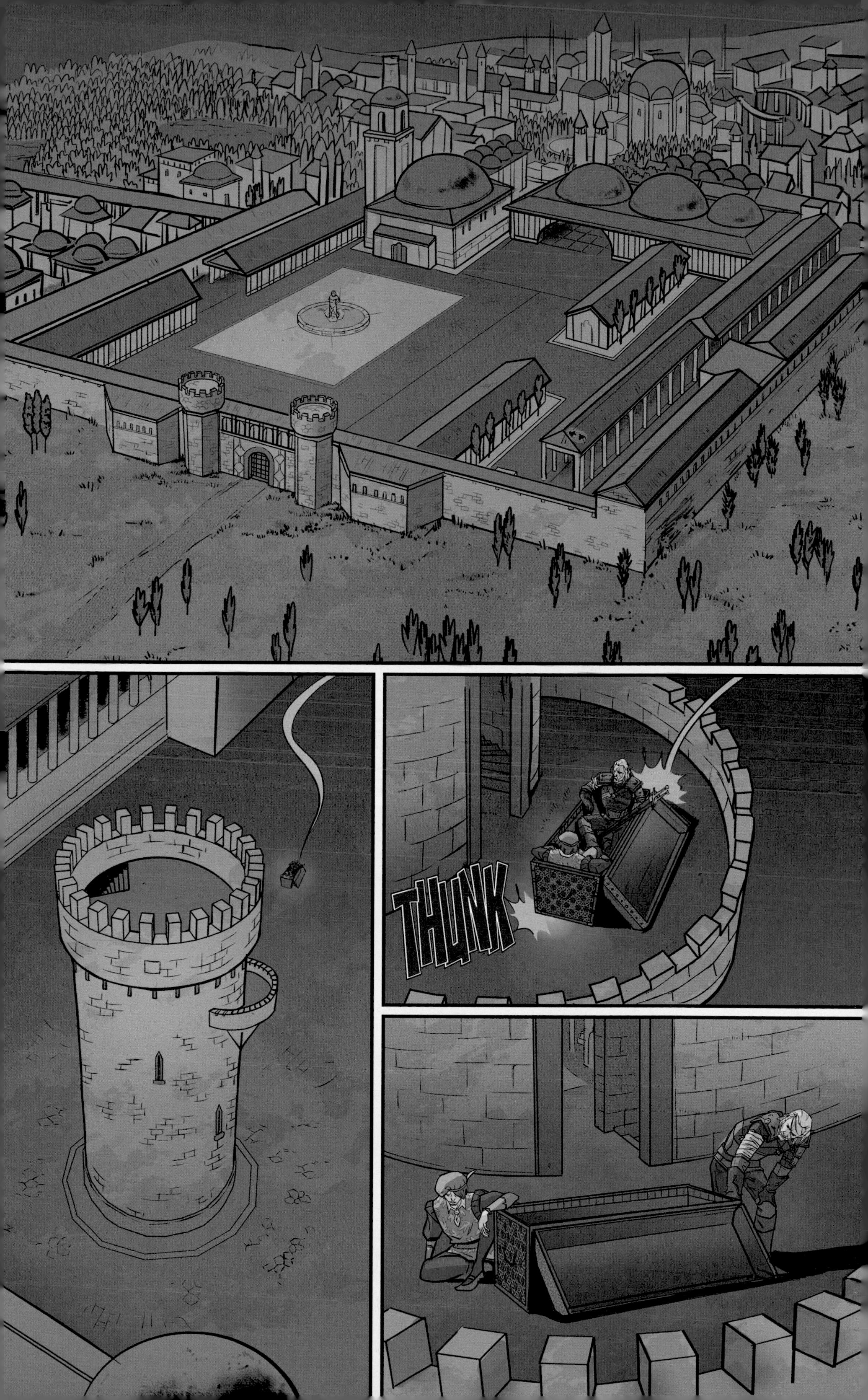
THUNK

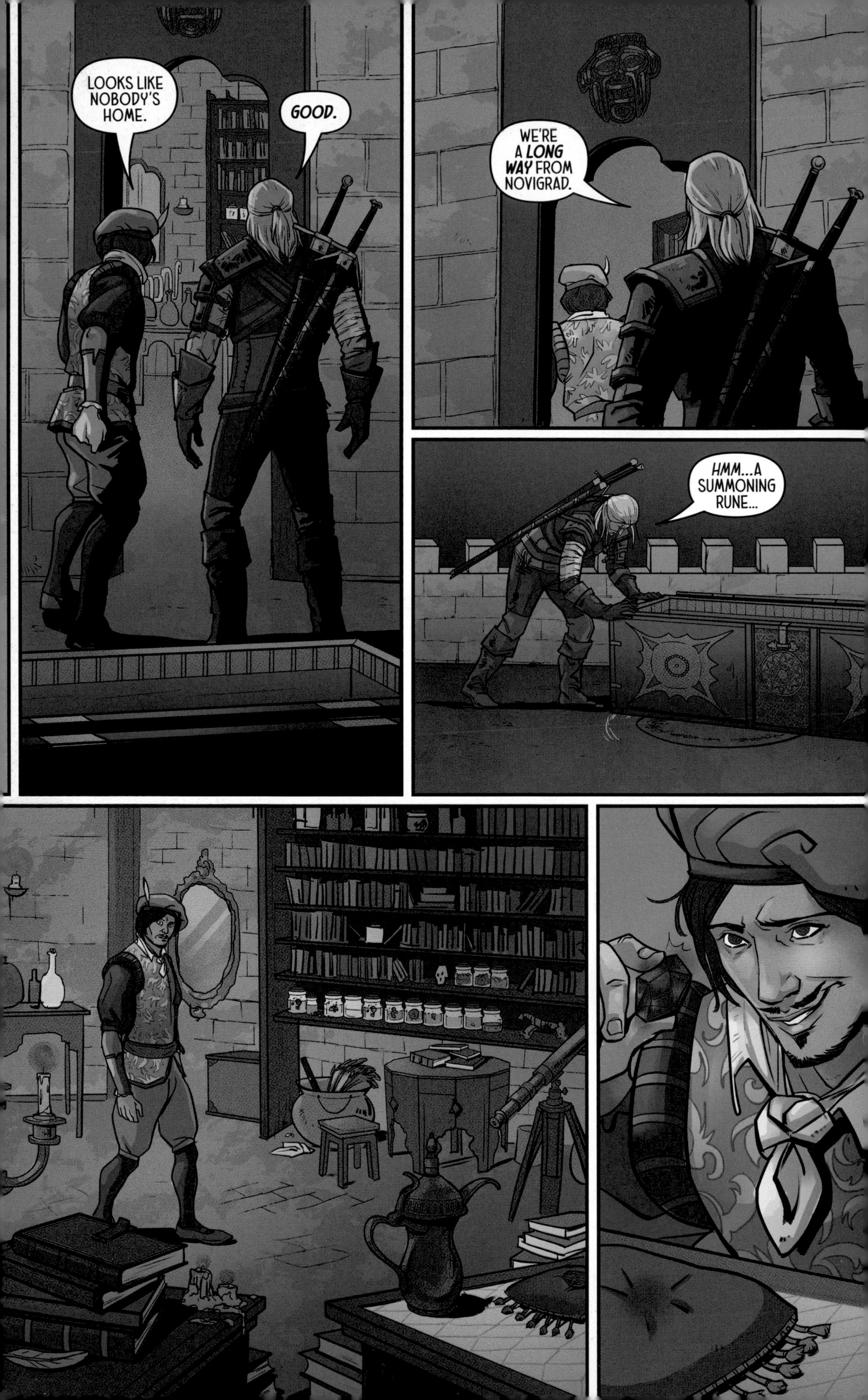
LOOKS LIKE NOBODY'S HOME.
GOOD.
WE'RE A LONG WAY FROM NOVIGRAD.
HMM...A SUMMONING RUNE...

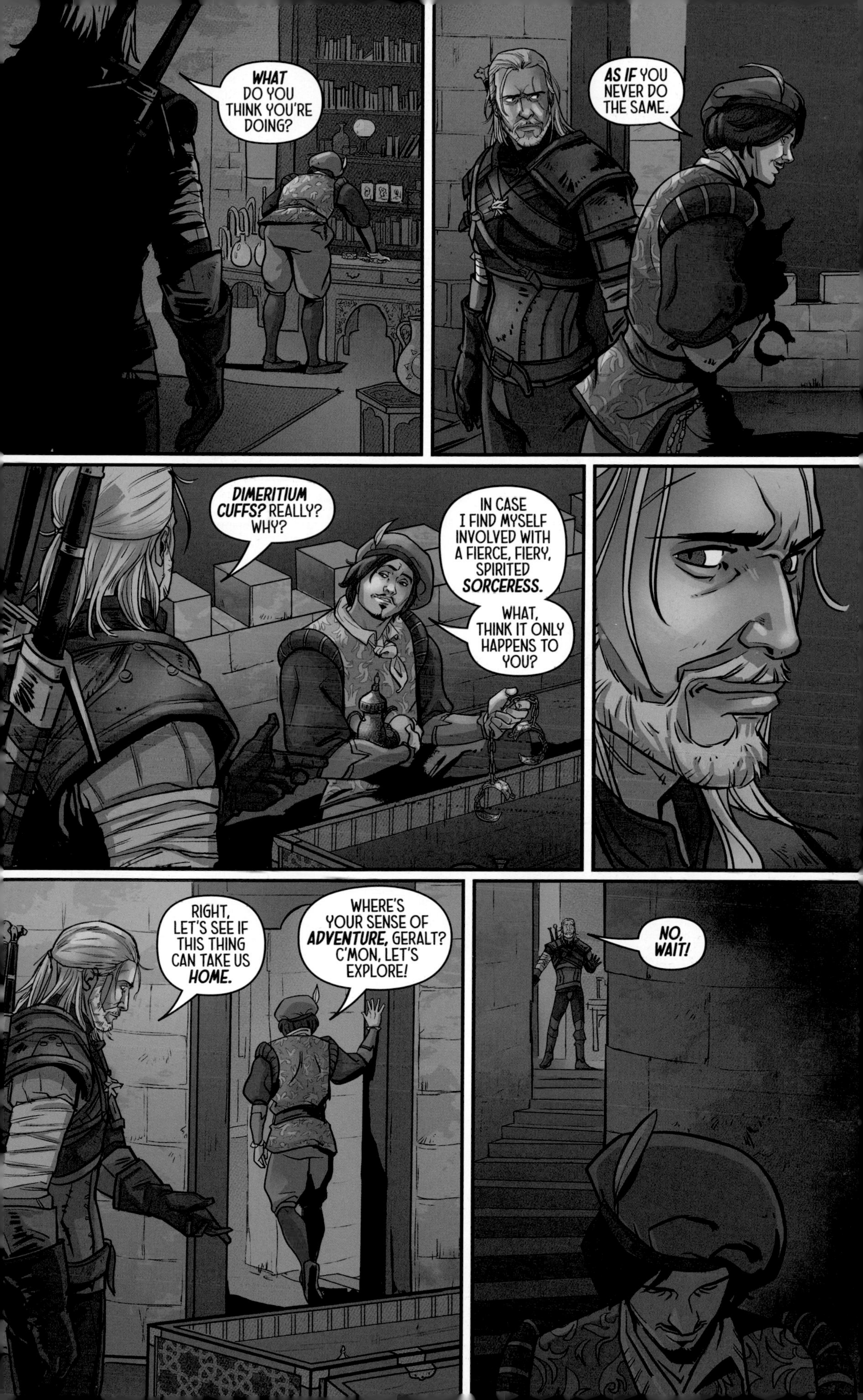

WHAT DO YOU THINK YOU'RE DOING?
AS IF YOU NEVER DO THE SAME.
DIMERITIUM CUFFS? REALLY? WHY?
IN CASE I FIND MYSELF INVOLVED WITH A FIERCE, FIERY, SPIRITED SORCERESS.
WHAT, THINK IT ONLY HAPPENS TO YOU?
RIGHT, LET'S SEE IF THIS THING CAN TAKE US HOME.
WHERE'S YOUR SENSE OF ADVENTURE, GERALT? C'MON, LET'S EXPLORE!
NO, WAIT!

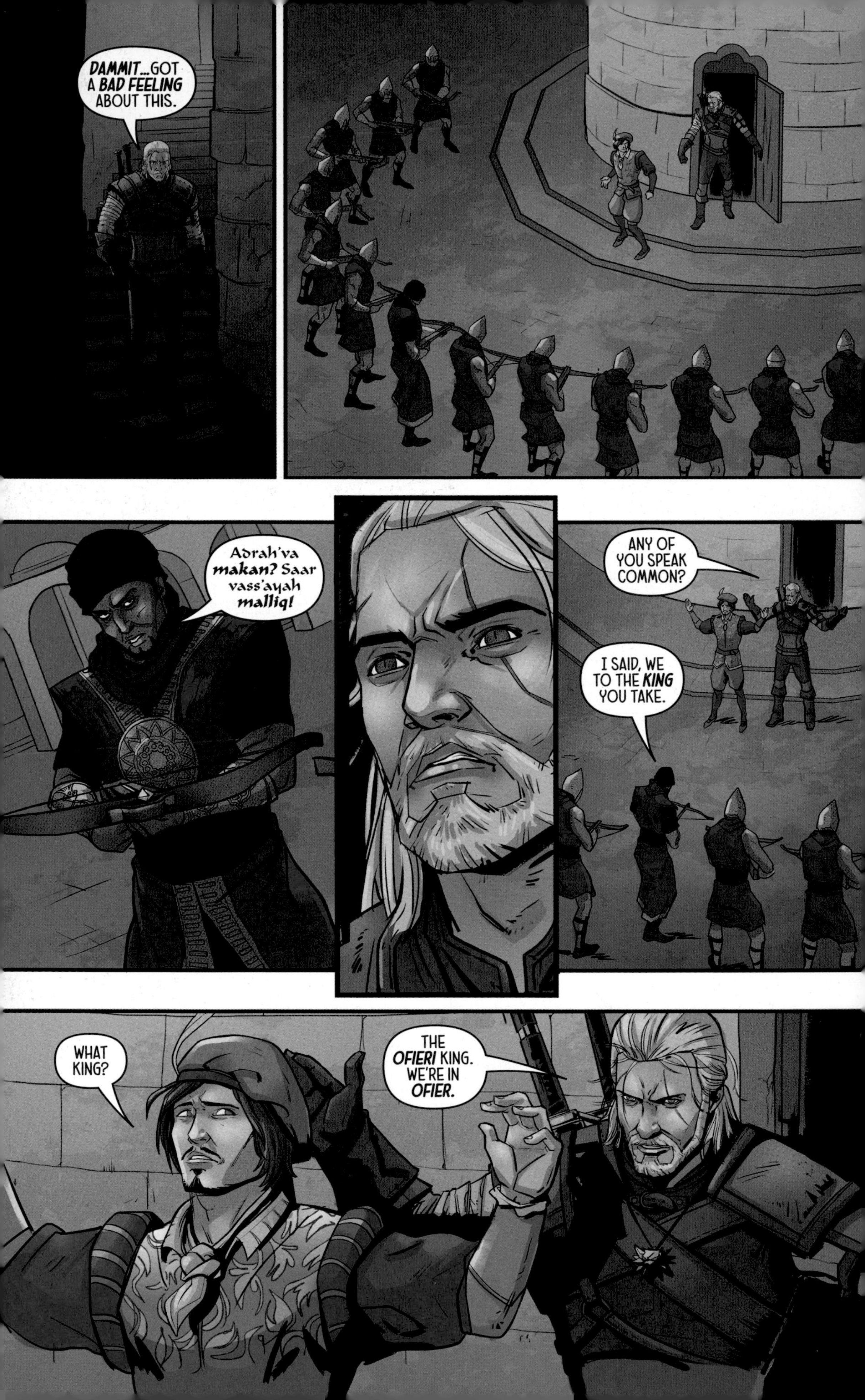
DAMMIT...GOT A BAD FEELING ABOUT THIS.
Adrah'va makan? Saar vass'ayah malliq!
ANY OF YOU SPEAK COMMON?
I SAID, WE TO THE KING YOU TAKE.
WHAT KING?
THE OFIERI KING. WE'RE IN OFIER.

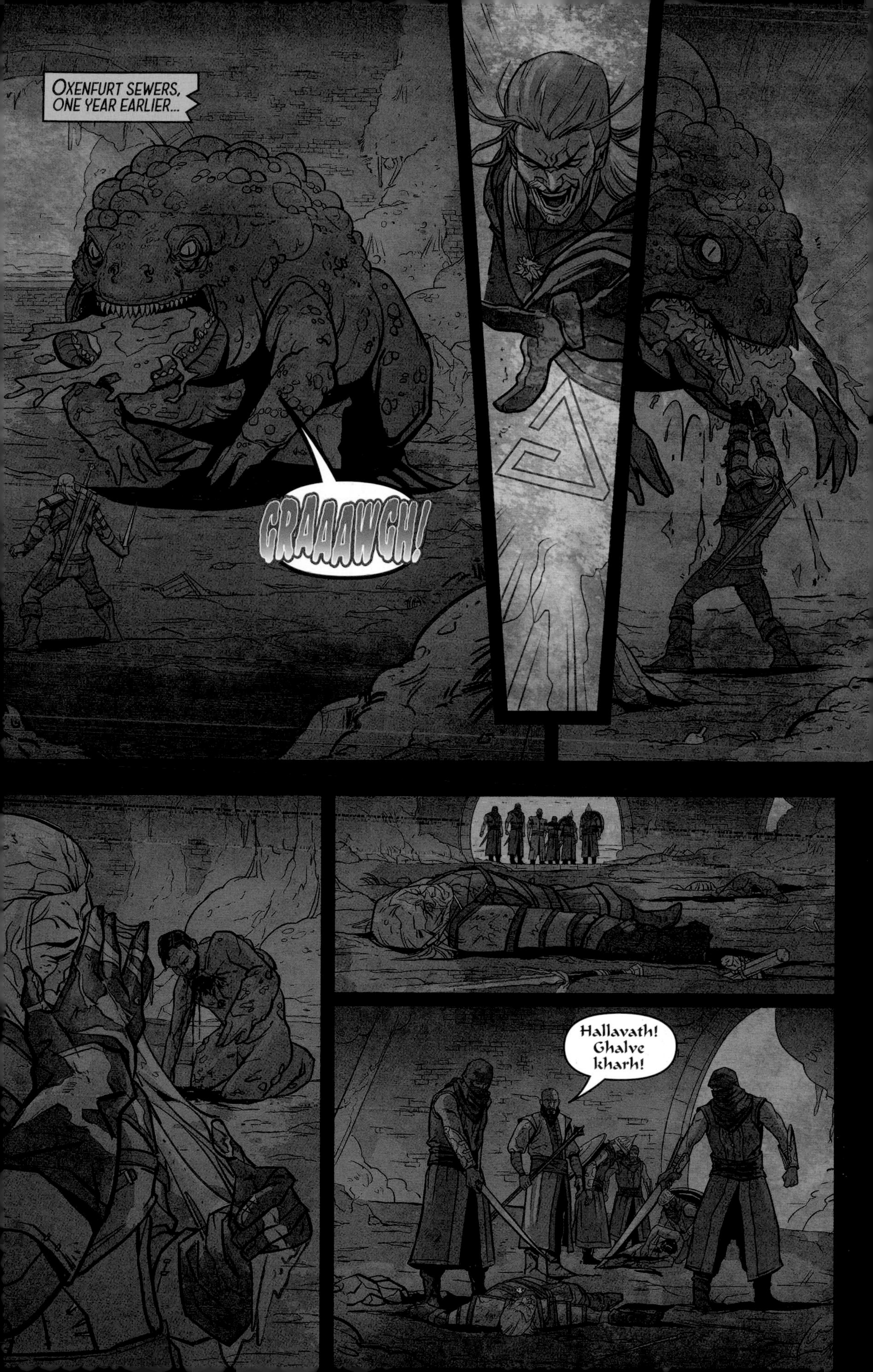
OXENFURT SEWERS, ONE YEAR EARLIER...
CRAAAWGH!
Hallavath! Ghalve kharh!

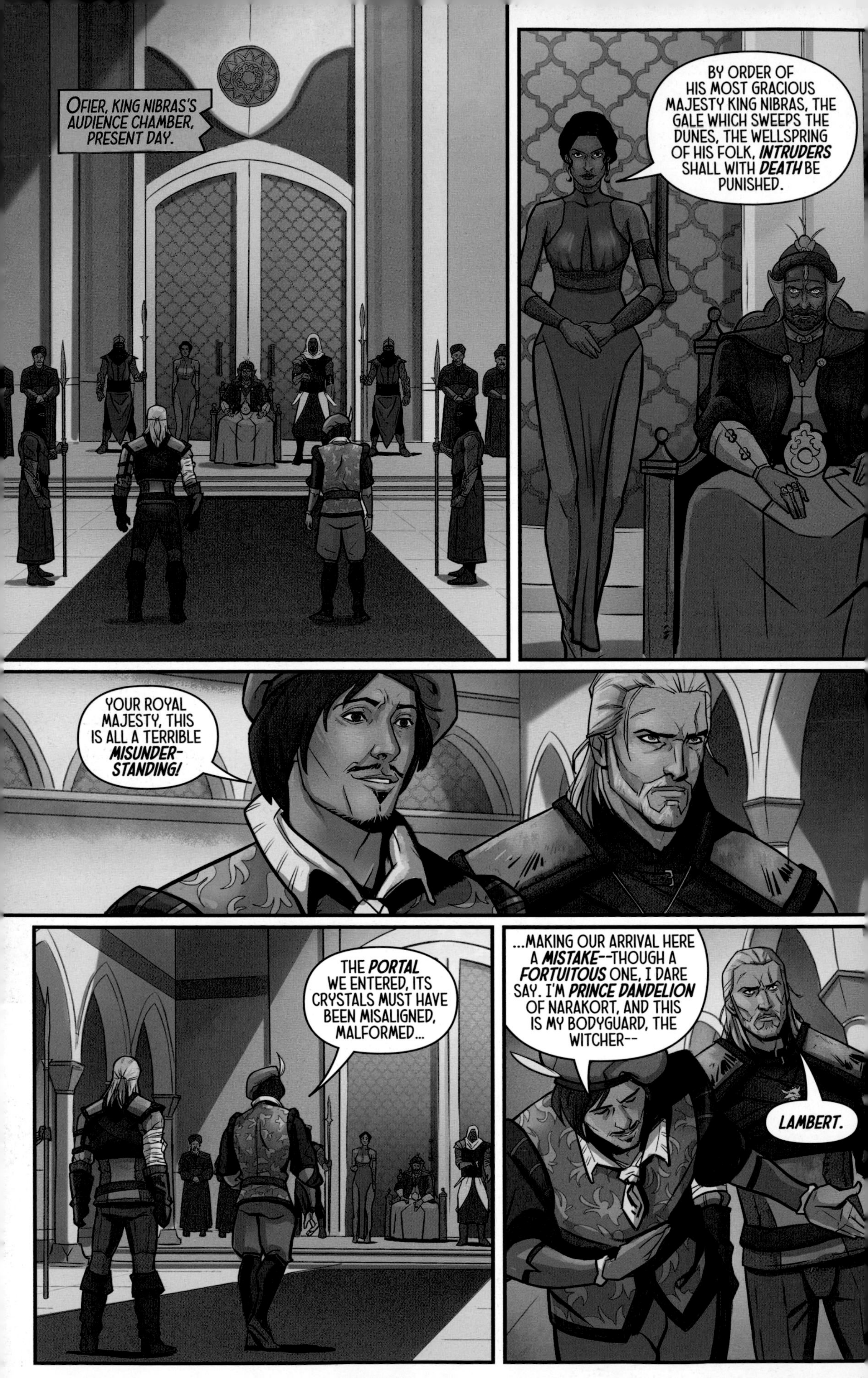
OFIER, KING NIBRAS'S AUDIENCE CHAMBER, PRESENT DAY.
BY ORDER OF HIS MOST GRACIOUS MAJESTY KING NIBRAS, THE GALE WHICH SWEEPS THE DUNES, THE WELLSPRING OF HIS FOLK, INTRUDERS SHALL WITH DEATH BE PUNISHED.
YOUR ROYAL MAJESTY, THIS IS ALL A TERRIBLE MISUNDER-STANDING!
THE PORTAL WE ENTERED, ITS CRYSTALS MUST HAVE BEEN MISALIGNED, MALFORMED...
...MAKING OUR ARRIVAL HERE A MISTAKE--THOUGH A FORTUITOUS ONE, I DARE SAY. I'M PRINCE DANDELION OF NARAKORT, AND THIS IS MY BODYGUARD, THE WITCHER--
LAMBERT.

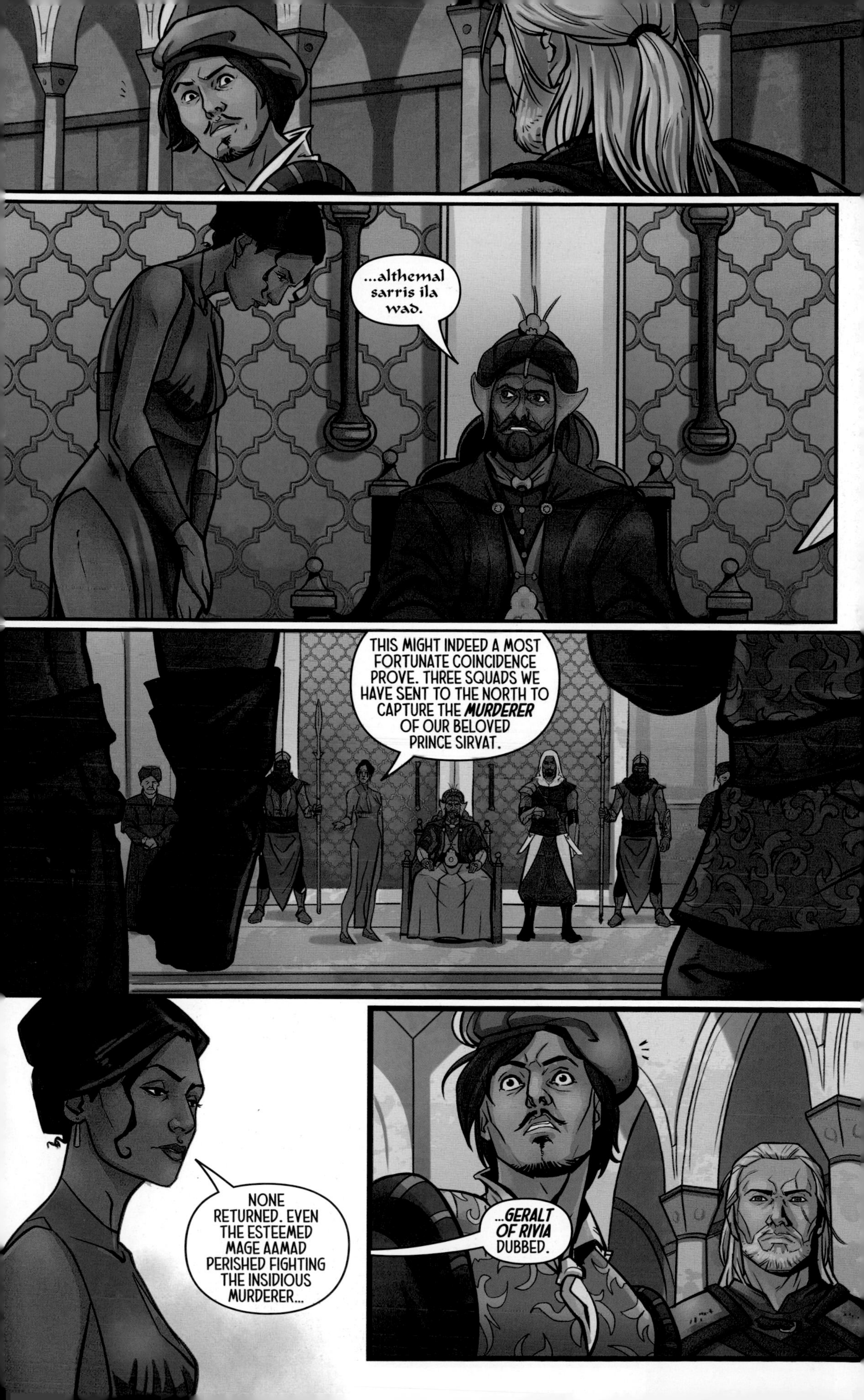
...althemal sarris ila wad.
THIS MIGHT INDEED A MOST FORTUNATE COINCIDENCE PROVE. THREE SQUADS WE HAVE SENT TO THE NORTH TO CAPTURE THE *MURDERER* OF OUR BELOVED PRINCE SIRVAT.
NONE RETURNED. EVEN THE ESTEEMED MAGE AAMAD PERISHED FIGHTING THE INSIDIOUS MURDERER...
...*GERALT OF RIVIA* DUBBED.

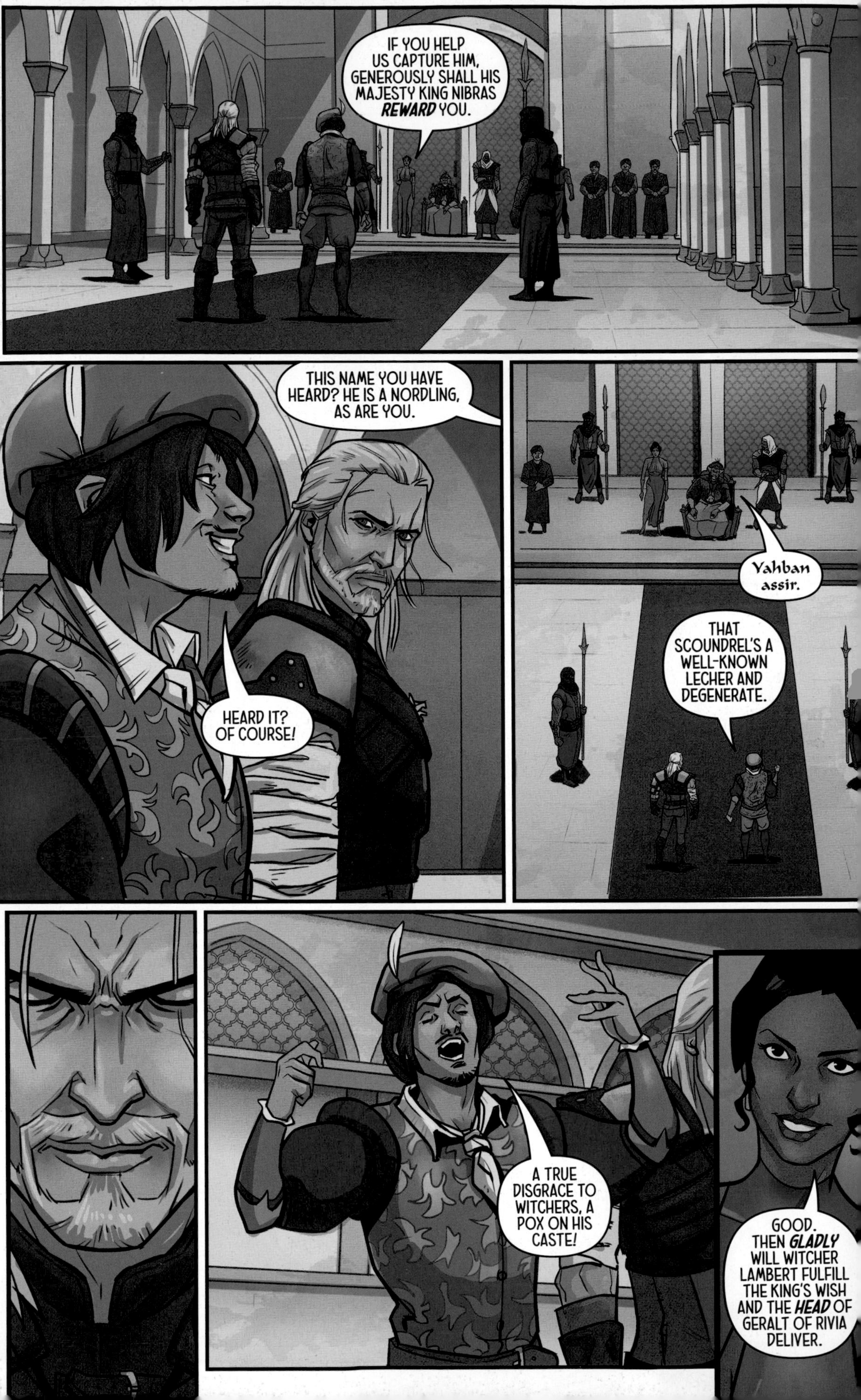
IF YOU HELP US CAPTURE HIM, GENEROUSLY SHALL HIS MAJESTY KING NIBRAS REWARD YOU.
THIS NAME YOU HAVE HEARD? HE IS A NORDLING, AS ARE YOU.
HEARD IT? OF COURSE!
Yahban assir.
THAT SCOUNDREL'S A WELL-KNOWN LECHER AND DEGENERATE.
A TRUE DISGRACE TO WITCHERS, A POX ON HIS CASTE!
GOOD. THEN GLADLY WILL WITCHER LAMBERT FULFILL THE KING'S WISH AND THE HEAD OF GERALT OF RIVIA DELIVER.

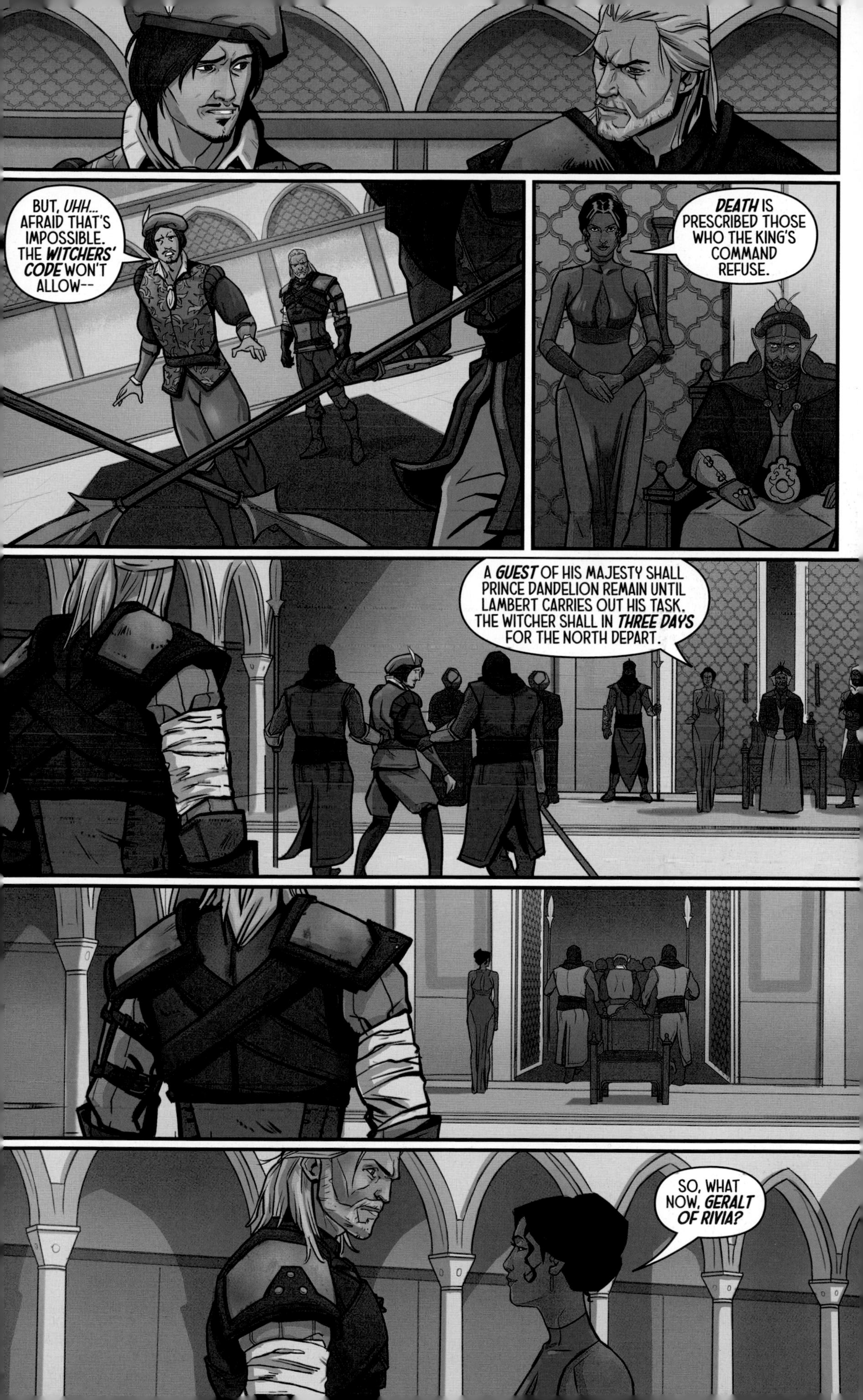
BUT, *UHH*... AFRAID THAT'S IMPOSSIBLE. THE ***WITCHERS' CODE*** WON'T ALLOW--
DEATH IS PRESCRIBED THOSE WHO THE KING'S COMMAND REFUSE.
A ***GUEST*** OF HIS MAJESTY SHALL PRINCE DANDELION REMAIN UNTIL LAMBERT CARRIES OUT HIS TASK. THE WITCHER SHALL IN ***THREE DAYS*** FOR THE NORTH DEPART.
SO, WHAT NOW, ***GERALT OF RIVIA?***

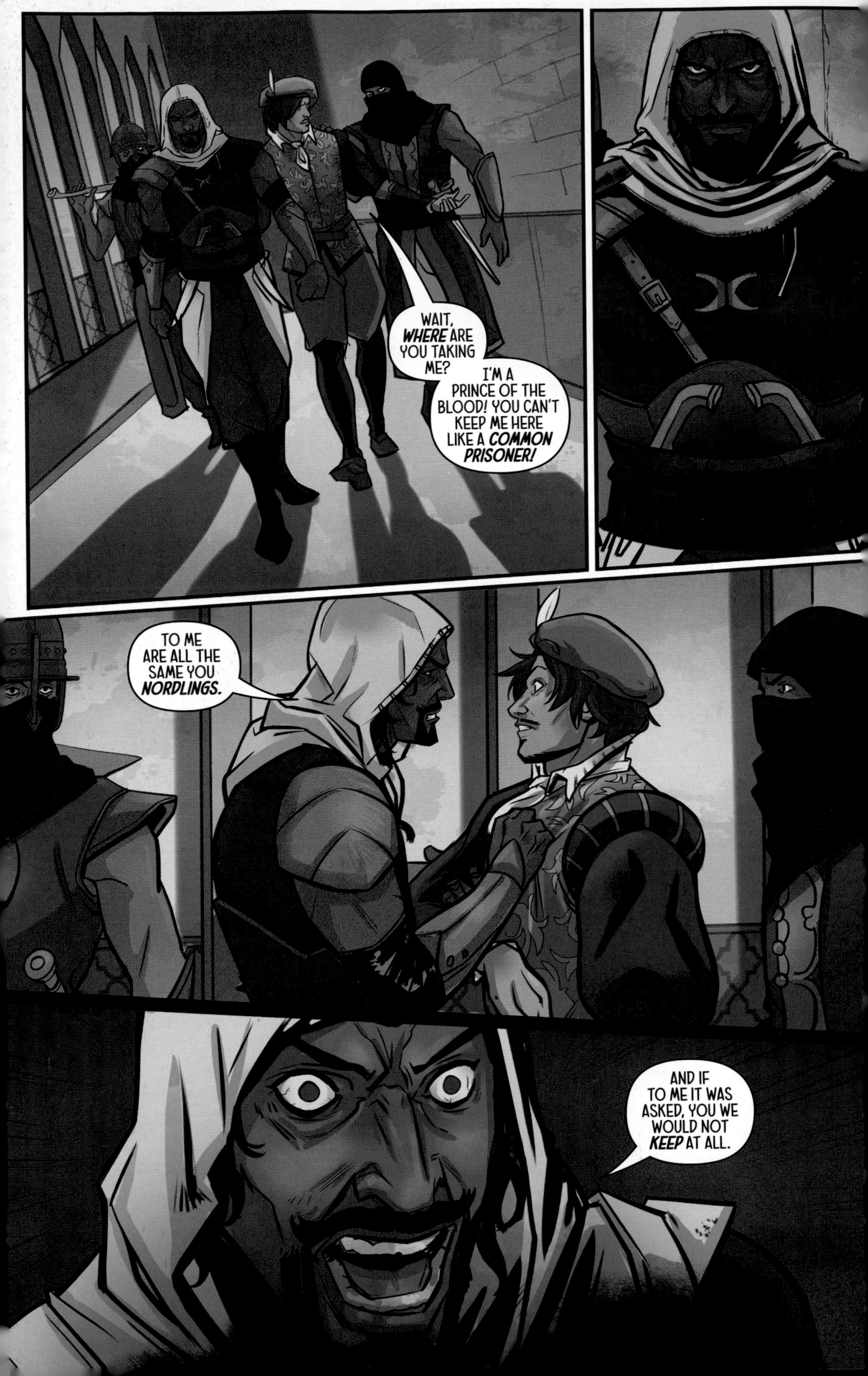
WAIT, *WHERE* ARE YOU TAKING ME?
I'M A PRINCE OF THE BLOOD! YOU CAN'T KEEP ME HERE LIKE A *COMMON PRISONER!*
TO ME ARE ALL THE SAME YOU *NORDLINGS.*
AND IF TO ME IT WAS ASKED, YOU WE WOULD NOT *KEEP* AT ALL.

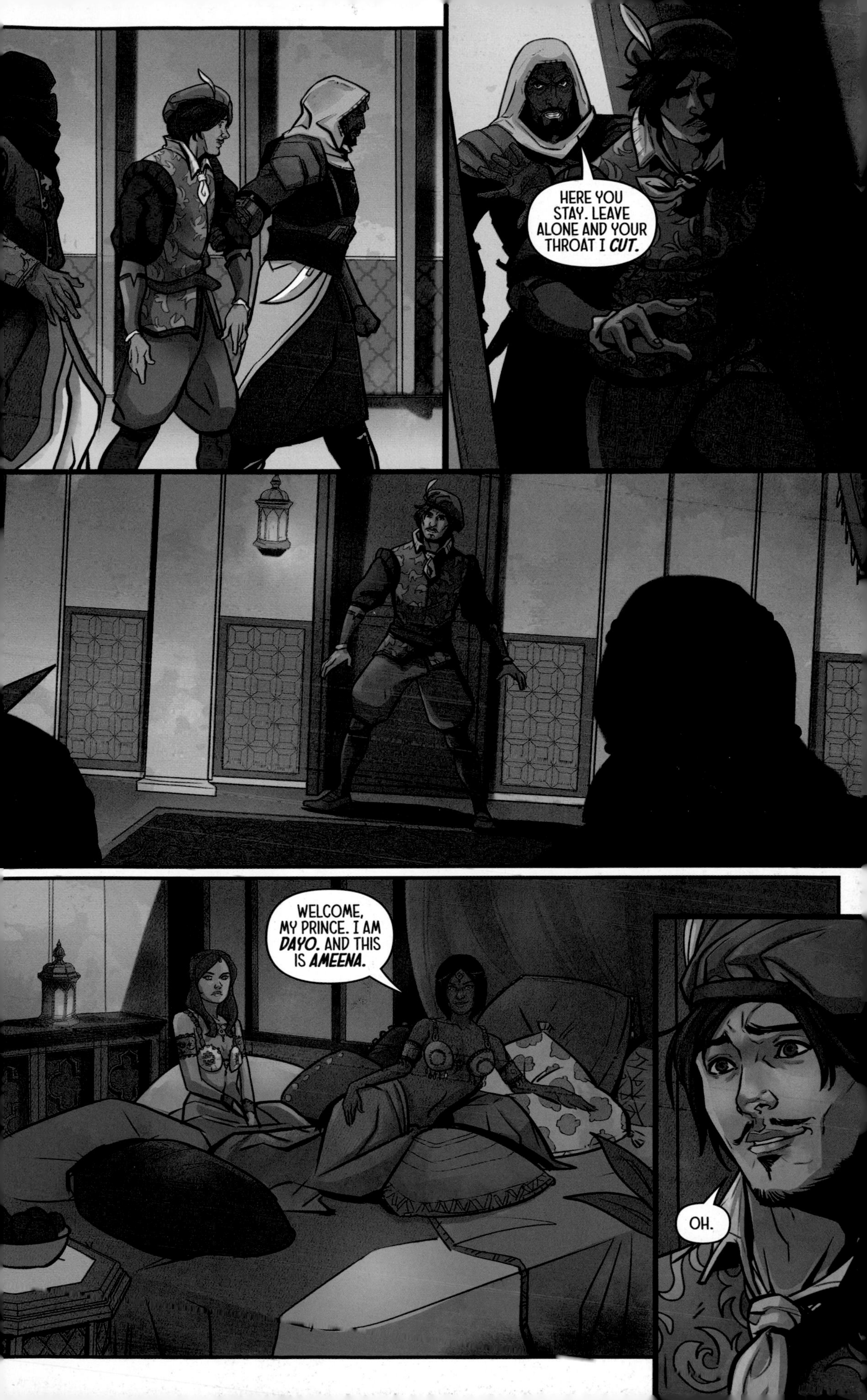
HERE YOU STAY. LEAVE ALONE AND YOUR THROAT I CUT.
WELCOME, MY PRINCE. I AM DAYO. AND THIS IS AMEENA.
OH.

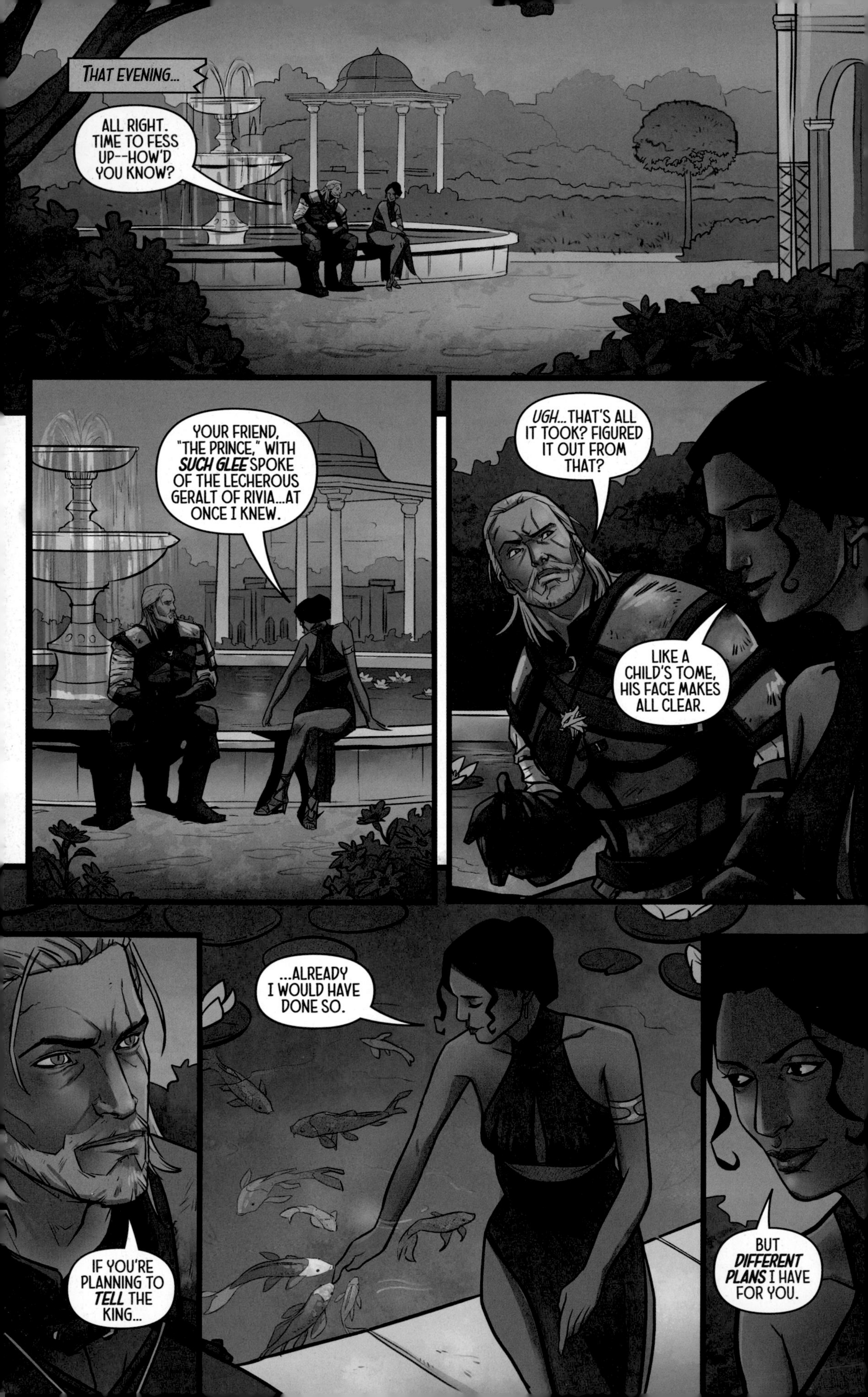
THAT EVENING...
ALL RIGHT. TIME TO FESS UP--HOW'D YOU KNOW?
YOUR FRIEND, "THE PRINCE," WITH SUCH GLEE SPOKE OF THE LECHEROUS GERALT OF RIVIA...AT ONCE I KNEW.
UGH...THAT'S ALL IT TOOK? FIGURED IT OUT FROM THAT?
LIKE A CHILD'S TOME, HIS FACE MAKES ALL CLEAR.
IF YOU'RE PLANNING TO TELL THE KING...
...ALREADY I WOULD HAVE DONE SO.
BUT DIFFERENT PLANS I HAVE FOR YOU.

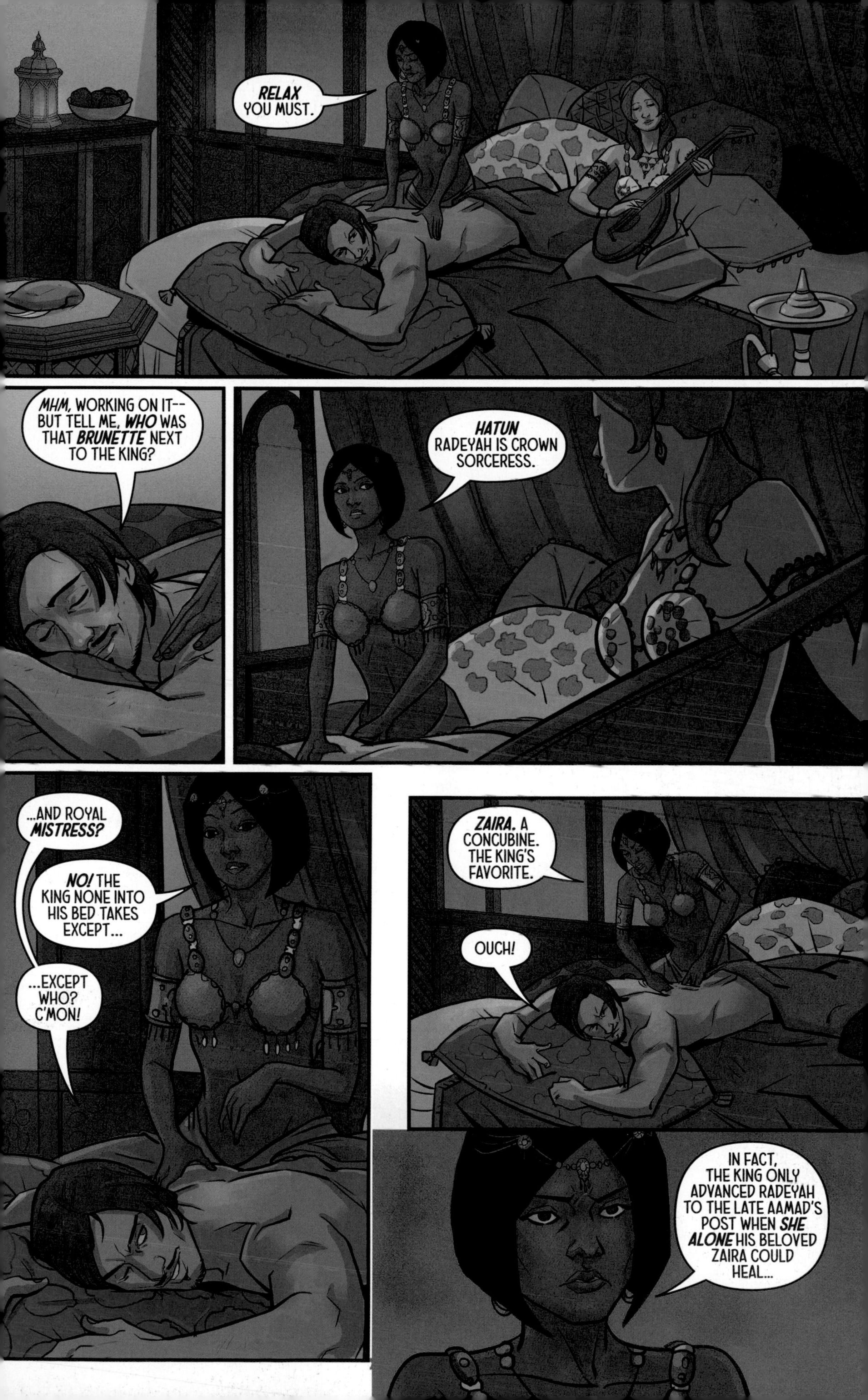
RELAX YOU MUST.
MHM, WORKING ON IT-- BUT TELL ME, WHO WAS THAT BRUNETTE NEXT TO THE KING?
HATUN RADEYAH IS CROWN SORCERESS.
...AND ROYAL MISTRESS?
NO! THE KING NONE INTO HIS BED TAKES EXCEPT...
...EXCEPT WHO? C'MON!
ZAIRA. A CONCUBINE. THE KING'S FAVORITE.
OUCH!
IN FACT, THE KING ONLY ADVANCED RADEYAH TO THE LATE AAMAD'S POST WHEN SHE ALONE HIS BELOVED ZAIRA COULD HEAL...

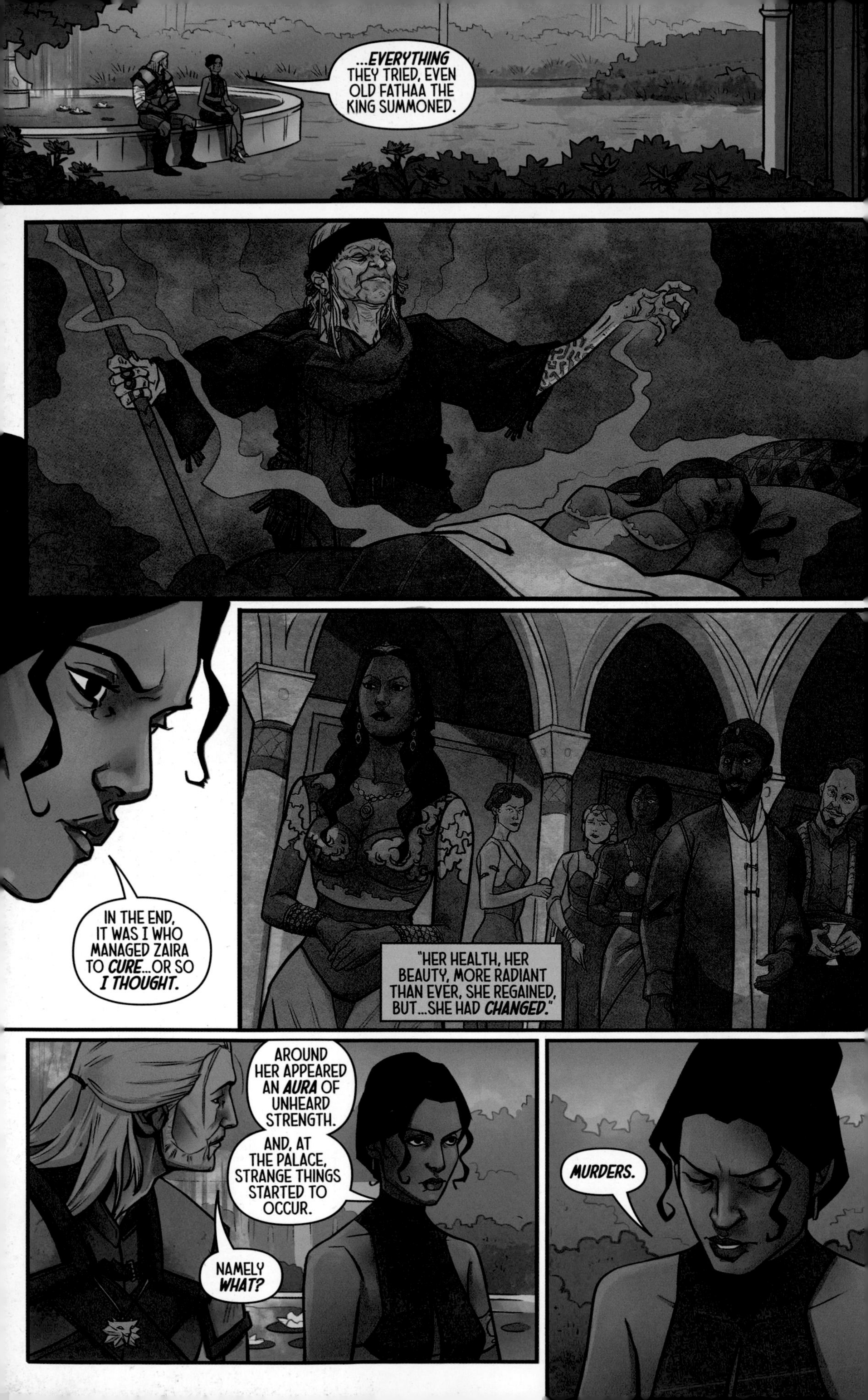

...*EVERYTHING* THEY TRIED, EVEN OLD FATHAA THE KING SUMMONED.
IN THE END, IT WAS I WHO MANAGED ZAIRA TO *CURE*...OR SO *I THOUGHT*.
"HER HEALTH, HER BEAUTY, MORE RADIANT THAN EVER, SHE REGAINED, BUT...SHE HAD *CHANGED*."
AROUND HER APPEARED AN *AURA* OF UNHEARD STRENGTH.
AND, AT THE PALACE, STRANGE THINGS STARTED TO OCCUR.
NAMELY *WHAT?*
MURDERS.

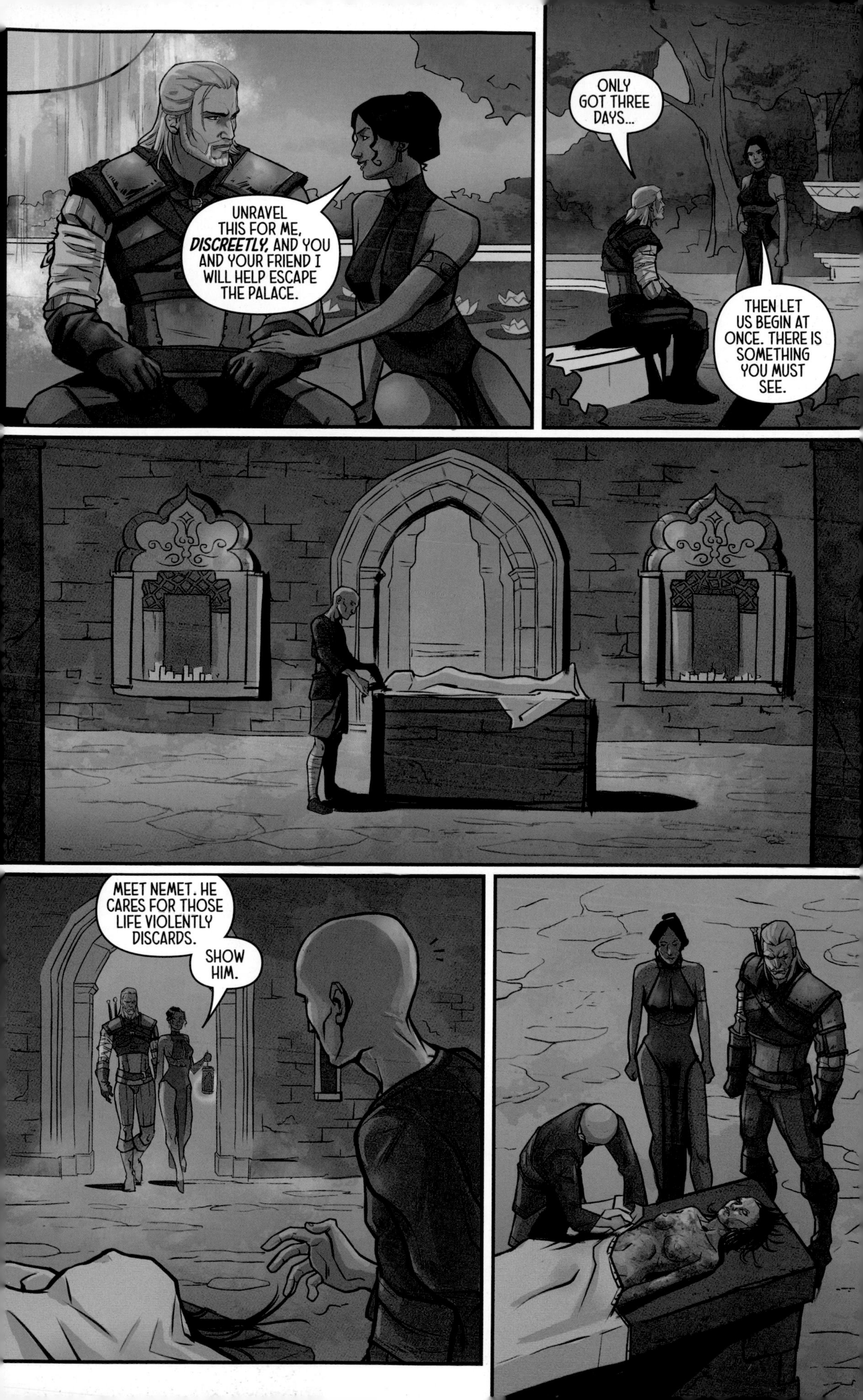
UNRAVEL THIS FOR ME, ***DISCREETLY,*** AND YOU AND YOUR FRIEND I WILL HELP ESCAPE THE PALACE.
ONLY GOT THREE DAYS...
THEN LET US BEGIN AT ONCE. THERE IS SOMETHING YOU MUST SEE.
MEET NEMET. HE CARES FOR THOSE LIFE VIOLENTLY DISCARDS.
SHOW HIM.

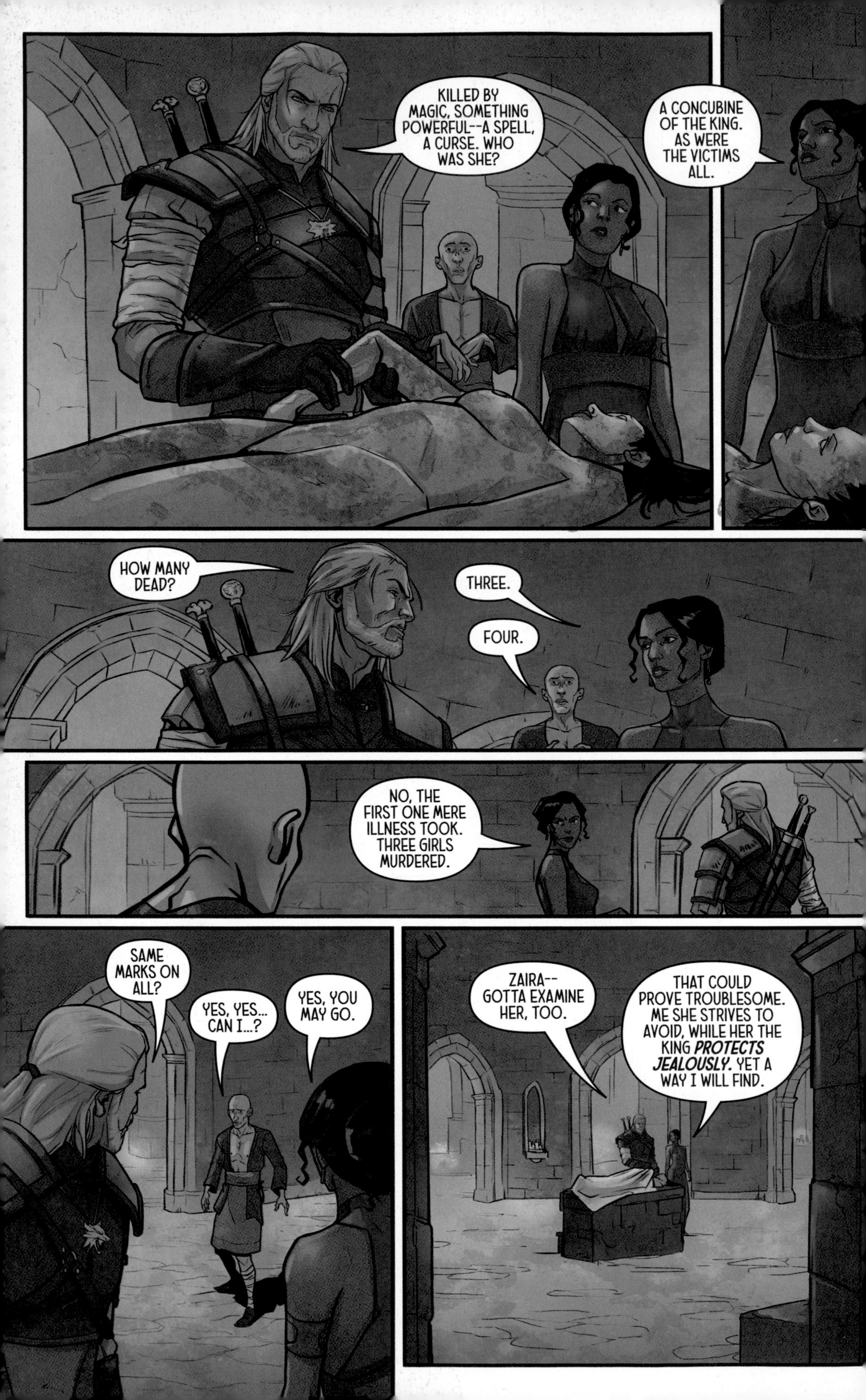
KILLED BY MAGIC, SOMETHING POWERFUL--A SPELL, A CURSE. WHO WAS SHE?
A CONCUBINE OF THE KING. AS WERE THE VICTIMS ALL.
HOW MANY DEAD?
THREE.
FOUR.
NO, THE FIRST ONE MERE ILLNESS TOOK. THREE GIRLS MURDERED.
SAME MARKS ON ALL?
YES, YES... CAN I...?
YES, YOU MAY GO.
ZAIRA-- GOTTA EXAMINE HER, TOO.
THAT COULD PROVE TROUBLESOME. ME SHE STRIVES TO AVOID, WHILE HER THE KING *PROTECTS JEALOUSLY.* YET A WAY I WILL FIND.

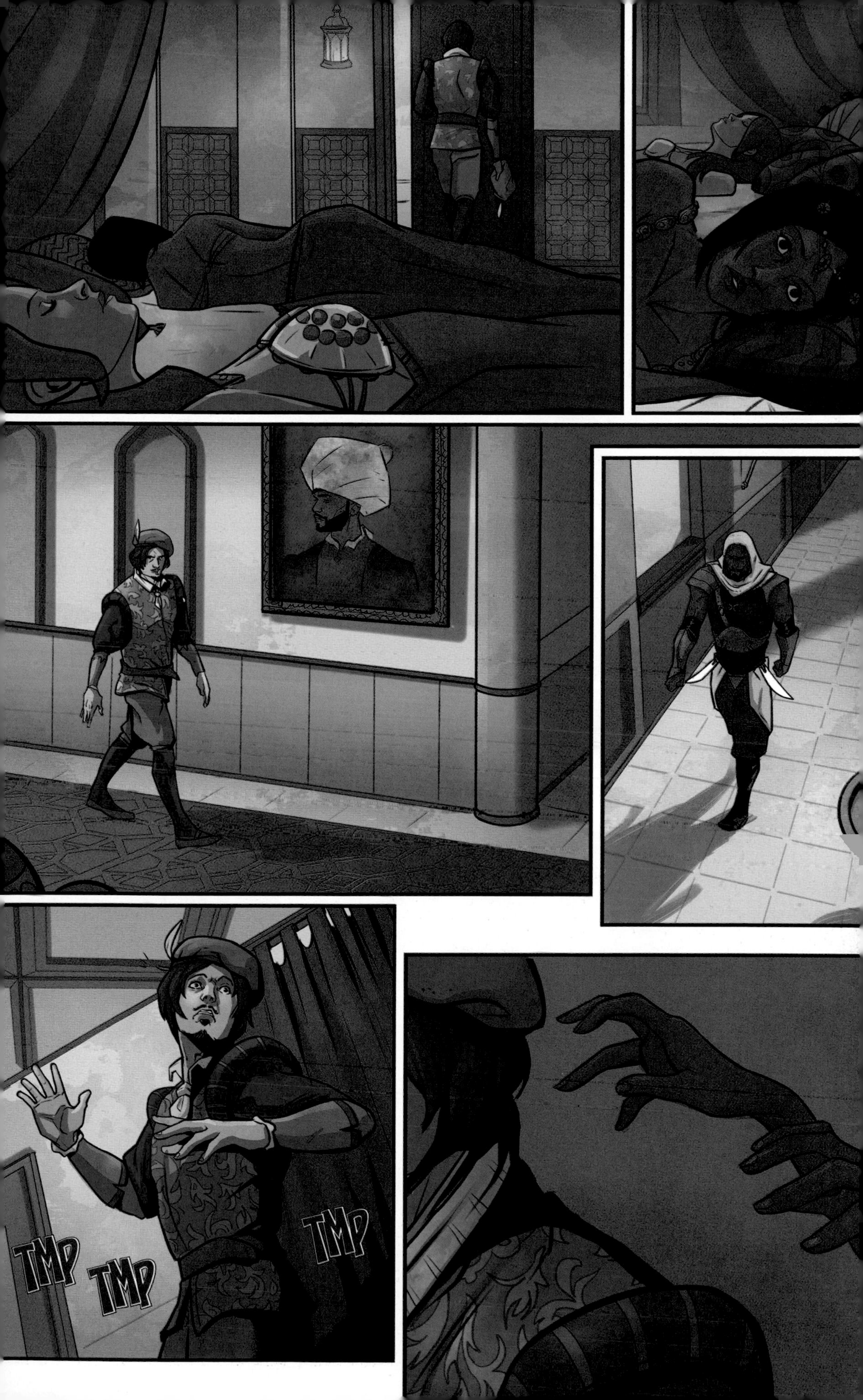
TMP
TMP
TMP

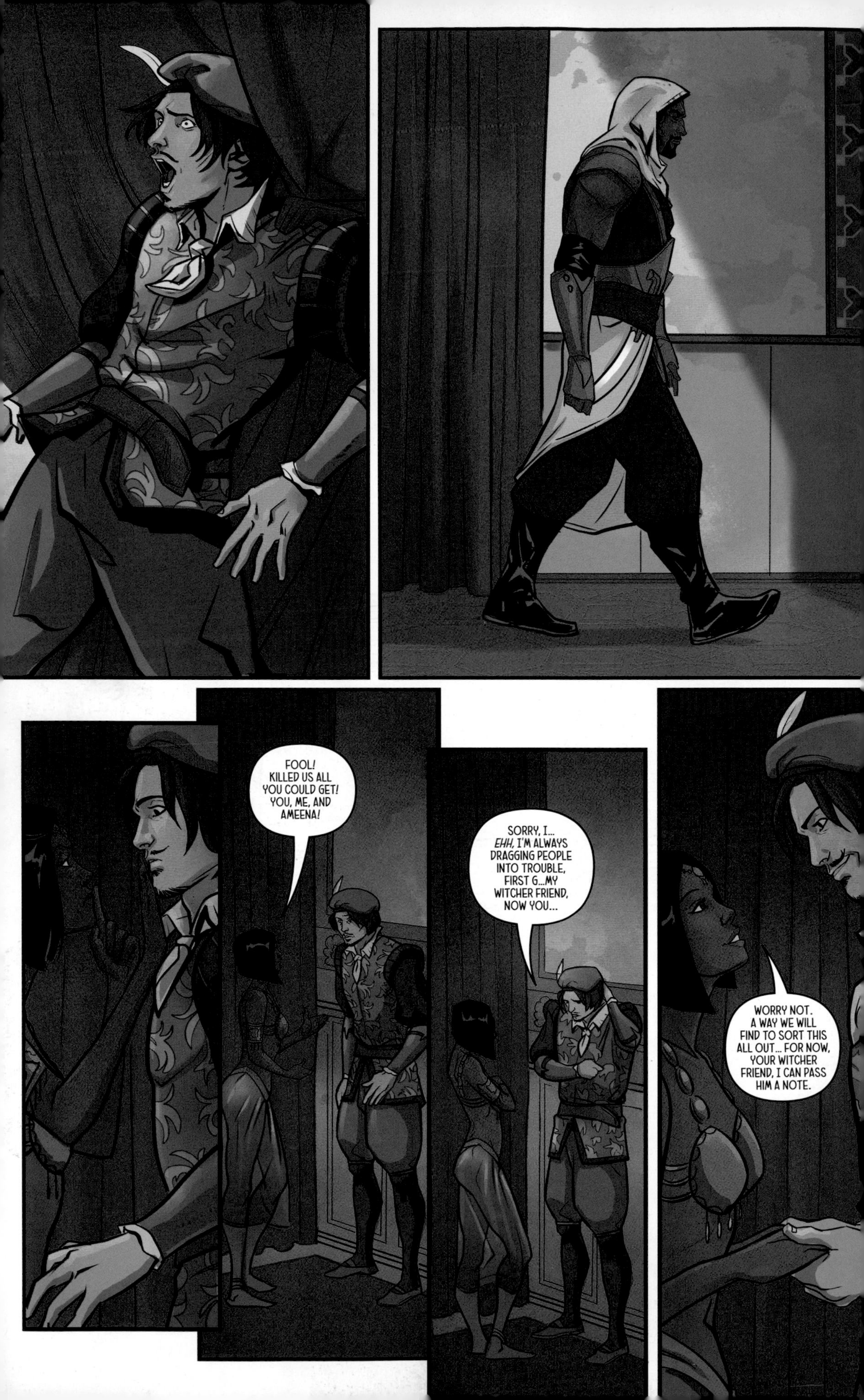
FOOL!
KILLED US ALL
YOU COULD GET!
YOU, ME, AND
AMEENA!
SORRY, I...
EHH, I'M ALWAYS
DRAGGING PEOPLE
INTO TROUBLE,
FIRST G...MY
WITCHER FRIEND,
NOW YOU...
WORRY NOT.
A WAY WE WILL
FIND TO SORT THIS
ALL OUT... FOR NOW,
YOUR WITCHER
FRIEND, I CAN PASS
HIM A NOTE.

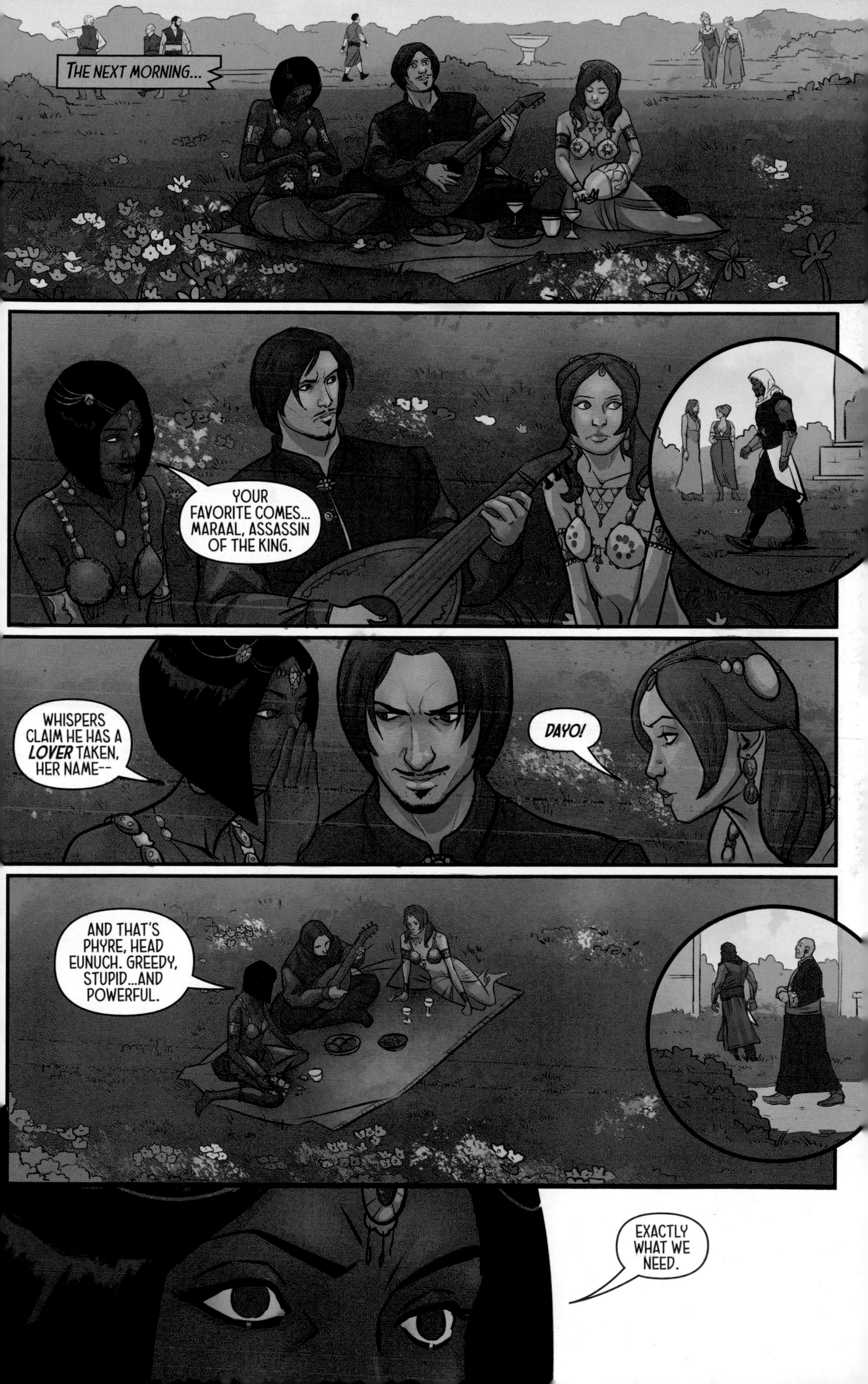
THE NEXT MORNING...
YOUR FAVORITE COMES... MARAAL, ASSASSIN OF THE KING.
WHISPERS CLAIM HE HAS A LOVER TAKEN, HER NAME--
DAYO!
AND THAT'S PHYRE, HEAD EUNUCH. GREEDY, STUPID...AND POWERFUL.
EXACTLY WHAT WE NEED.

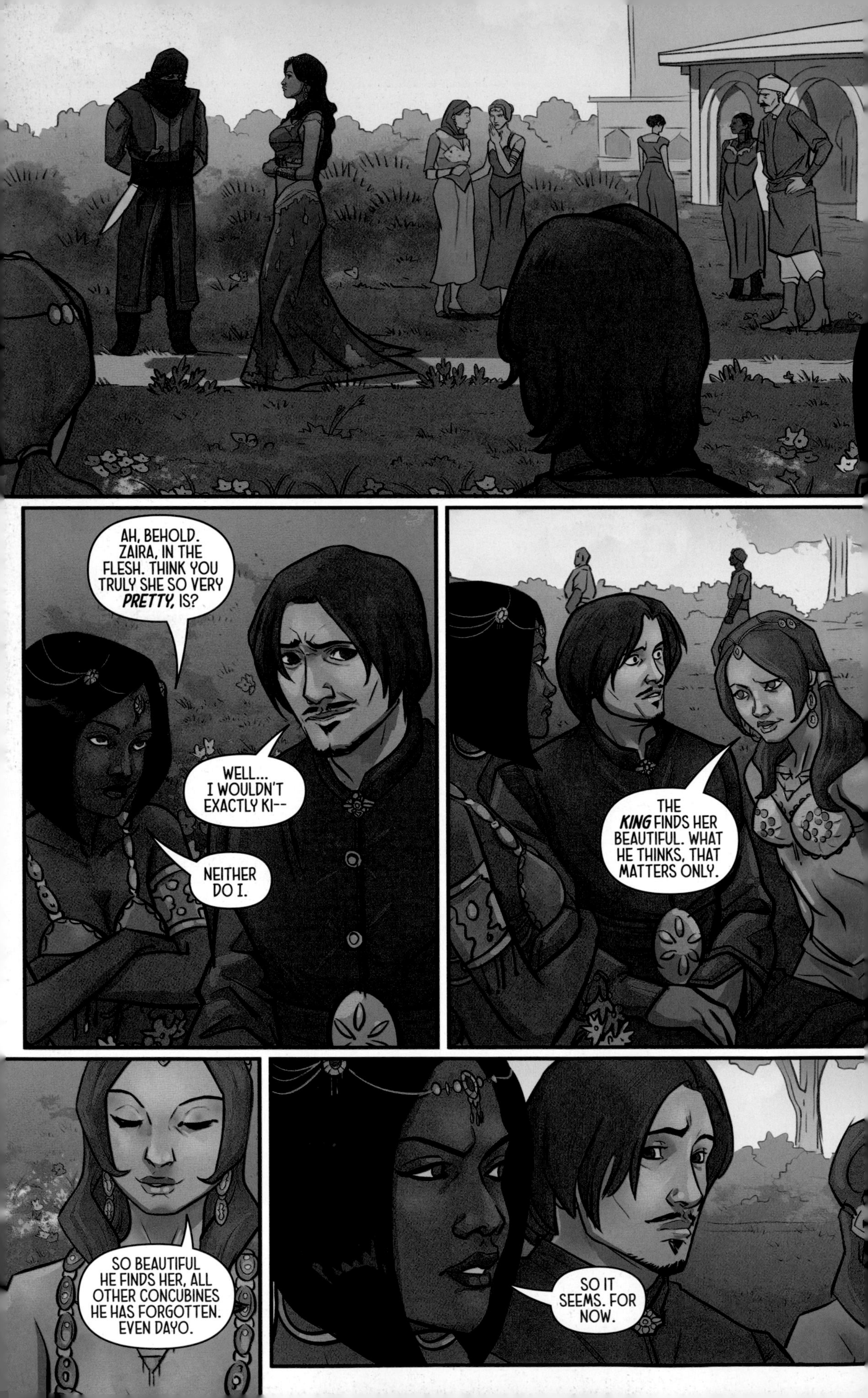
AH, BEHOLD. ZAIRA, IN THE FLESH. THINK YOU TRULY SHE SO VERY *PRETTY,* IS?
WELL... I WOULDN'T EXACTLY KI--
NEITHER DO I.
THE *KING* FINDS HER BEAUTIFUL. WHAT HE THINKS, THAT MATTERS ONLY.
SO BEAUTIFUL HE FINDS HER, ALL OTHER CONCUBINES HE HAS FORGOTTEN. EVEN DAYO.
SO IT SEEMS. FOR NOW.

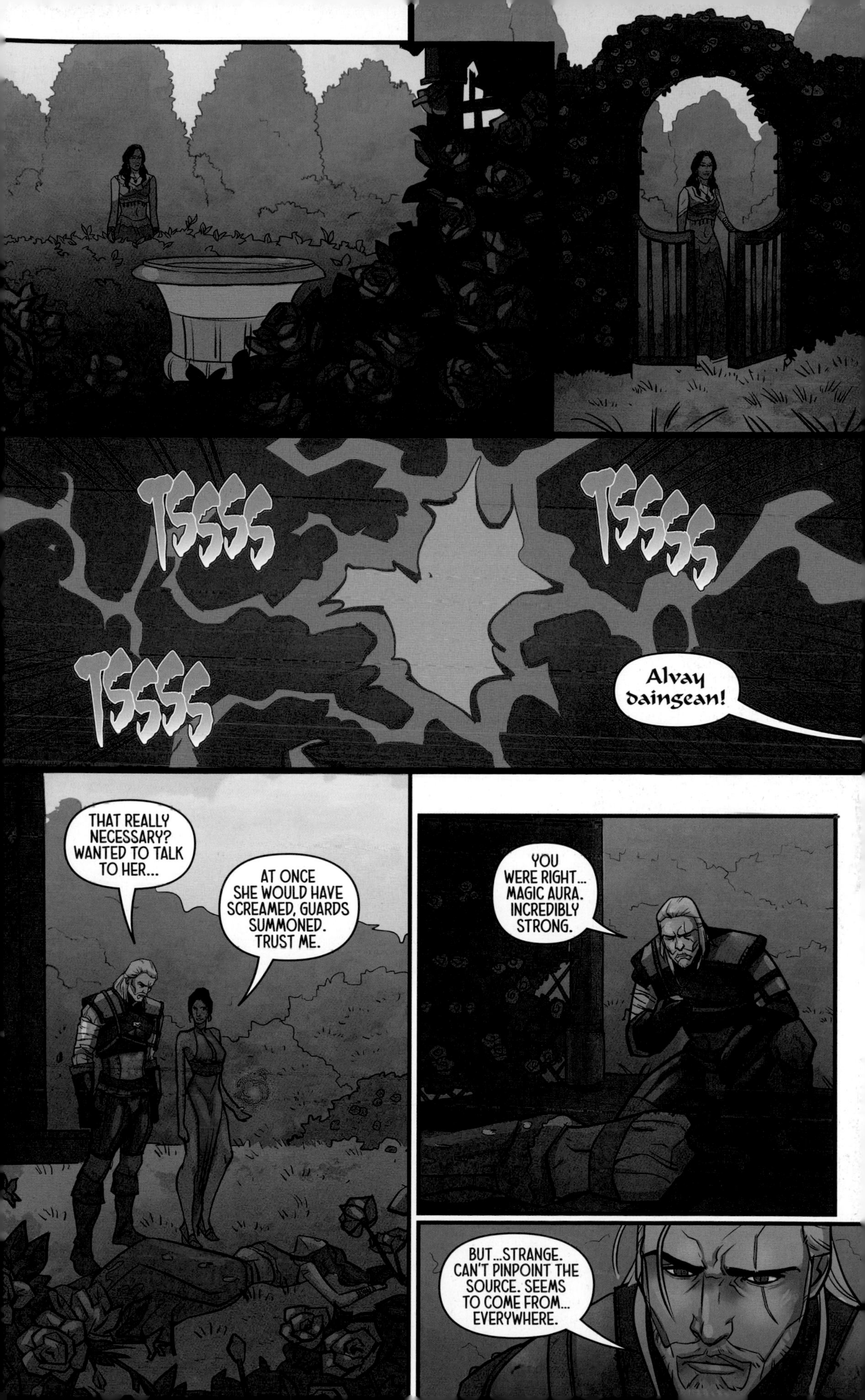
TSSSS
TSSSS
TSSSS
Alvay daingean!
THAT REALLY NECESSARY? WANTED TO TALK TO HER...
AT ONCE SHE WOULD HAVE SCREAMED, GUARDS SUMMONED. TRUST ME.
YOU WERE RIGHT... MAGIC AURA. INCREDIBLY STRONG.
BUT...STRANGE. CAN'T PINPOINT THE SOURCE. SEEMS TO COME FROM... EVERYWHERE.

WHAT'S THAT?

EYE OF NEHALENI. DISPELS MAGIC ILLUSIONS. LET'S SEE...

CRACK!

OH NO. HAVE YOU OTHERS?

WHAT THE...? NO. *HM*, BRACELETS SEEM UNUSUAL.

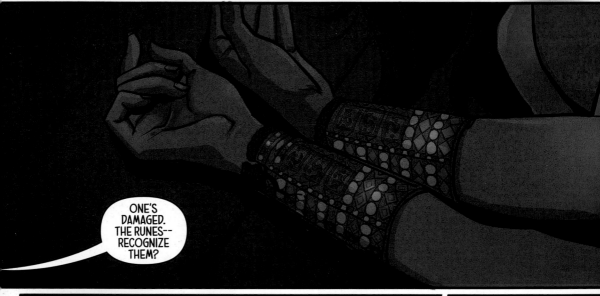

ONE'S DAMAGED. THE RUNES-- RECOGNIZE THEM?

CHARMS, MERELY. FOR GOOD LUCK. IN OFIER ALL WEAR THEM.

SOMEONE COMES. QUICKLY!

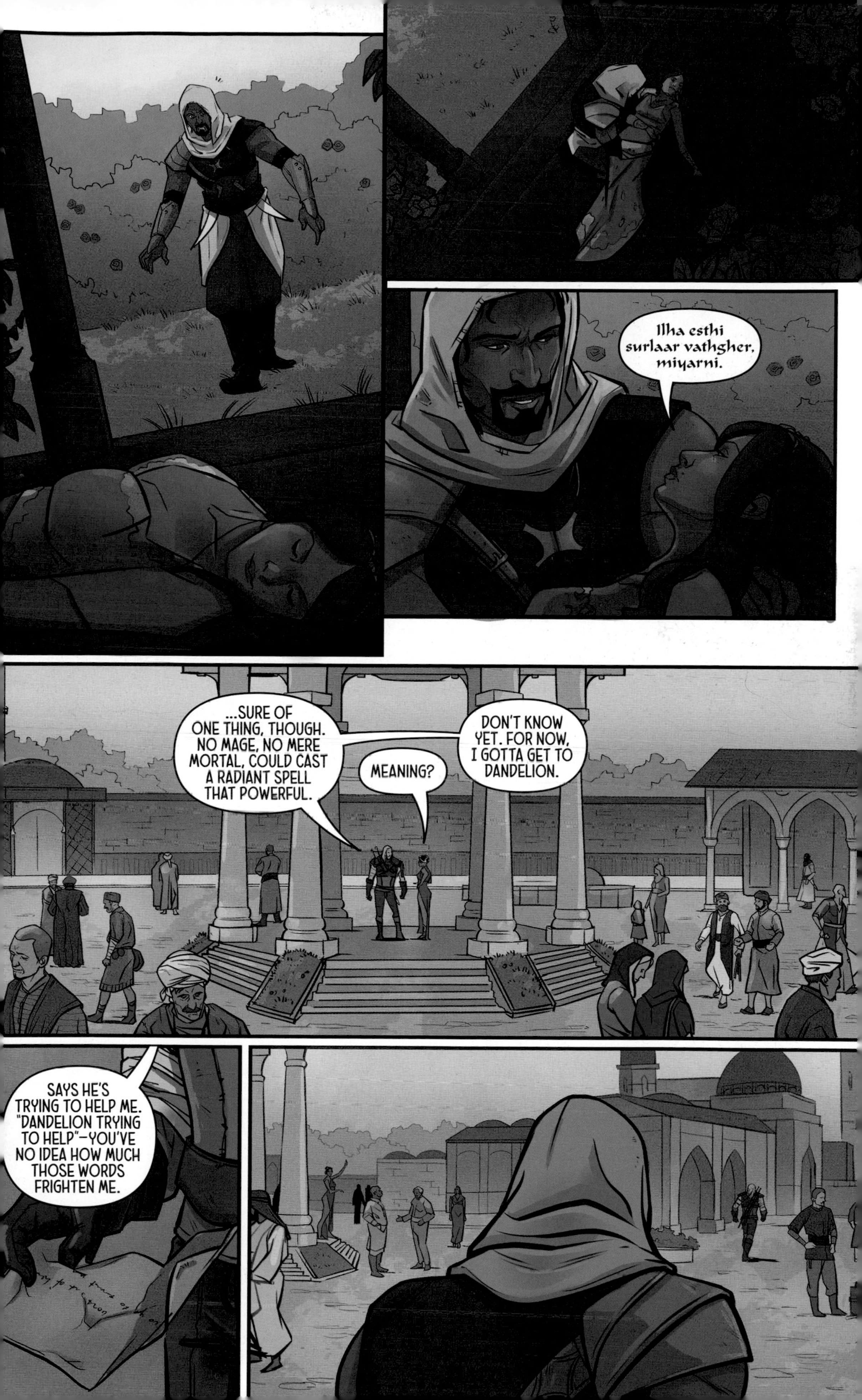
Ilha esthi surlaar vathgher, miyarni.
...SURE OF ONE THING, THOUGH. NO MAGE, NO MERE MORTAL, COULD CAST A RADIANT SPELL THAT POWERFUL.
MEANING?
DON'T KNOW YET. FOR NOW, I GOTTA GET TO DANDELION.
SAYS HE'S TRYING TO HELP ME. "DANDELION TRYING TO HELP"—YOU'VE NO IDEA HOW MUCH THOSE WORDS FRIGHTEN ME.

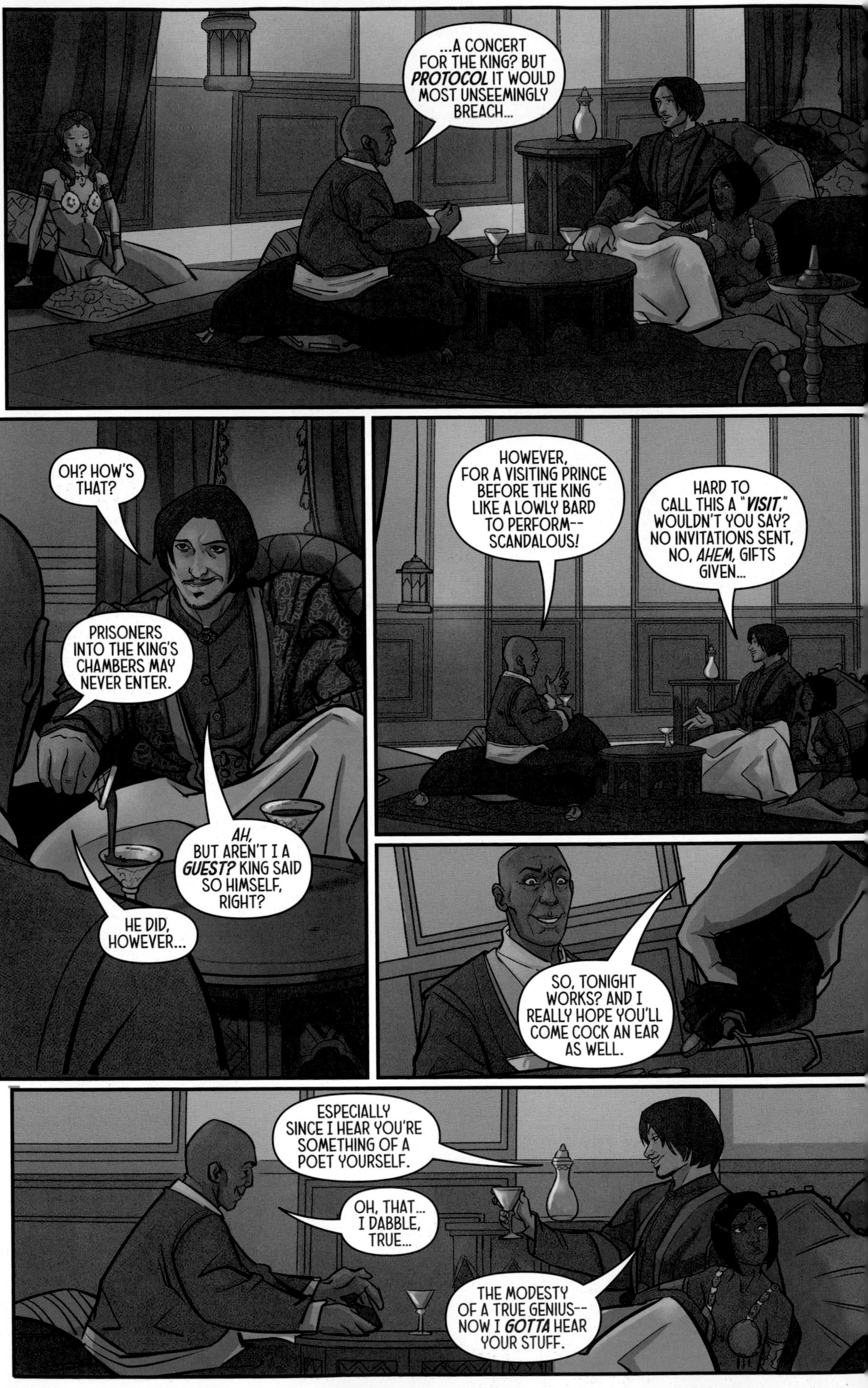
...A CONCERT FOR THE KING? BUT PROTOCOL IT WOULD MOST UNSEEMINGLY BREACH...
OH? HOW'S THAT?
PRISONERS INTO THE KING'S CHAMBERS MAY NEVER ENTER.
AH, BUT AREN'T I A GUEST? KING SAID SO HIMSELF, RIGHT?
HE DID, HOWEVER...
HOWEVER, FOR A VISITING PRINCE BEFORE THE KING LIKE A LOWLY BARD TO PERFORM-- SCANDALOUS!
HARD TO CALL THIS A "VISIT," WOULDN'T YOU SAY? NO INVITATIONS SENT, NO, AHEM, GIFTS GIVEN...
SO, TONIGHT WORKS? AND I REALLY HOPE YOU'LL COME COCK AN EAR AS WELL.
ESPECIALLY SINCE I HEAR YOU'RE SOMETHING OF A POET YOURSELF.
OH, THAT... I DABBLE, TRUE...
THE MODESTY OF A TRUE GENIUS-- NOW I GOTTA HEAR YOUR STUFF.

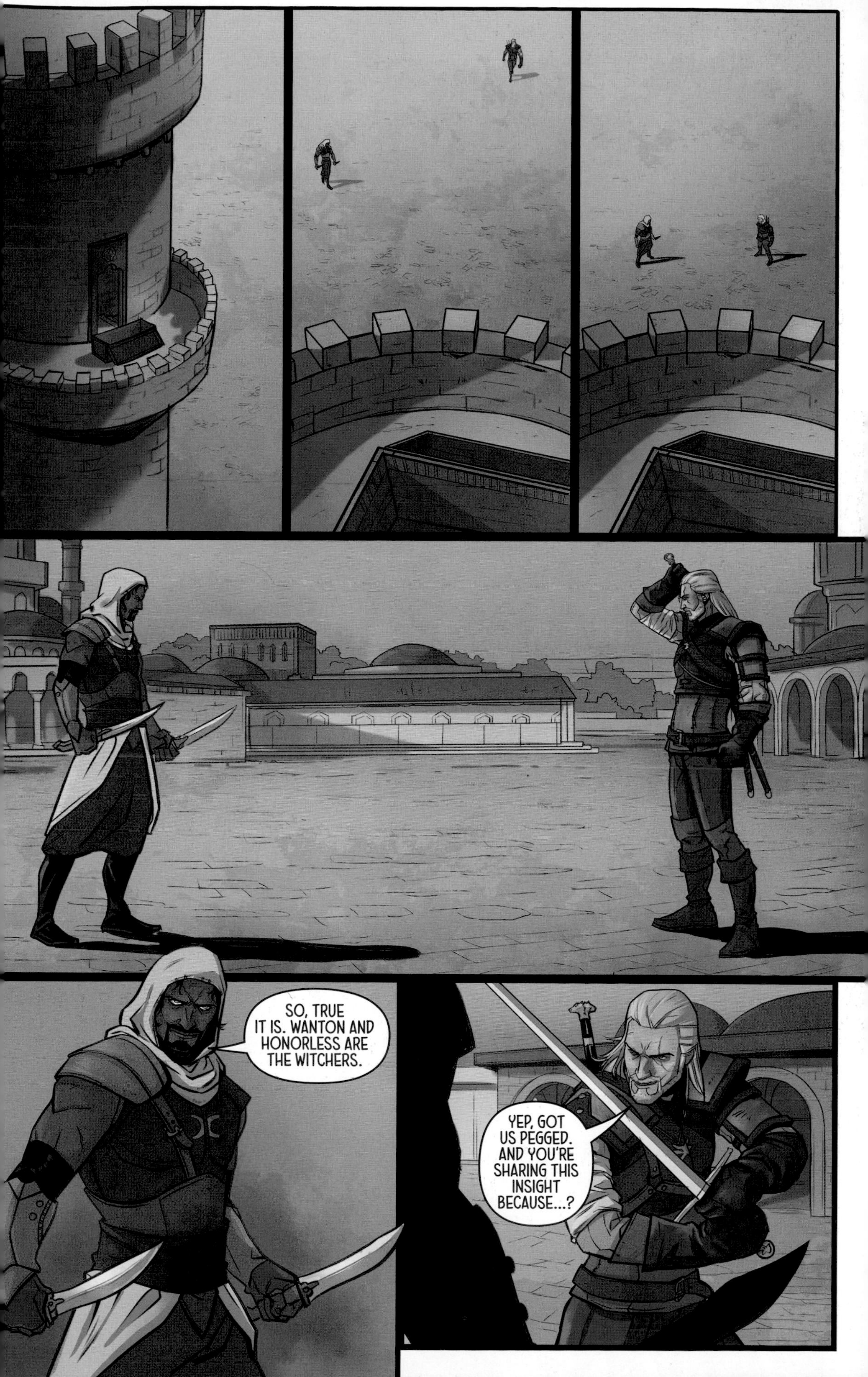
SO, TRUE
IT IS. WANTON AND
HONORLESS ARE
THE WITCHERS.
YEP, GOT
US PEGGED.
AND YOU'RE
SHARING THIS
INSIGHT
BECAUSE...?

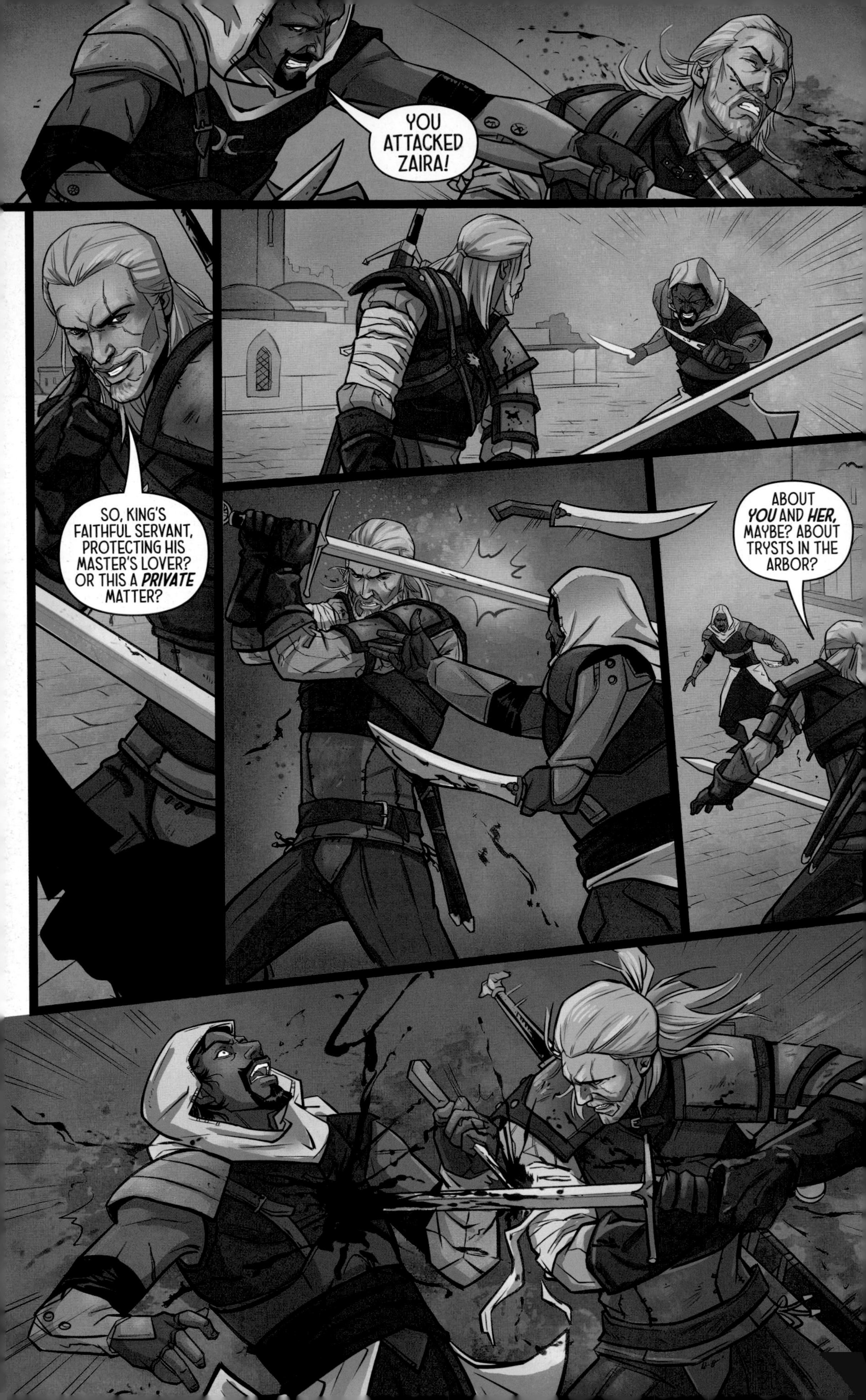
YOU ATTACKED ZAIRA!
SO, KING'S FAITHFUL SERVANT, PROTECTING HIS MASTER'S LOVER? OR THIS A *PRIVATE* MATTER?
ABOUT *YOU* AND *HER,* MAYBE? ABOUT TRYSTS IN THE ARBOR?

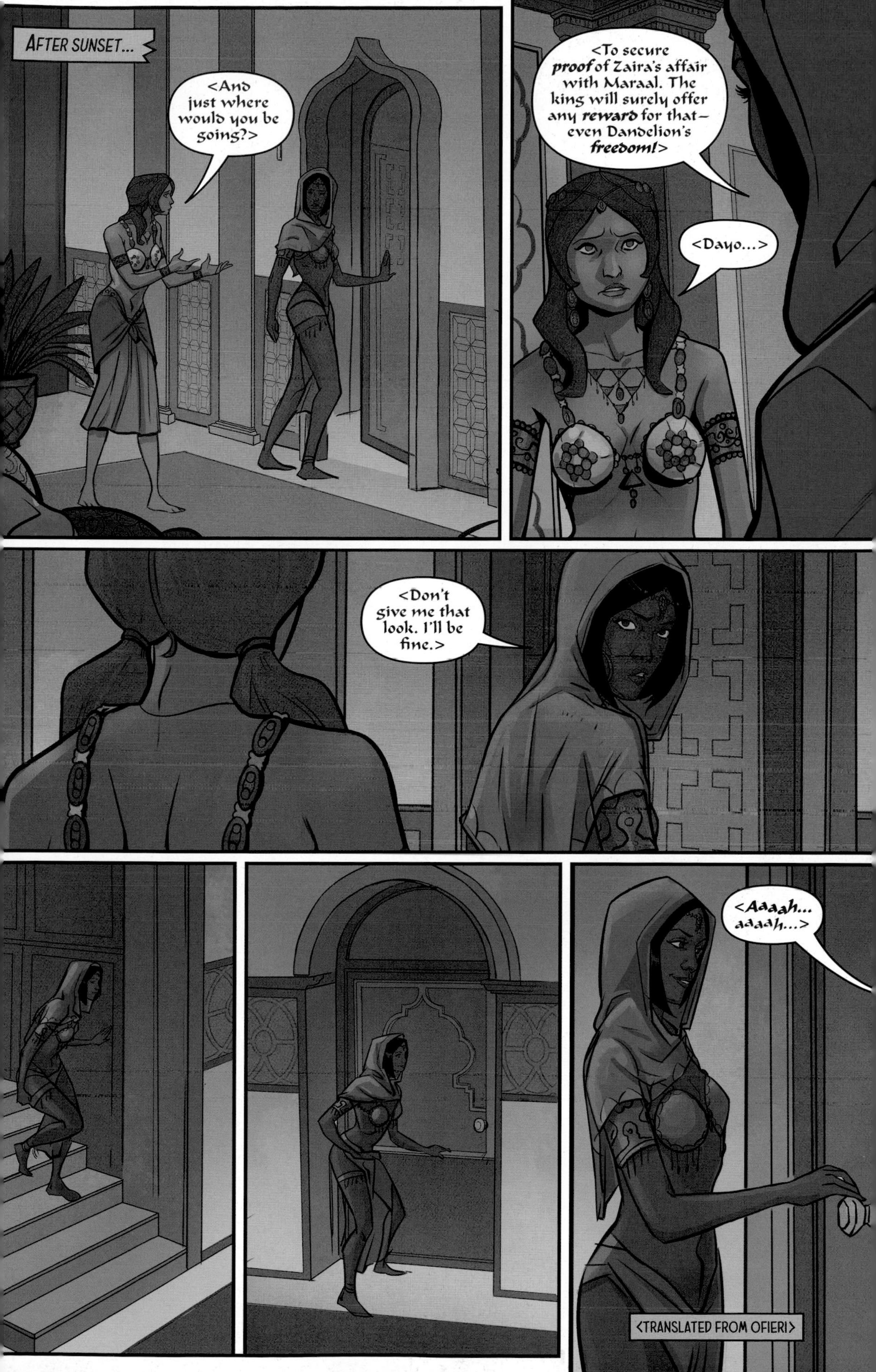
AFTER SUNSET...
<And just where would you be going?>
<To secure proof of Zaira's affair with Maraal. The king will surely offer any reward for that—even Dandelion's freedom!>
<Dayo...>
<Don't give me that look. I'll be fine.>
<Aaaah... aaaah...>
<TRANSLATED FROM OFIERI>

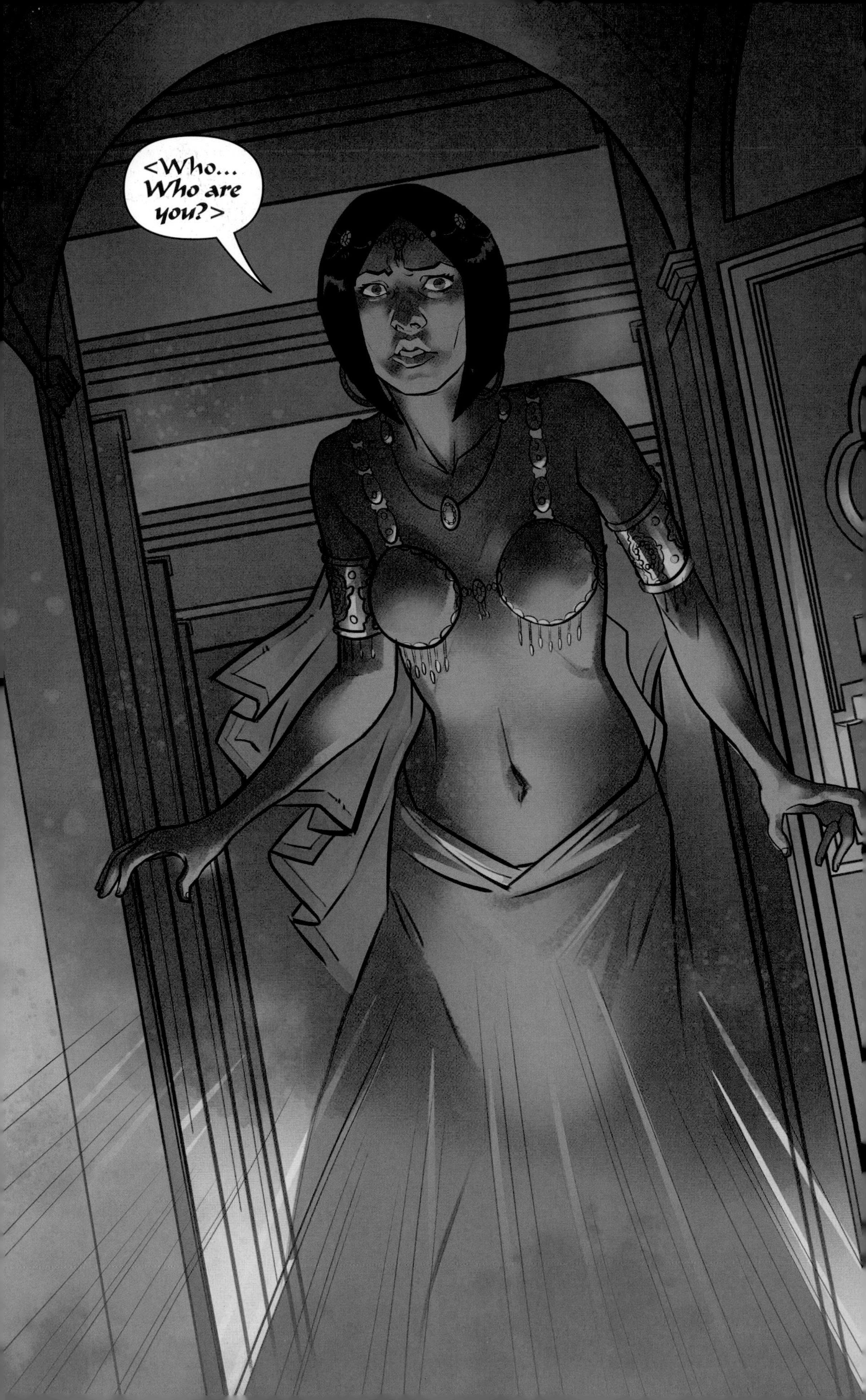
<Who... Who are you?>

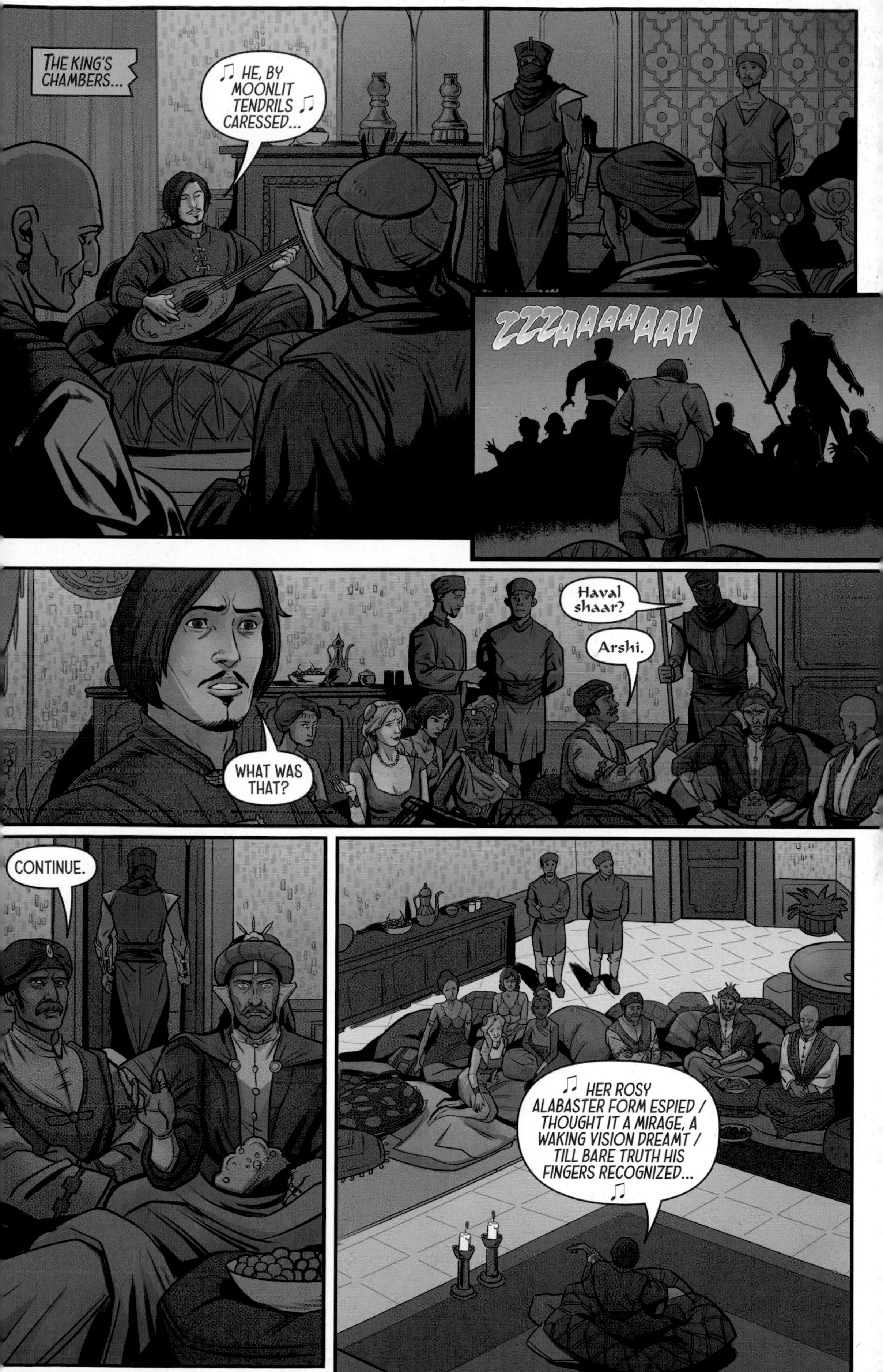
THE KING'S CHAMBERS...
♫ HE, BY MOONLIT TENDRILS ♫ CARESSED...
ZZZAAAAAAH
Haval shaar?
Arshi.
WHAT WAS THAT?
CONTINUE.
♫ HER ROSY ALABASTER FORM ESPIED / THOUGHT IT A MIRAGE, A WAKING VISION DREAMT / TILL BARE TRUTH HIS FINGERS RECOGNIZED... ♫

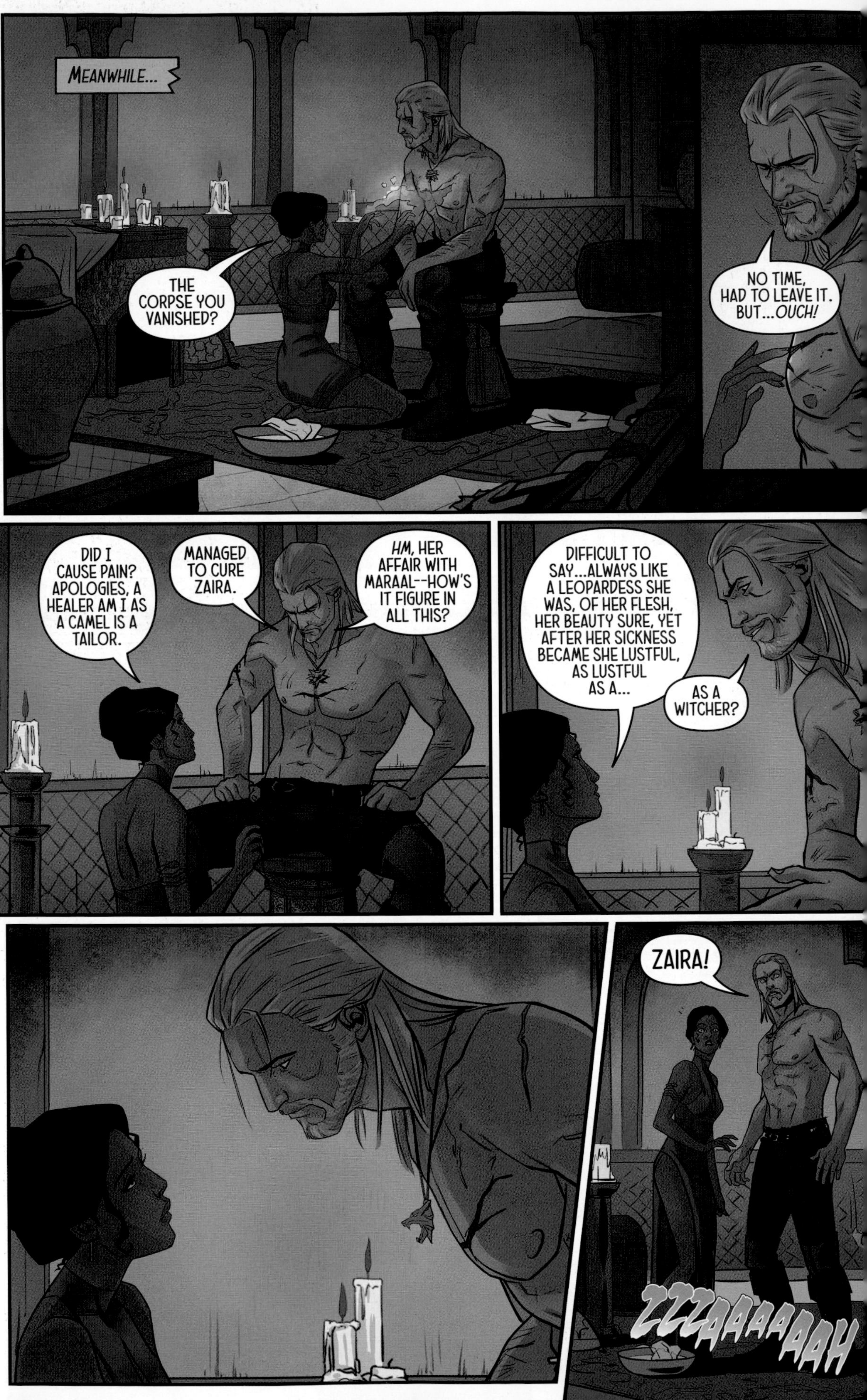
MEANWHILE...
THE CORPSE YOU VANISHED?
NO TIME, HAD TO LEAVE IT. BUT...*OUCH!*
DID I CAUSE PAIN? APOLOGIES, A HEALER AM I AS A CAMEL IS A TAILOR.
MANAGED TO CURE ZAIRA.
HM, HER AFFAIR WITH MARAAL--HOW'S IT FIGURE IN ALL THIS?
DIFFICULT TO SAY...ALWAYS LIKE A LEOPARDESS SHE WAS, OF HER FLESH, HER BEAUTY SURE, YET AFTER HER SICKNESS BECAME SHE LUSTFUL, AS LUSTFUL AS A...
AS A WITCHER?
ZAIRA!
ZZZAAAAAAAH

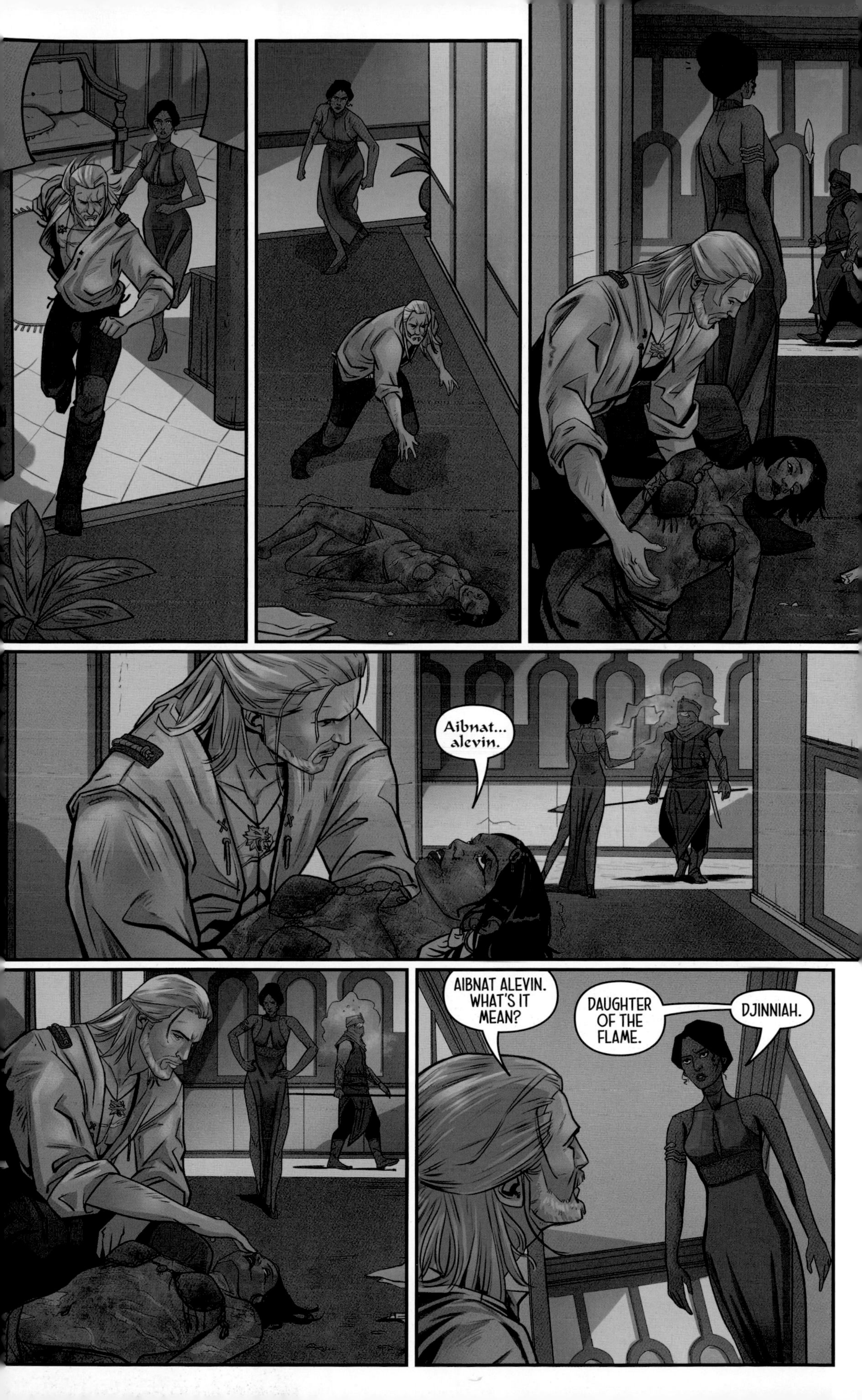
Aibnat... alevin.
AIBNAT ALEVIN. WHAT'S IT MEAN?
DAUGHTER OF THE FLAME.
DJINNIAH.

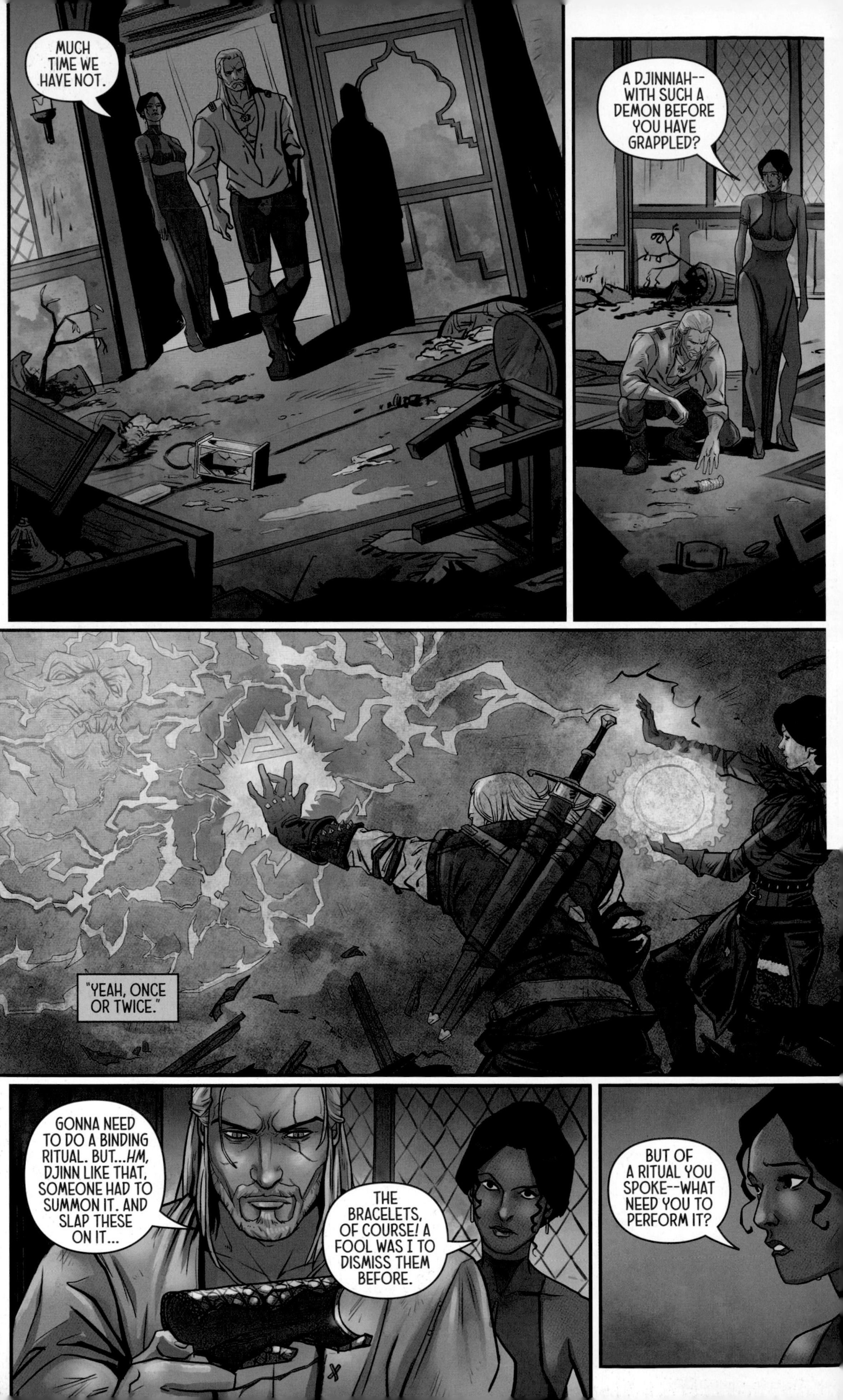
MUCH TIME WE HAVE NOT.
A DJINNIAH-- WITH SUCH A DEMON BEFORE YOU HAVE GRAPPLED?
"YEAH, ONCE OR TWICE."
GONNA NEED TO DO A BINDING RITUAL. BUT...HM, DJINN LIKE THAT, SOMEONE HAD TO SUMMON IT. AND SLAP THESE ON IT...
THE BRACELETS, OF COURSE! A FOOL WAS I TO DISMISS THEM BEFORE.
BUT OF A RITUAL YOU SPOKE--WHAT NEED YOU TO PERFORM IT?

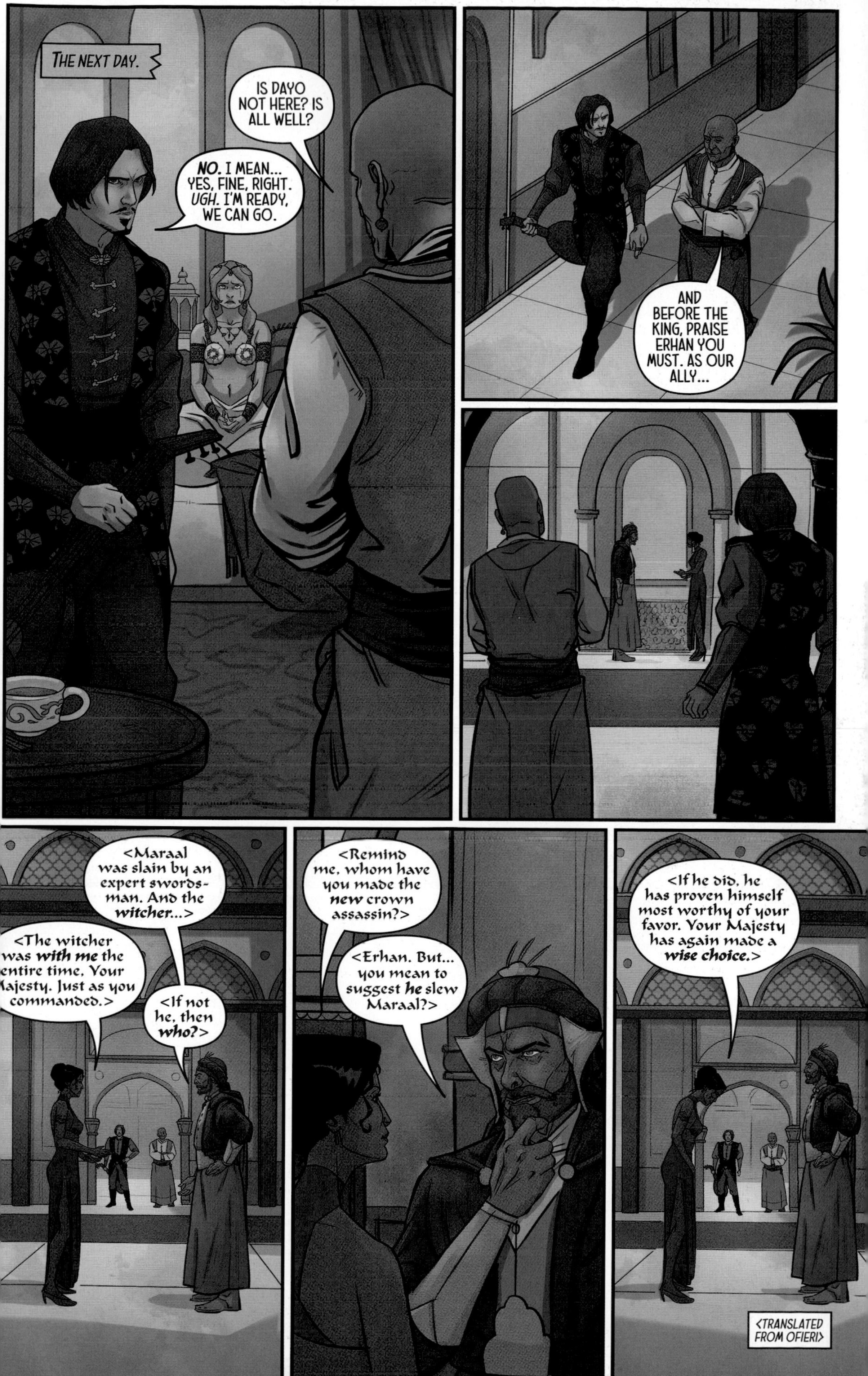
THE NEXT DAY.
IS DAYO NOT HERE? IS ALL WELL?
NO. I MEAN... YES, FINE, RIGHT. UGH. I'M READY, WE CAN GO.
AND BEFORE THE KING, PRAISE ERHAN YOU MUST. AS OUR ALLY...
<Maraal was slain by an expert swordsman. And the witcher...>
<The witcher was with me the entire time. Your Majesty. Just as you commanded.>
<If not he, then who?>
<Remind me, whom have you made the new crown assassin?>
<Erhan. But... you mean to suggest he slew Maraal?>
<If he did, he has proven himself most worthy of your favor. Your Majesty has again made a wise choice.>
<TRANSLATED FROM OFIERI>

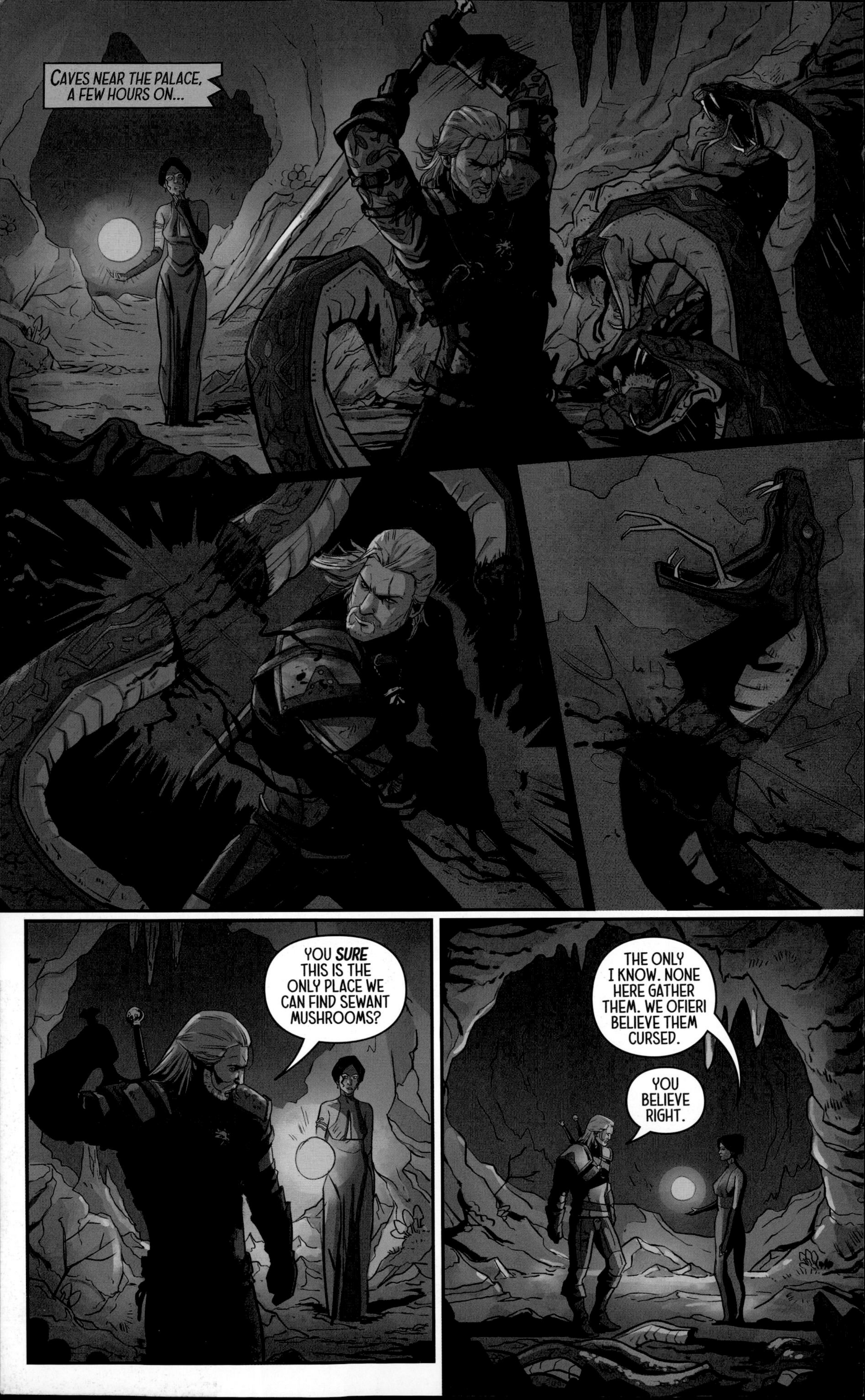
CAVES NEAR THE PALACE, A FEW HOURS ON...
YOU SURE THIS IS THE ONLY PLACE WE CAN FIND SEWANT MUSHROOMS?
THE ONLY I KNOW. NONE HERE GATHER THEM. WE OFIERI BELIEVE THEM CURSED.
YOU BELIEVE RIGHT.

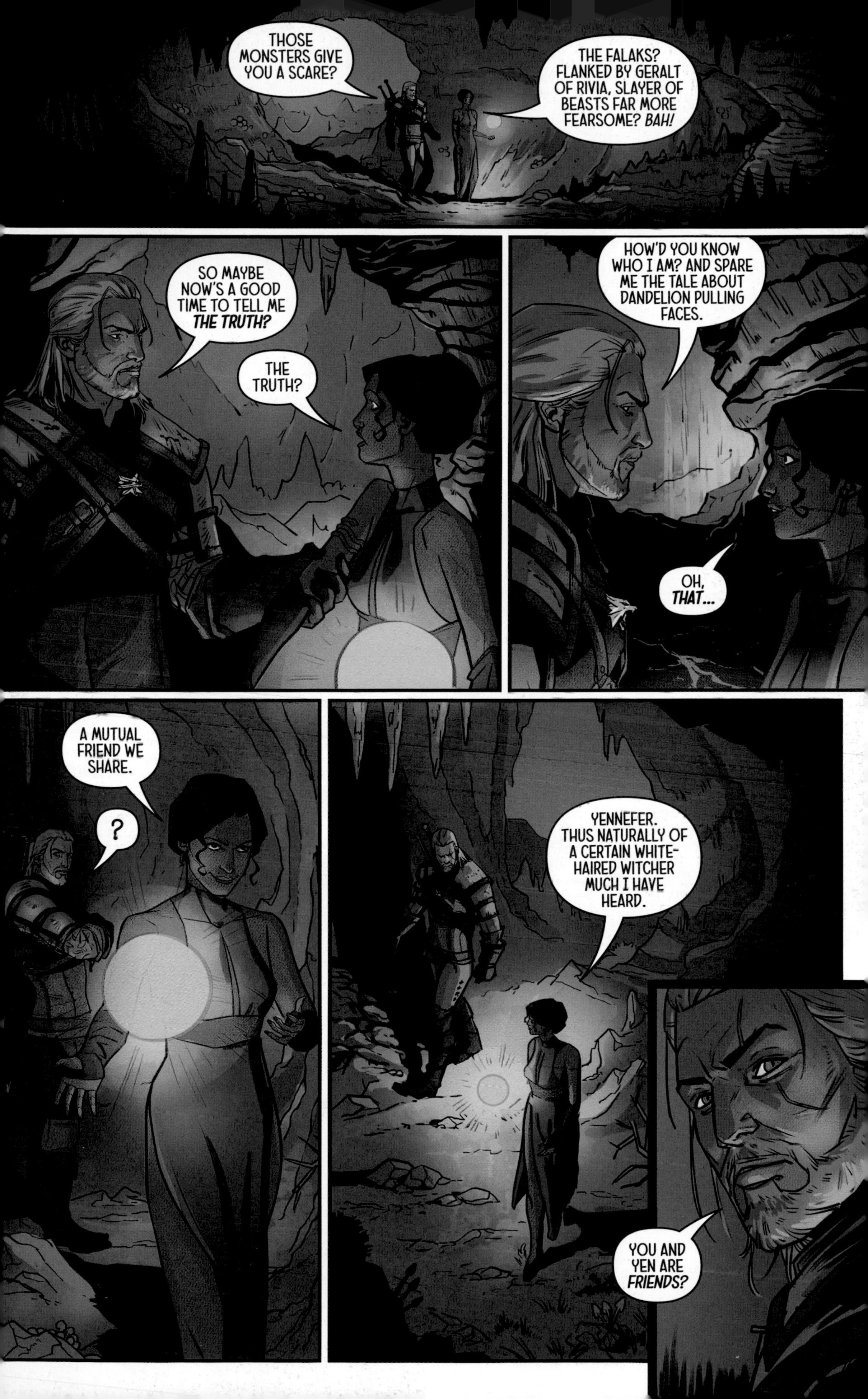
THOSE MONSTERS GIVE YOU A SCARE?
THE FALAKS? FLANKED BY GERALT OF RIVIA, SLAYER OF BEASTS FAR MORE FEARSOME? *BAH!*
SO MAYBE NOW'S A GOOD TIME TO TELL ME *THE TRUTH?*
THE TRUTH?
HOW'D YOU KNOW WHO I AM? AND SPARE ME THE TALE ABOUT DANDELION PULLING FACES.
OH, *THAT...*
A MUTUAL FRIEND WE SHARE.
?
YENNEFER. THUS NATURALLY OF A CERTAIN WHITE-HAIRED WITCHER MUCH I HAVE HEARD.
YOU AND YEN ARE *FRIENDS?*

"FRIENDS? NO, WELL, NOT *EXACTLY*.

"IN TRUTH, WHEN LAST WE MET, FROM HER I SNATCHED AN ARTIFACT OF RARE MAGIC...AND THE MAGE WITH WHOM SHE SLEPT."

THUS TO SEE HER AGAIN SOON I DO NOT *CRAVE*. SHE IS QUITE...

...*UNFORGIVING.* YEAH. I KNOW.

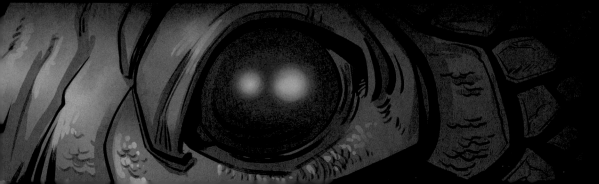

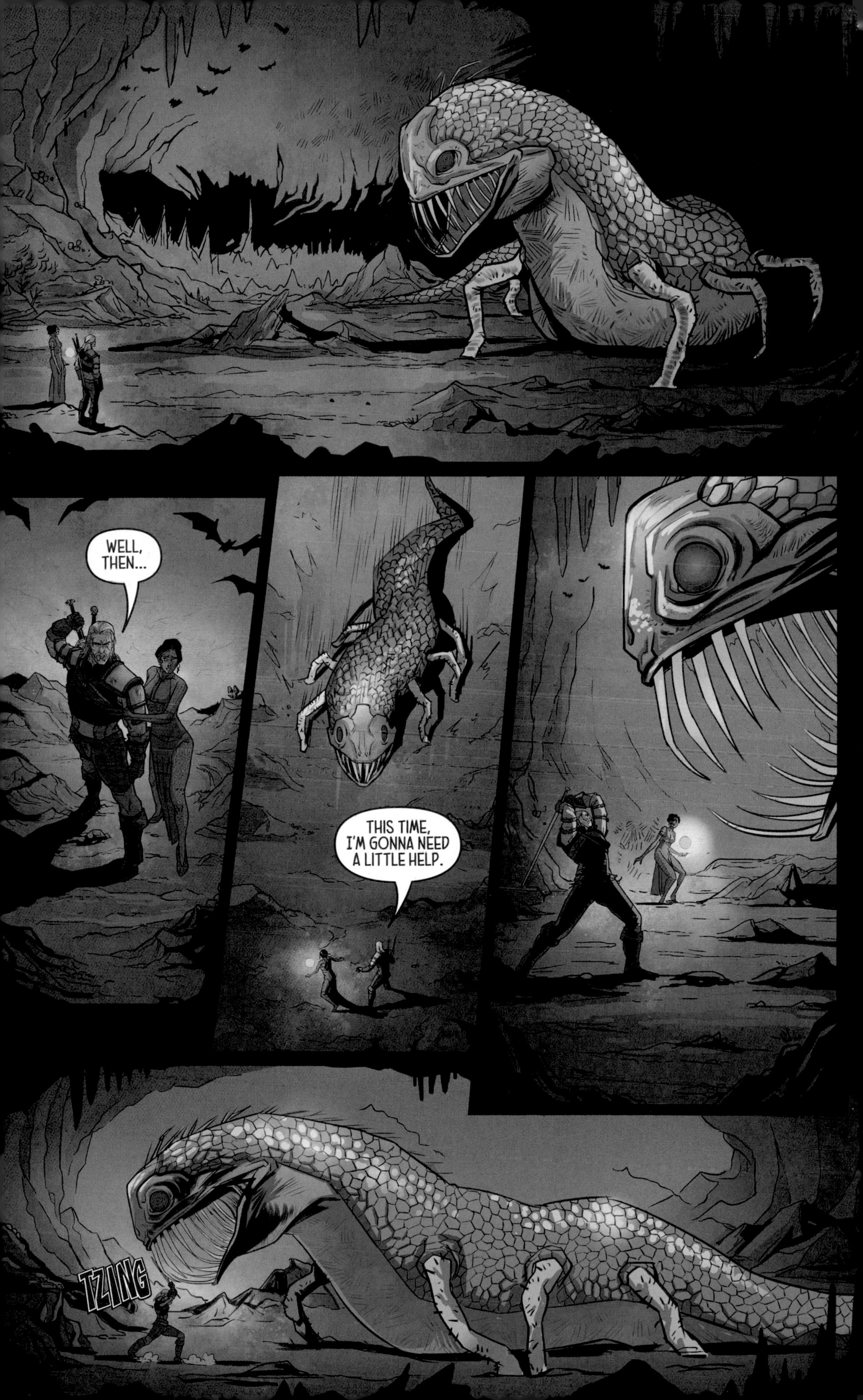
WELL, THEN...
THIS TIME, I'M GONNA NEED A LITTLE HELP.
TZING

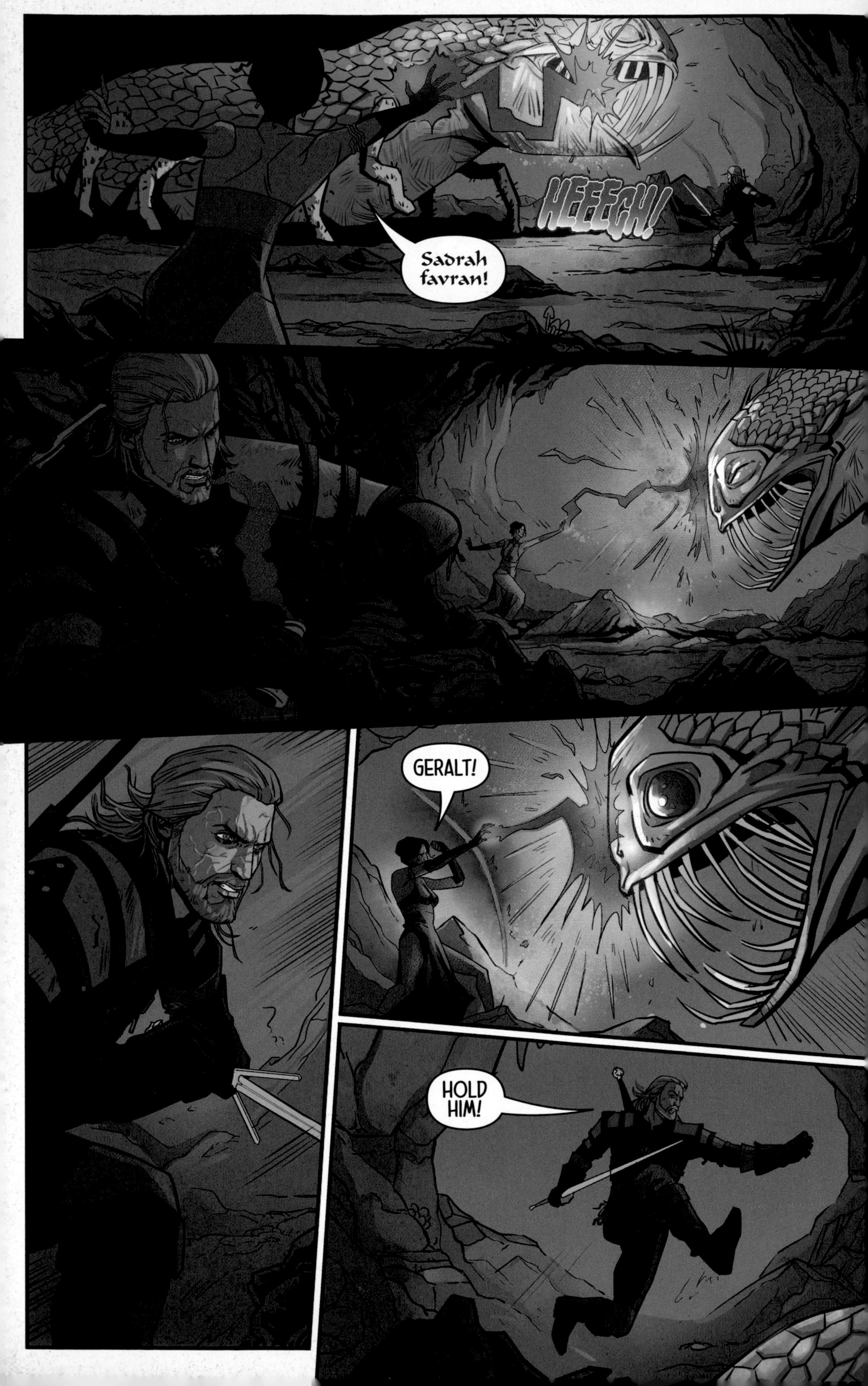
HEEECH!
Sadrah favran!
GERALT!
HOLD HIM!

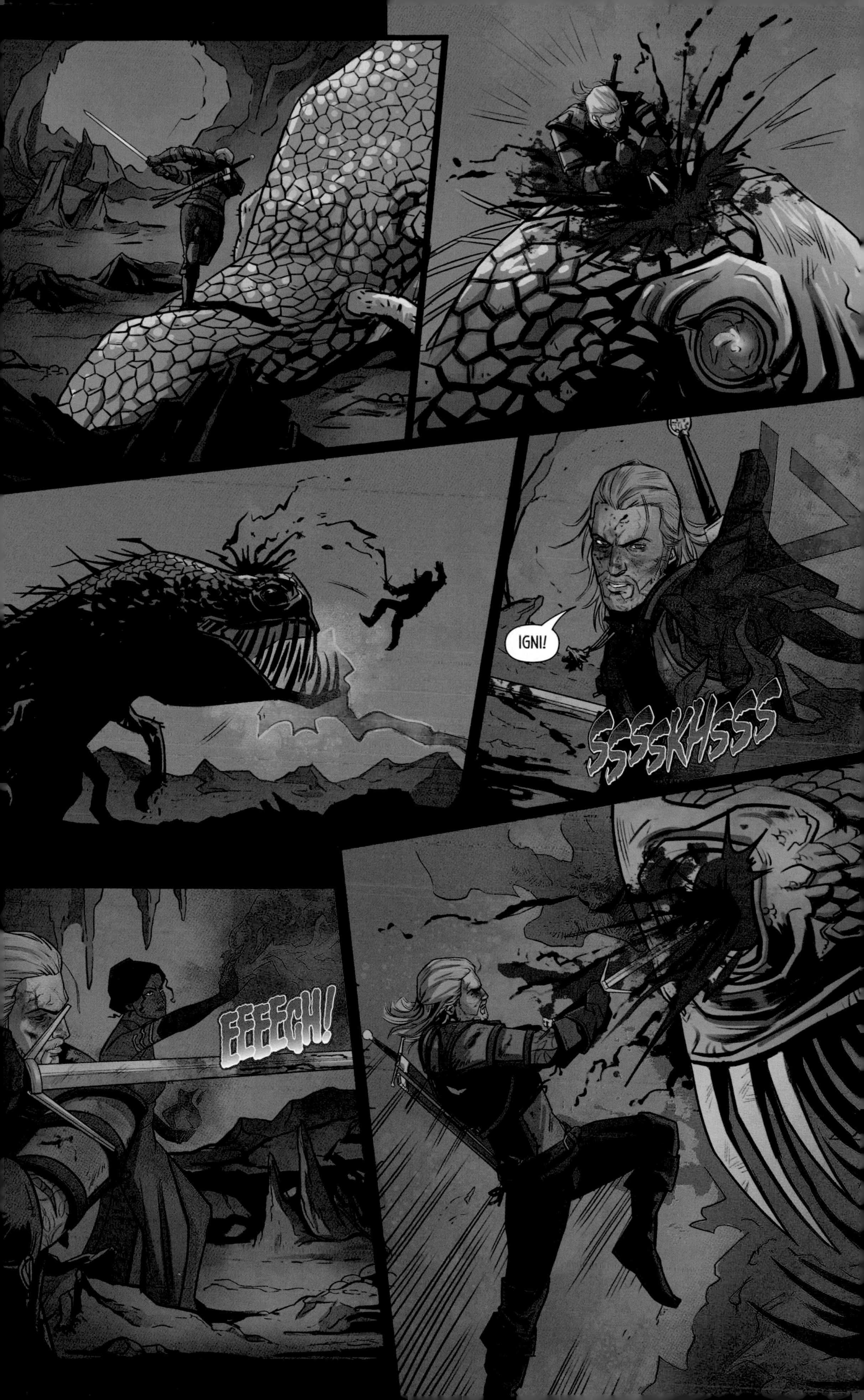
IGNI!
SSSSKHSSS
EEEECH!

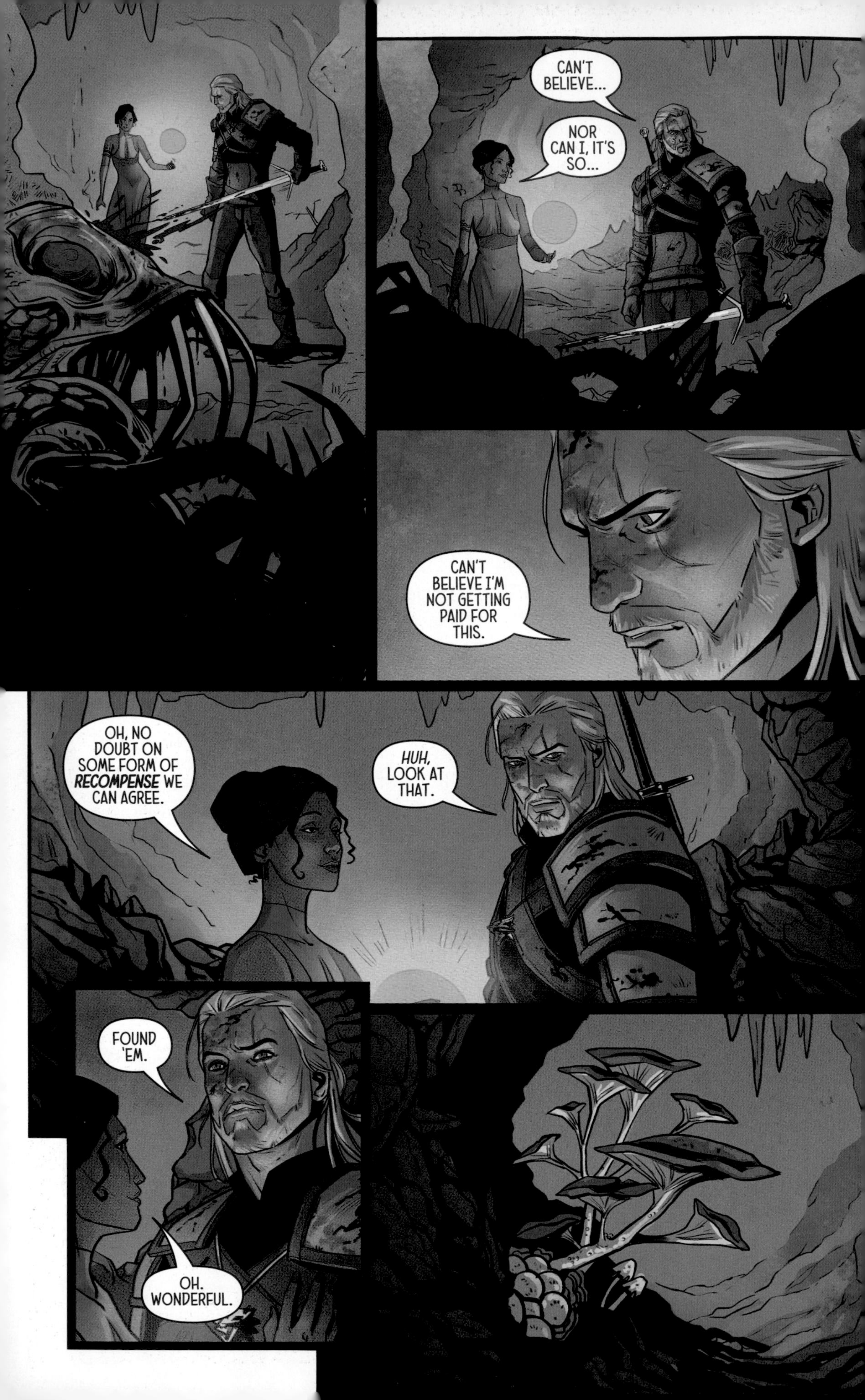
CAN'T BELIEVE...
NOR CAN I, IT'S SO...
CAN'T BELIEVE I'M NOT GETTING PAID FOR THIS.
OH, NO DOUBT ON SOME FORM OF *RECOMPENSE* WE CAN AGREE.
HUH, LOOK AT THAT.
FOUND 'EM.
OH. WONDERFUL.

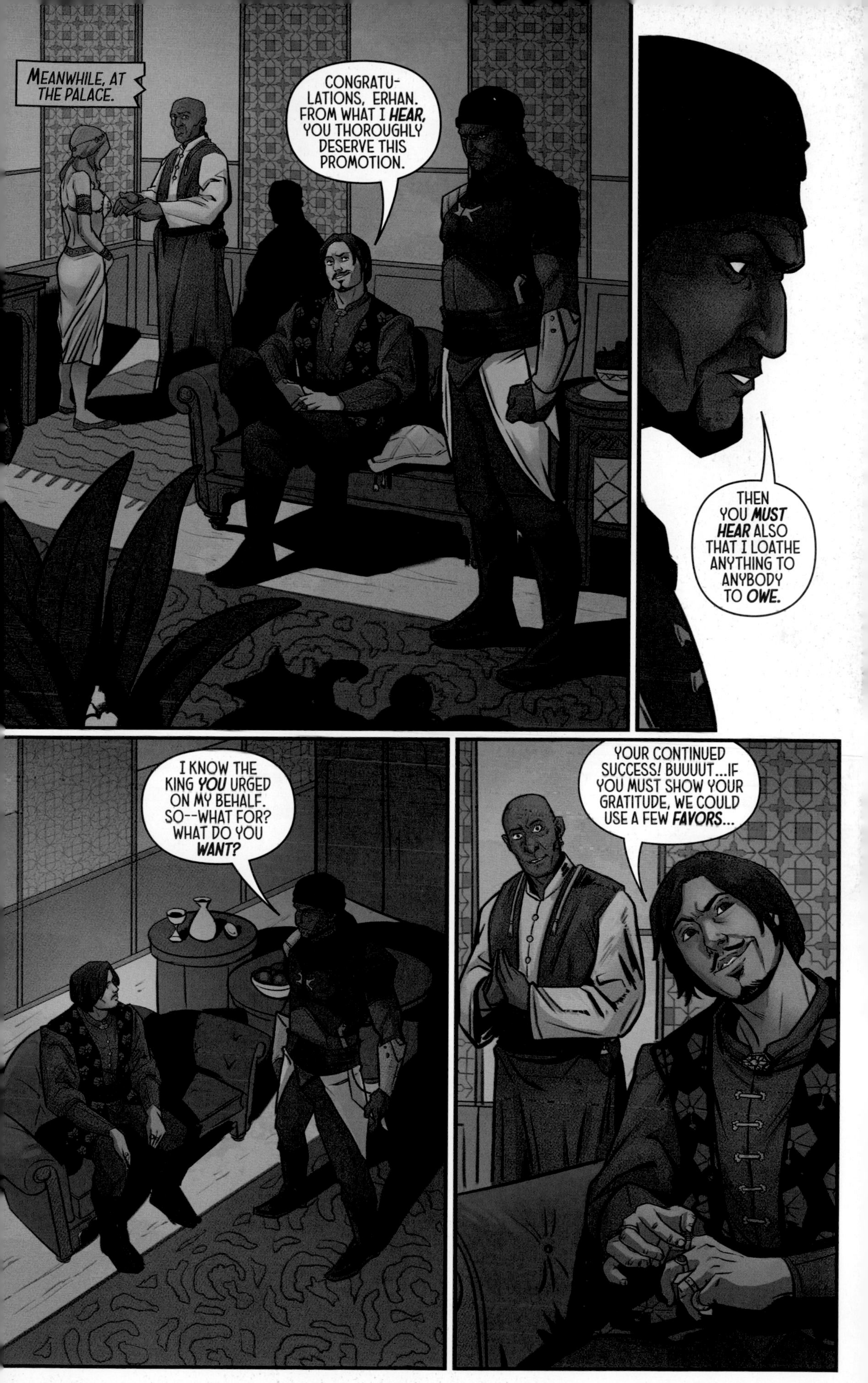
MEANWHILE, AT THE PALACE.
CONGRATULATIONS, ERHAN. FROM WHAT I HEAR, YOU THOROUGHLY DESERVE THIS PROMOTION.
THEN YOU MUST HEAR ALSO THAT I LOATHE ANYTHING TO ANYBODY TO OWE.
I KNOW THE KING YOU URGED ON MY BEHALF. SO--WHAT FOR? WHAT DO YOU WANT?
YOUR CONTINUED SUCCESS! BUUUUT...IF YOU MUST SHOW YOUR GRATITUDE, WE COULD USE A FEW FAVORS...

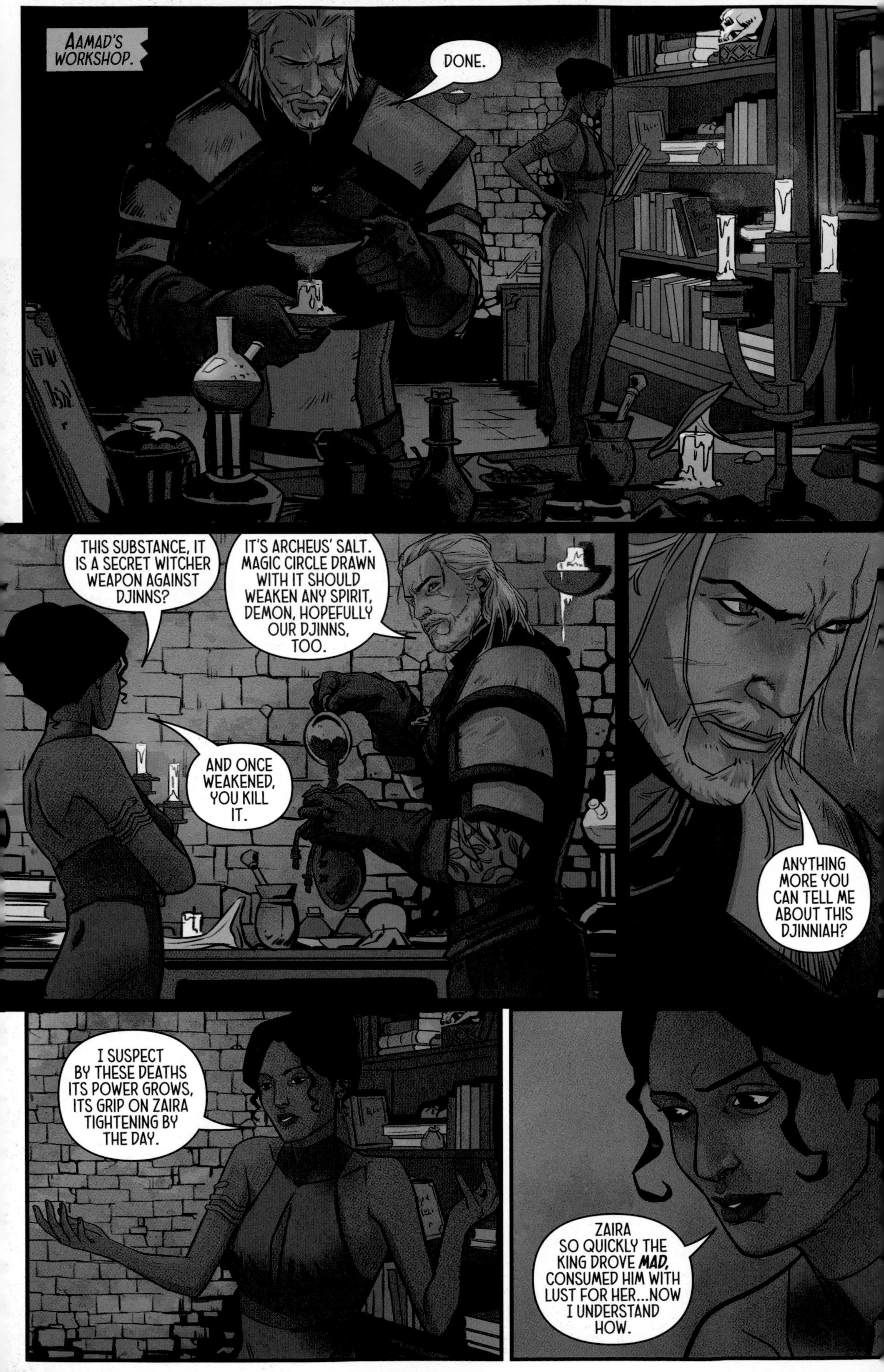
AAMAD'S WORKSHOP.
DONE.
THIS SUBSTANCE, IT IS A SECRET WITCHER WEAPON AGAINST DJINNS?
IT'S ARCHEUS' SALT. MAGIC CIRCLE DRAWN WITH IT SHOULD WEAKEN ANY SPIRIT, DEMON, HOPEFULLY OUR DJINNS, TOO.
AND ONCE WEAKENED, YOU KILL IT.
ANYTHING MORE YOU CAN TELL ME ABOUT THIS DJINNIAH?
I SUSPECT BY THESE DEATHS ITS POWER GROWS, ITS GRIP ON ZAIRA TIGHTENING BY THE DAY.
ZAIRA SO QUICKLY THE KING DROVE ***MAD,*** CONSUMED HIM WITH LUST FOR HER...NOW I UNDERSTAND HOW.

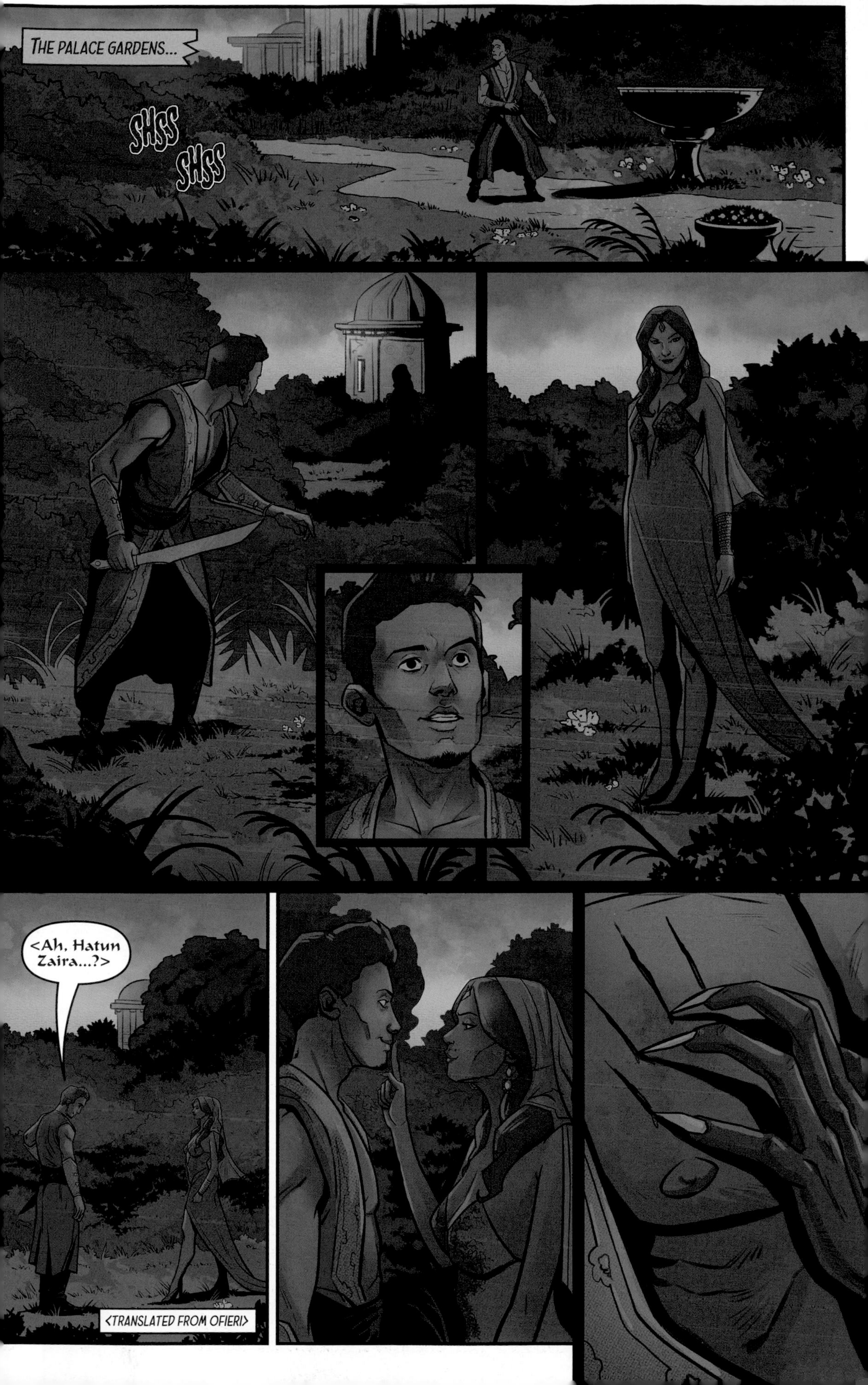
THE PALACE GARDENS...
SHSS
SHSS
<Ah, Hatun Zaira...?>
<TRANSLATED FROM OFIERI>

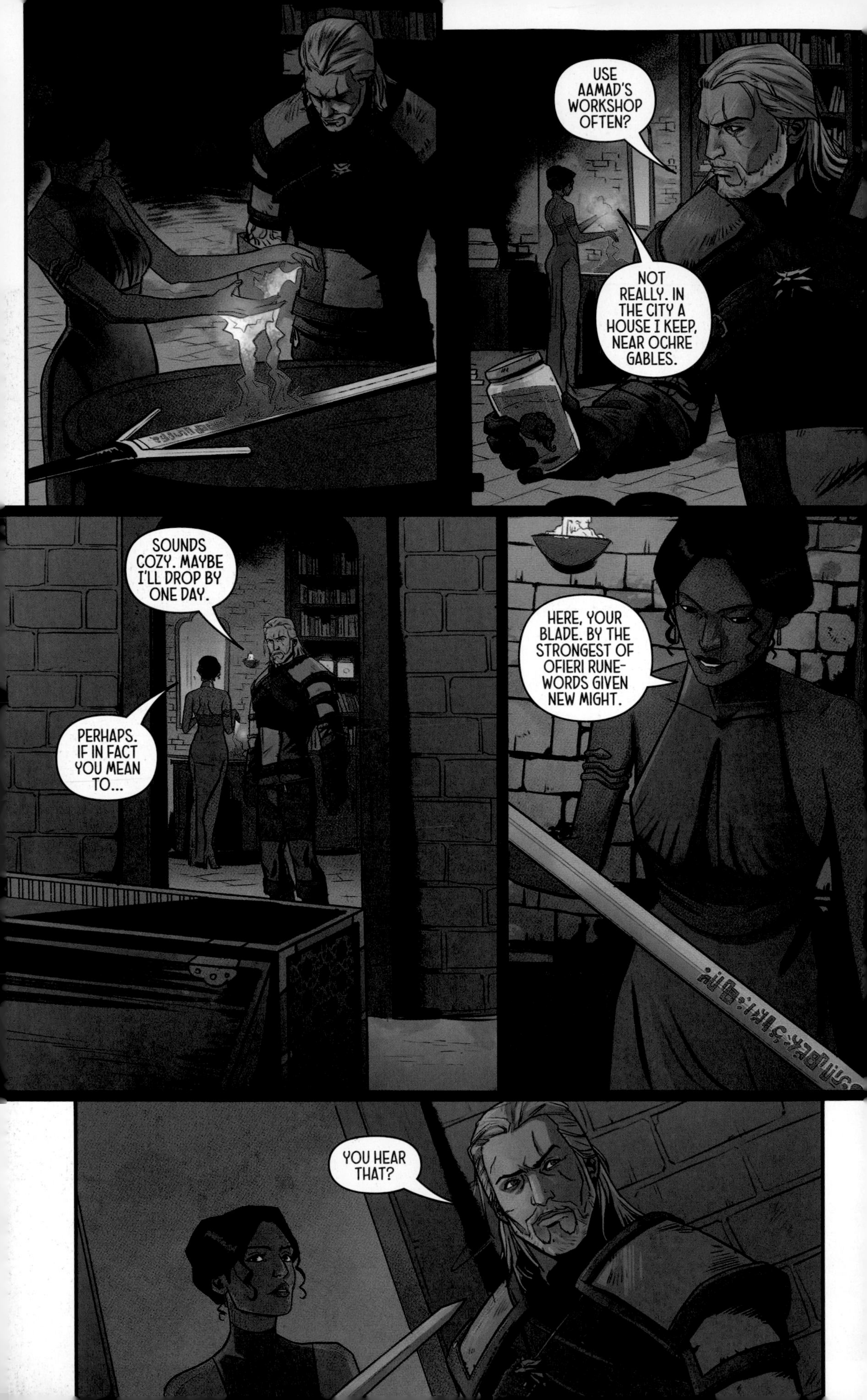
USE AAMAD'S WORKSHOP OFTEN?
NOT REALLY. IN THE CITY A HOUSE I KEEP, NEAR OCHRE GABLES.
SOUNDS COZY. MAYBE I'LL DROP BY ONE DAY.
PERHAPS. IF IN FACT YOU MEAN TO...
HERE, YOUR BLADE. BY THE STRONGEST OF OFIERI RUNE-WORDS GIVEN NEW MIGHT.
YOU HEAR THAT?

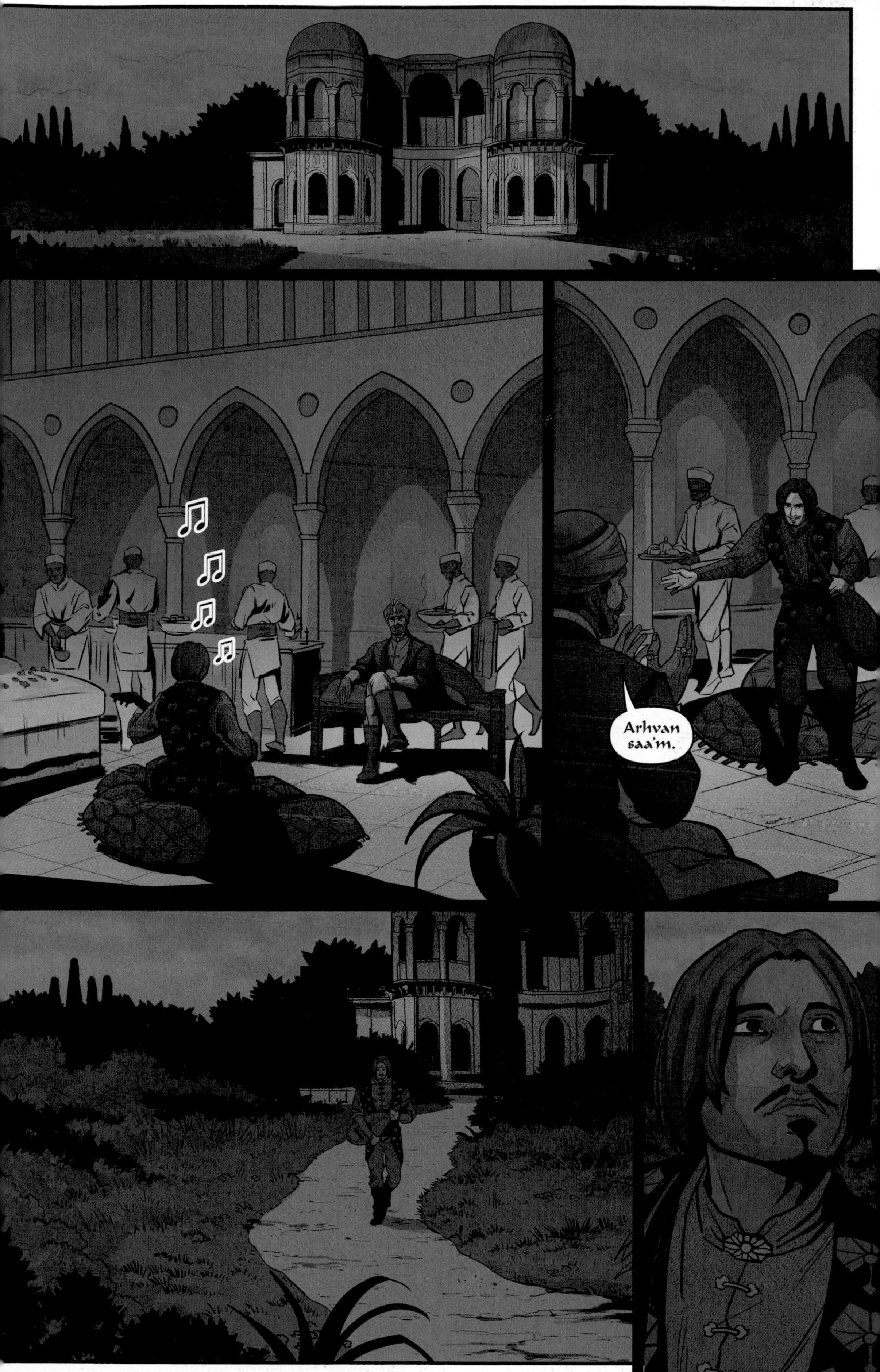
Arhvan saa'm.

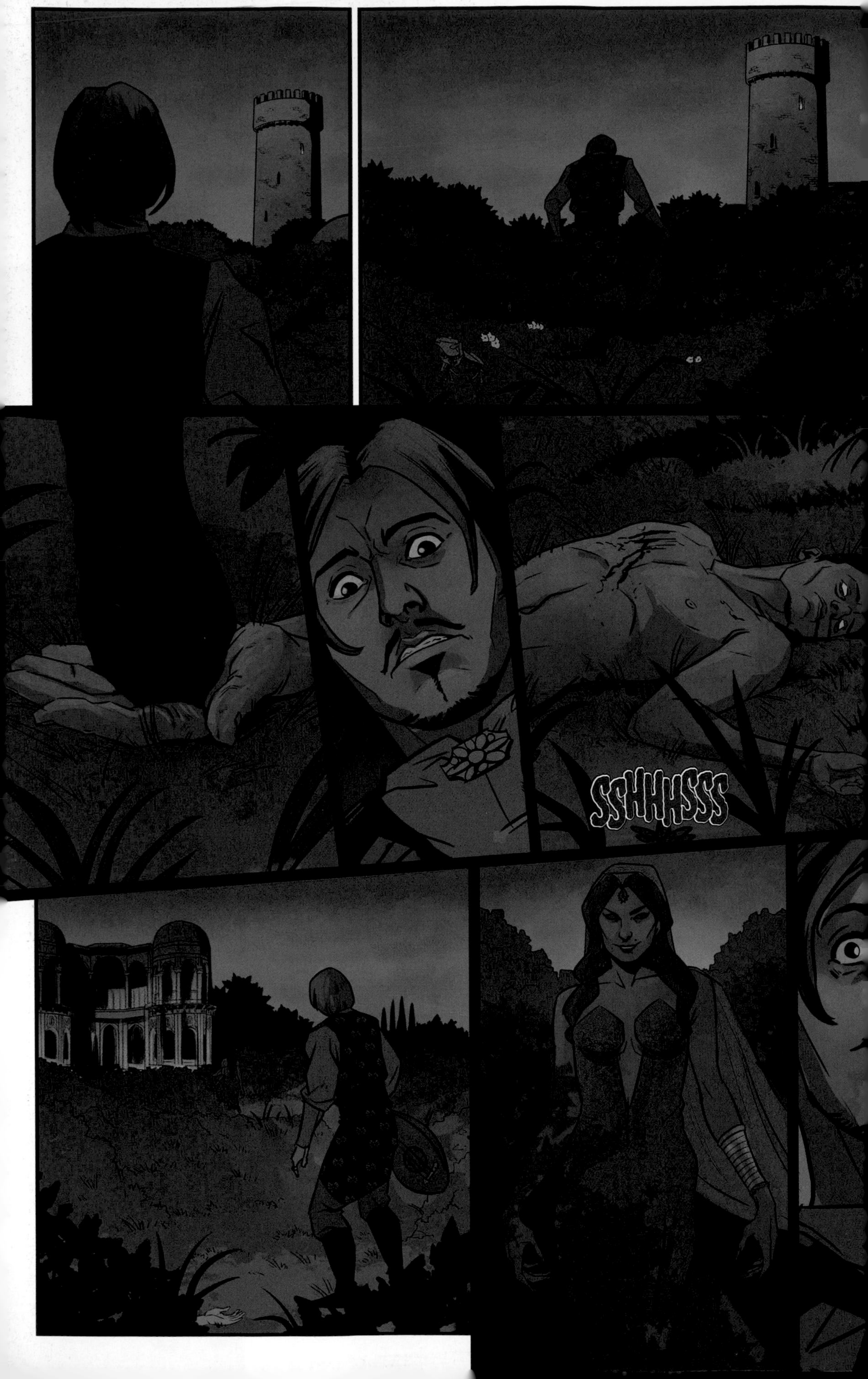
SSHHHSSS

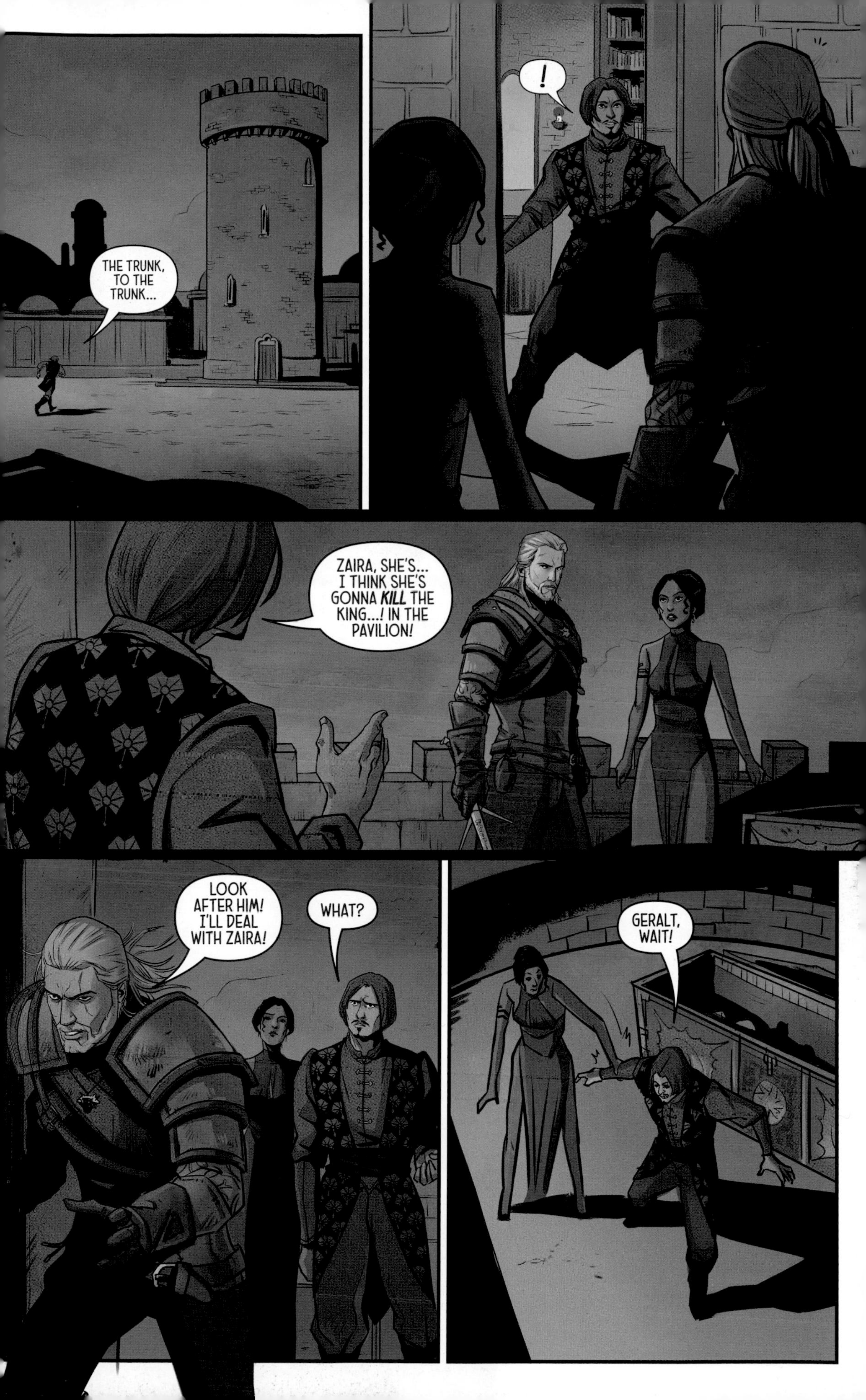
THE TRUNK, TO THE TRUNK...
!
ZAIRA, SHE'S... I THINK SHE'S GONNA **KILL** THE KING...! IN THE PAVILION!
LOOK AFTER HIM! I'LL DEAL WITH ZAIRA!
WHAT?
GERALT, WAIT!

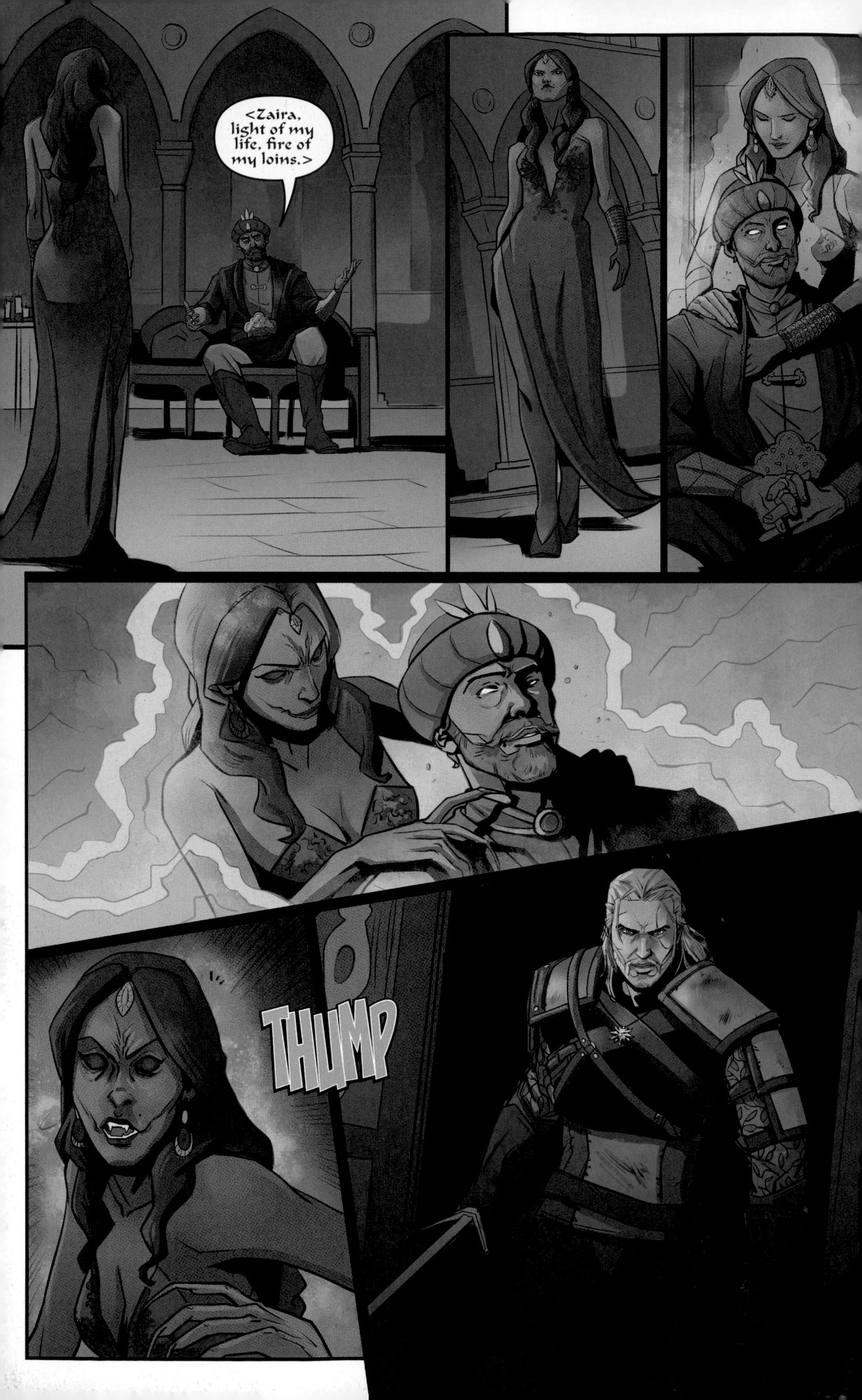
<Zaira, light of my life, fire of my loins.>
THUMP

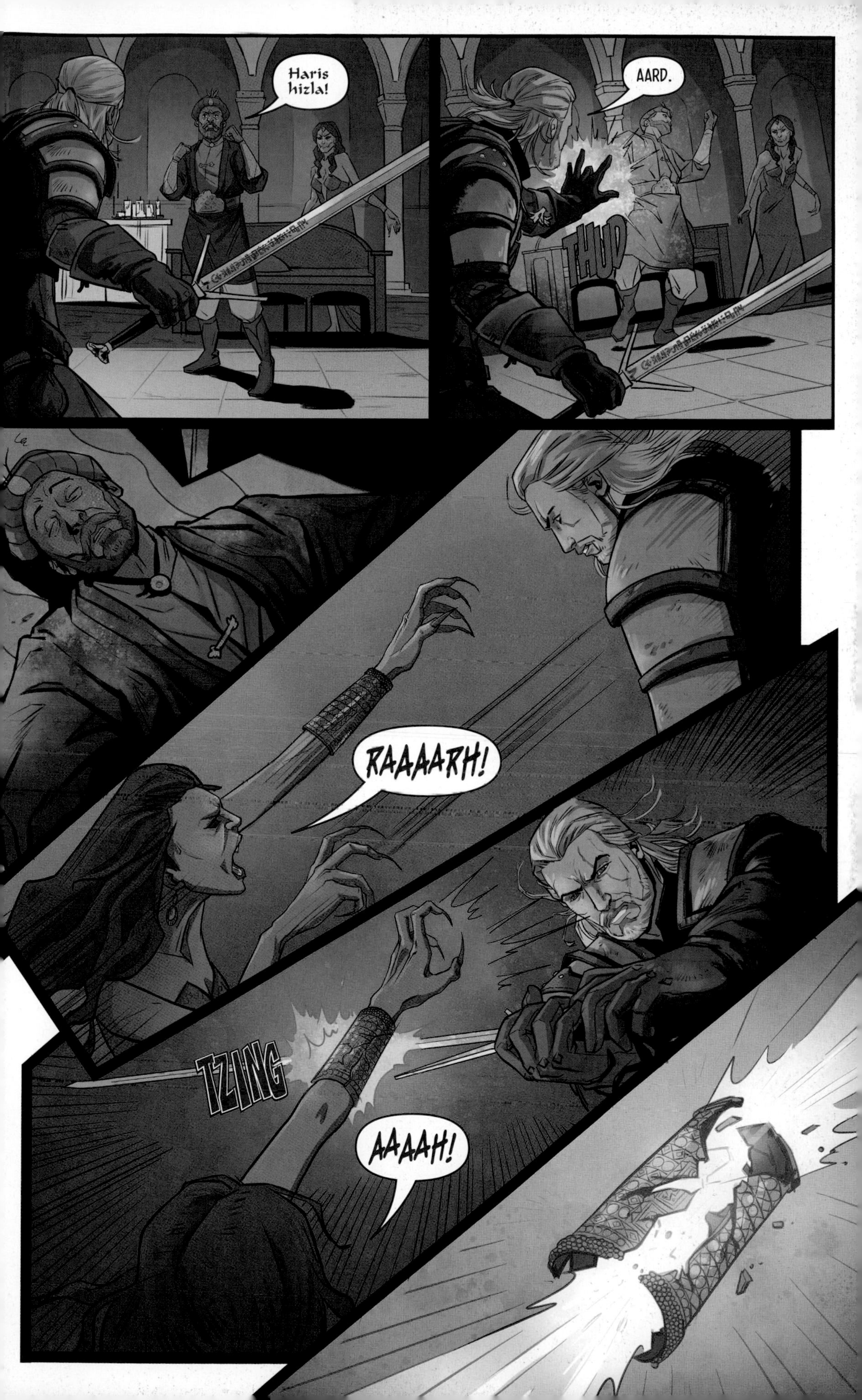
Haris hizla!
AARD.
THUD
RAAAARH!
TZING
AAAAH!

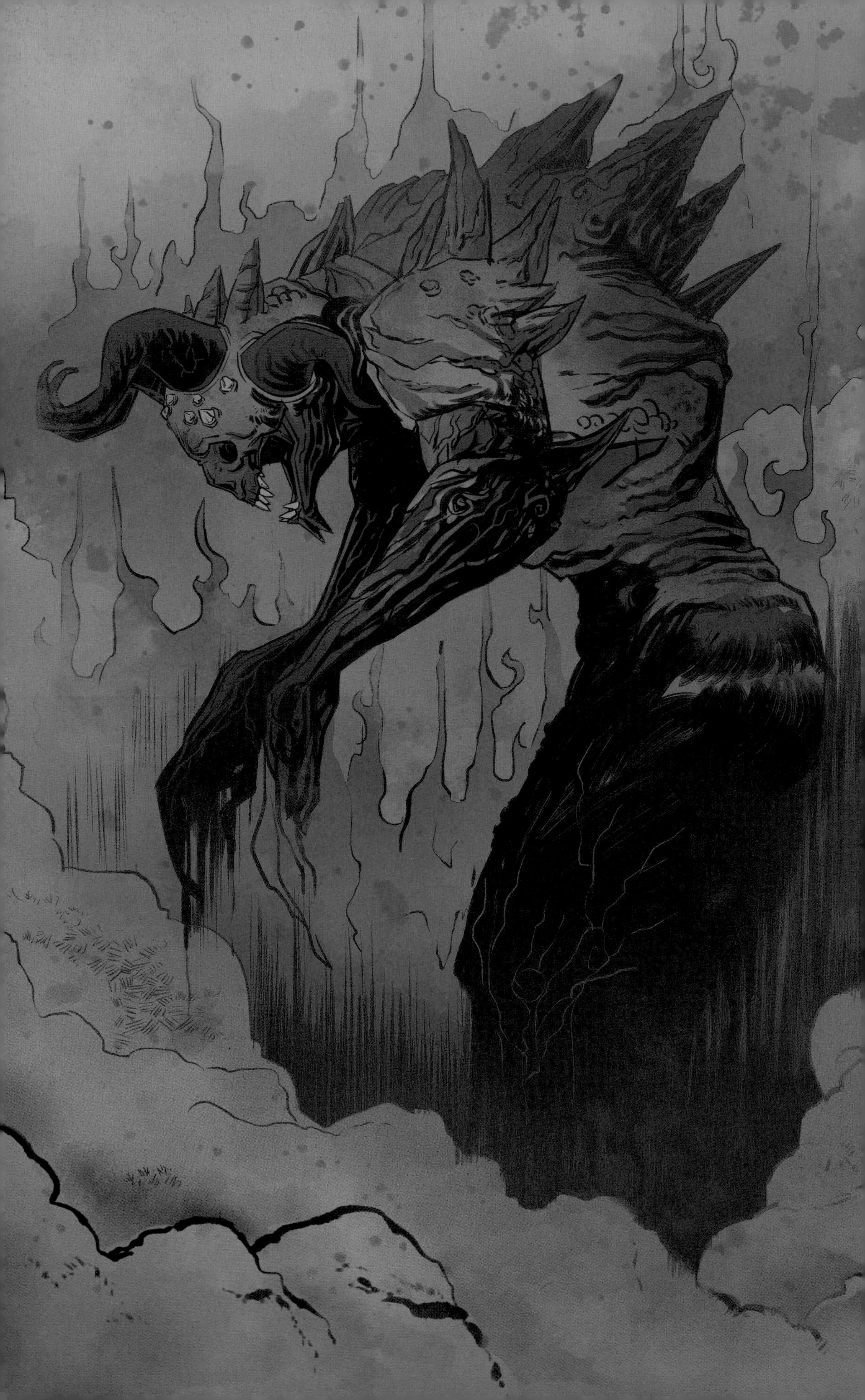

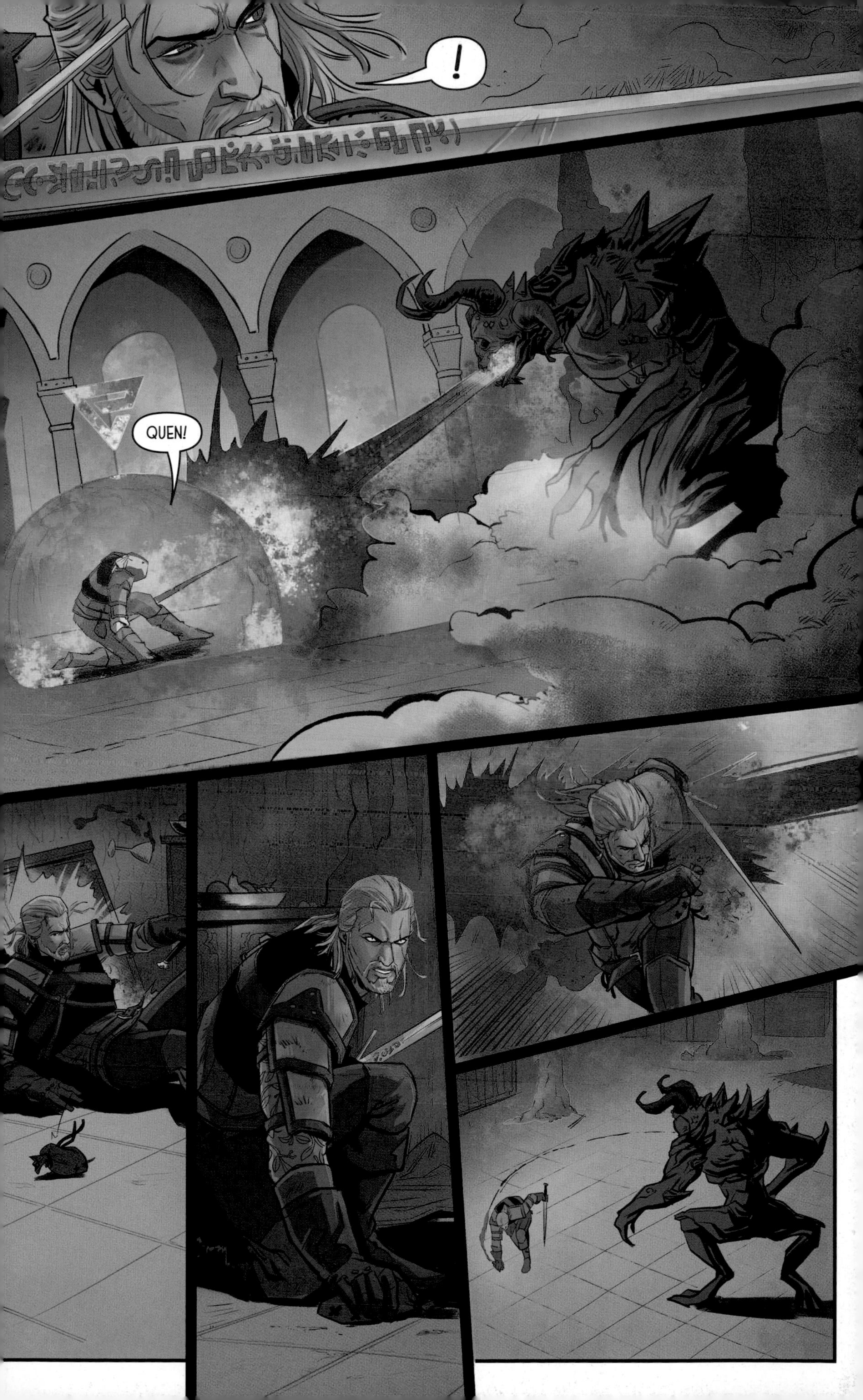
!
QUEN!

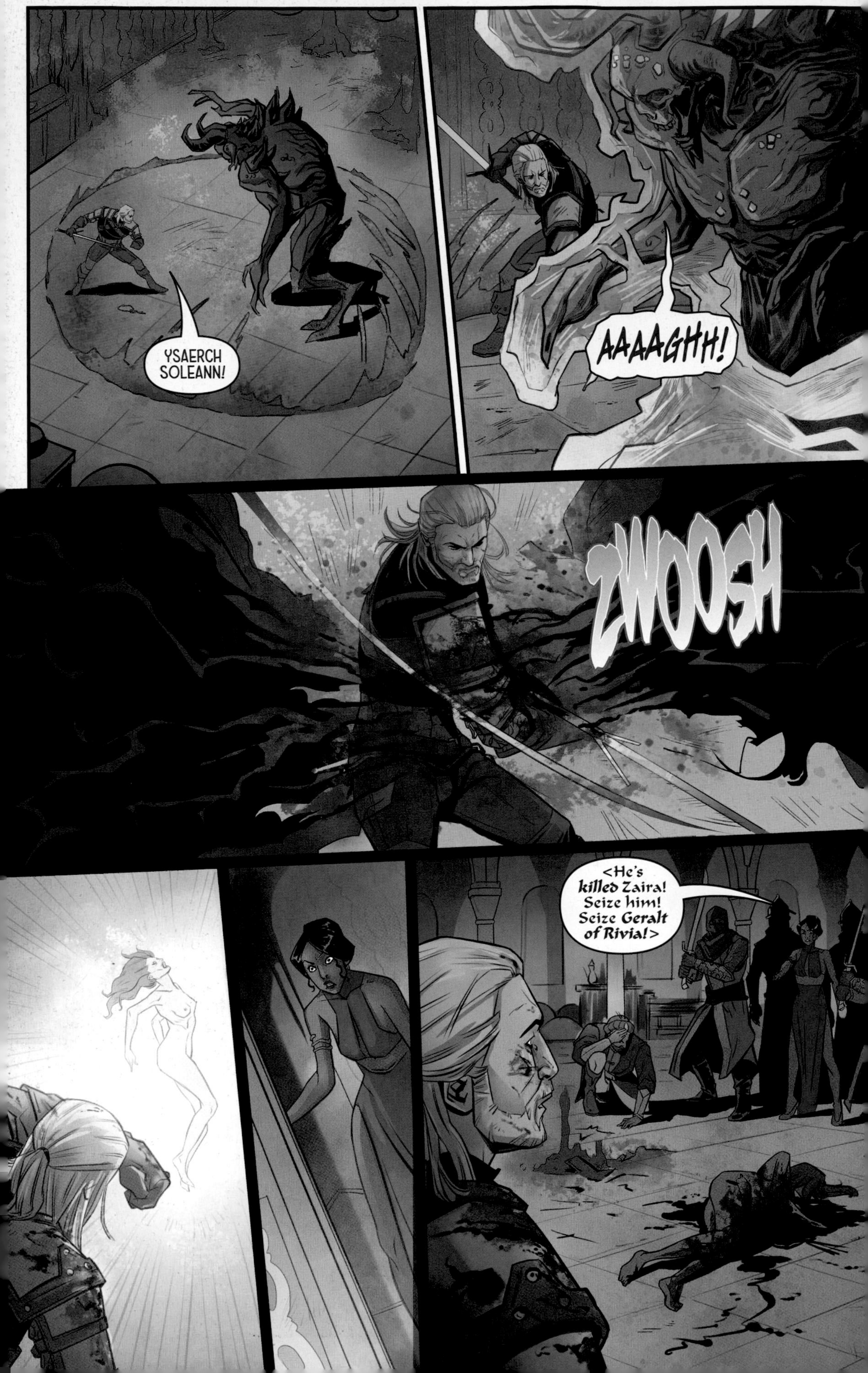
YSAERCH SOLEANN!
AAAAGHH!
ZWOOSH
<He's killed Zaira! Seize him! Seize Geralt of Rivia!>

GERALT OF RIVIA, OF THE *MURDERS* OF PRINCE SIRAT, BELOVED OF THE REALM, AND OF ZAIRA, THE CROWN CONCUBINE, THE KING FINDS YOU *GUILTY*.

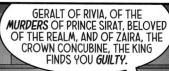
DIDN'T TAKE LONG.

AND TO *DEATH* YOU CONDEMNS, YOUR SKIN TO BE FLAYED FROM YOU LIKE A HOG AT SLAUGHTER, THEN YOUR LIMBS BY WILD HORSES TO BE RIPPED INTO FOUR.

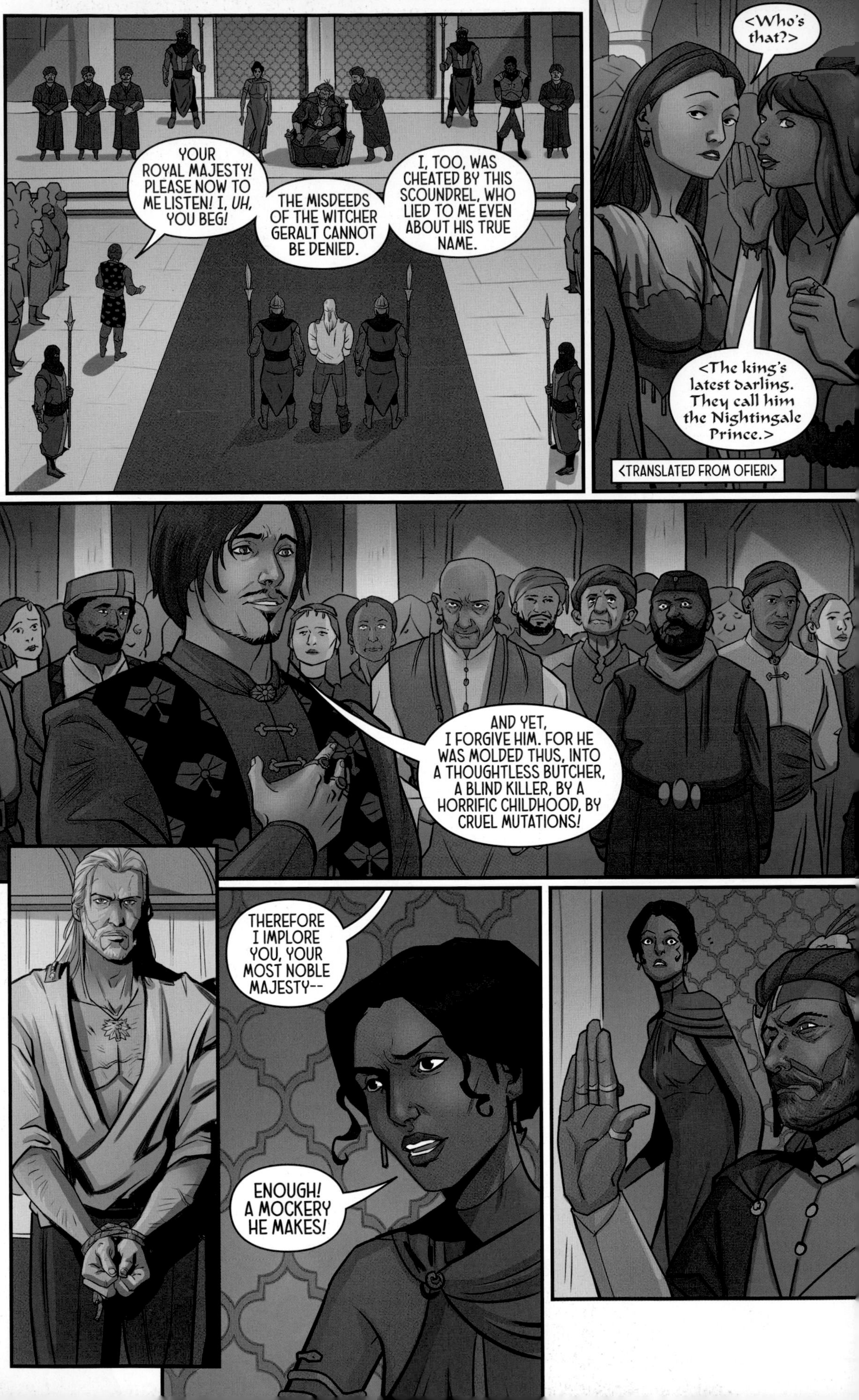

YOUR ROYAL MAJESTY! PLEASE NOW TO ME LISTEN! I, *UH*, YOU BEG!
THE MISDEEDS OF THE WITCHER GERALT CANNOT BE DENIED.
I, TOO, WAS CHEATED BY THIS SCOUNDREL, WHO LIED TO ME EVEN ABOUT HIS TRUE NAME.
<Who's that?>
<The king's latest darling. They call him the Nightingale Prince.>
<TRANSLATED FROM OFIERI>
AND YET, I FORGIVE HIM. FOR HE WAS MOLDED THUS, INTO A THOUGHTLESS BUTCHER, A BLIND KILLER, BY A HORRIFIC CHILDHOOD, BY CRUEL MUTATIONS!
THEREFORE I IMPLORE YOU, YOUR MOST NOBLE MAJESTY--
ENOUGH! A MOCKERY HE MAKES!

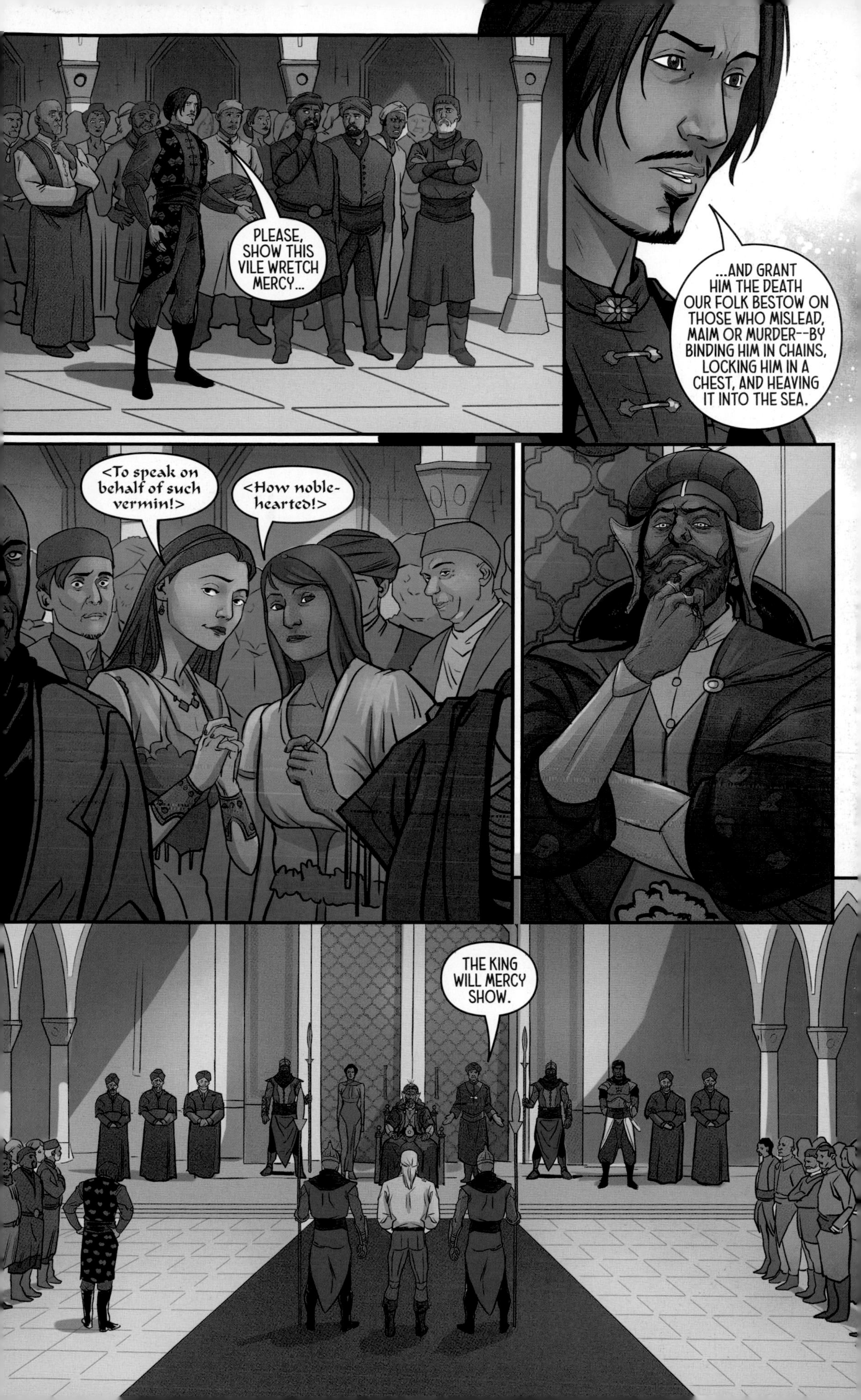

PLEASE, SHOW THIS VILE WRETCH MERCY...
...AND GRANT HIM THE DEATH OUR FOLK BESTOW ON THOSE WHO MISLEAD, MAIM OR MURDER--BY BINDING HIM IN CHAINS, LOCKING HIM IN A CHEST, AND HEAVING IT INTO THE SEA.
<To speak on behalf of such vermin!>
<How noble-hearted!>
THE KING WILL MERCY SHOW.

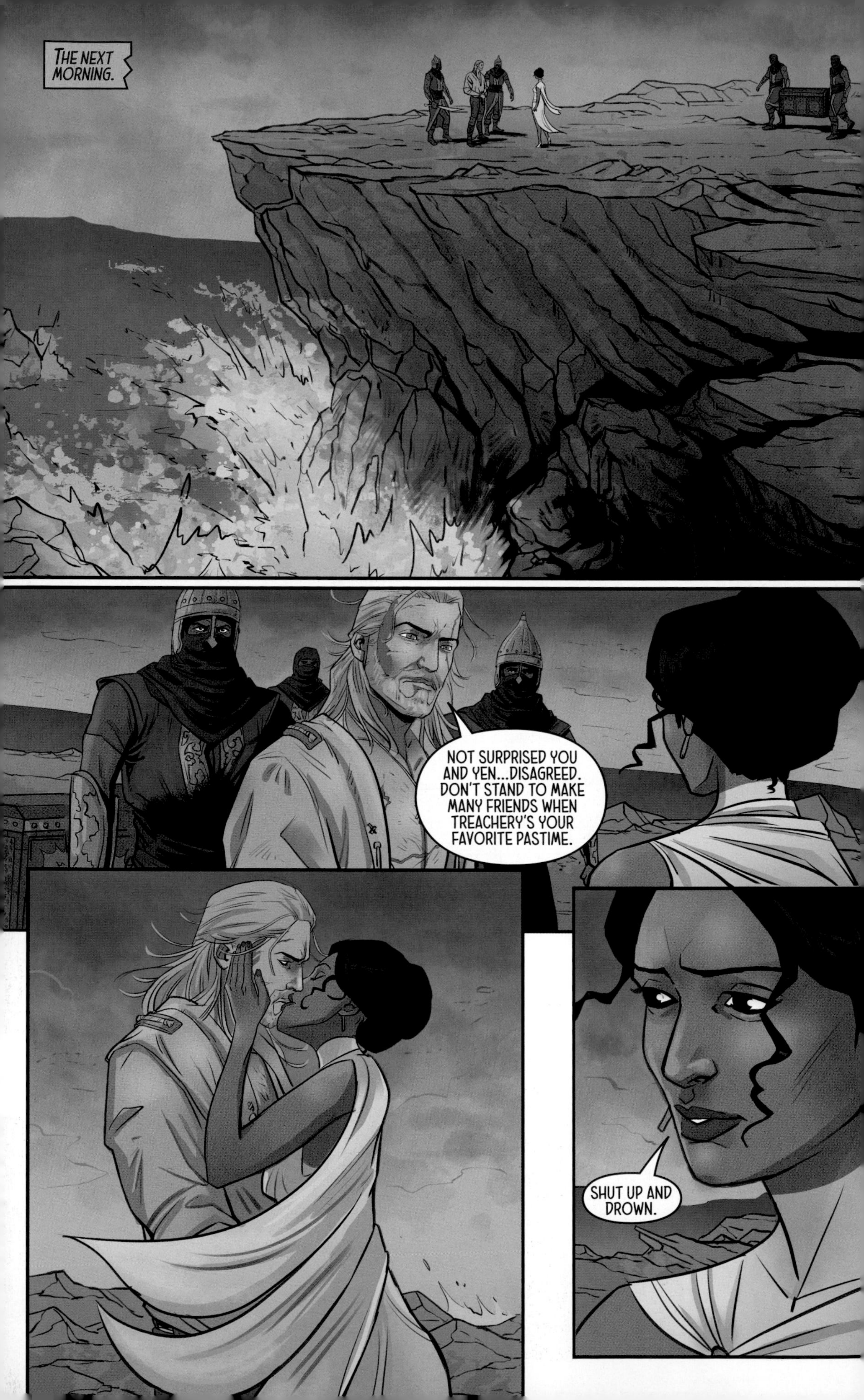
THE NEXT MORNING.
NOT SURPRISED YOU AND YEN...DISAGREED. DON'T STAND TO MAKE MANY FRIENDS WHEN TREACHERY'S YOUR FAVORITE PASTIME.
SHUT UP AND DROWN.

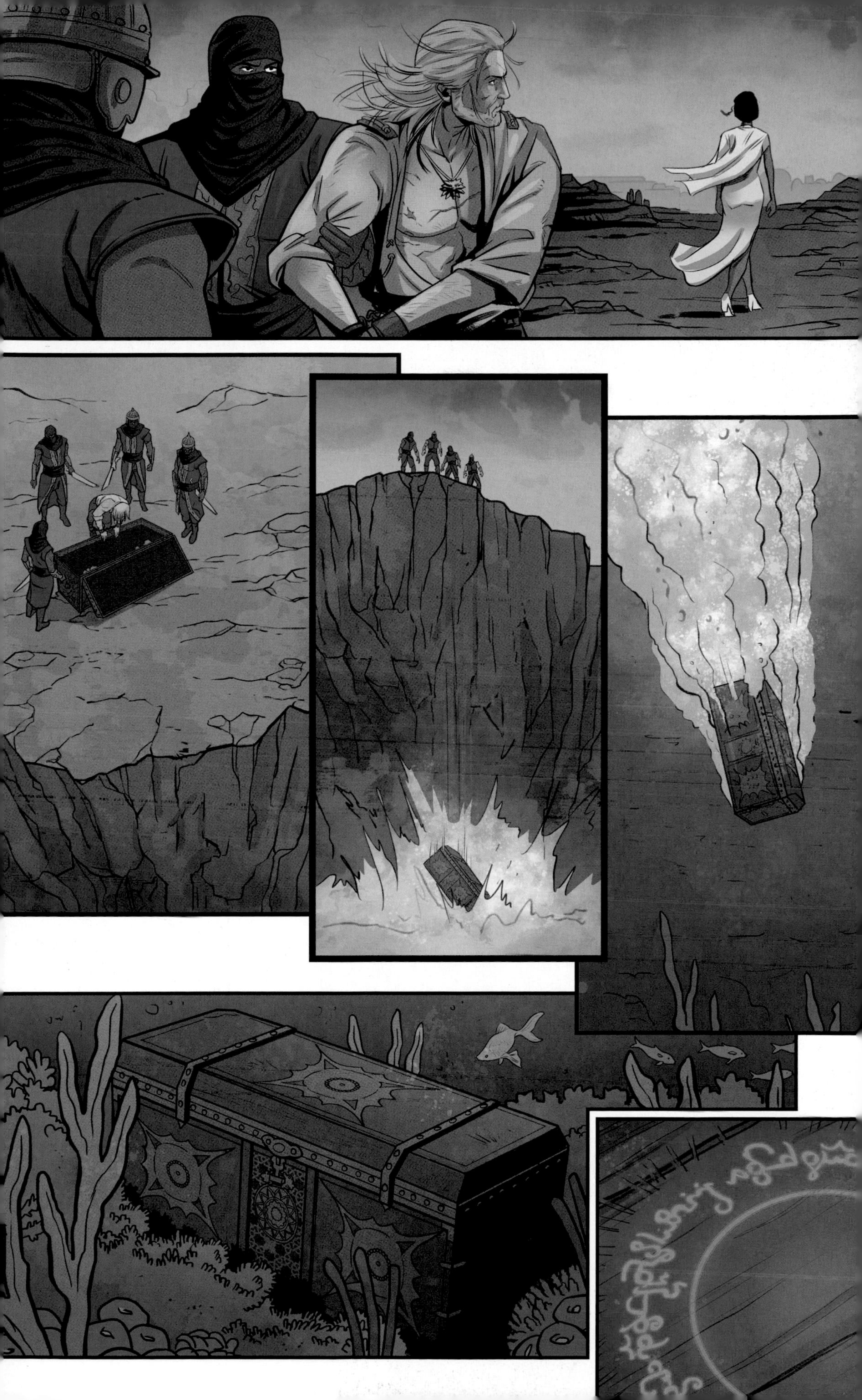

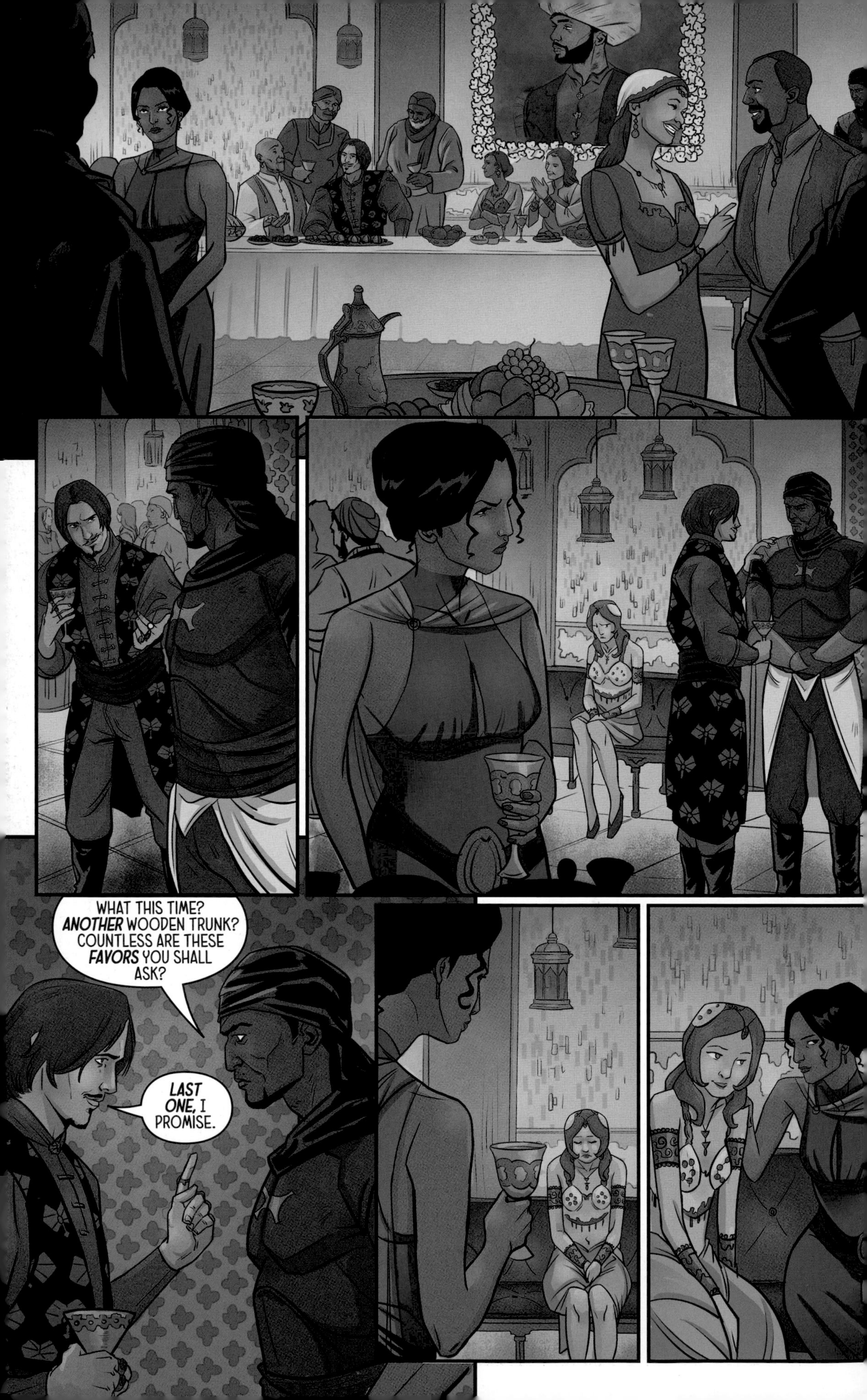
WHAT THIS TIME? ANOTHER WOODEN TRUNK? COUNTLESS ARE THESE FAVORS YOU SHALL ASK?
LAST ONE, I PROMISE.

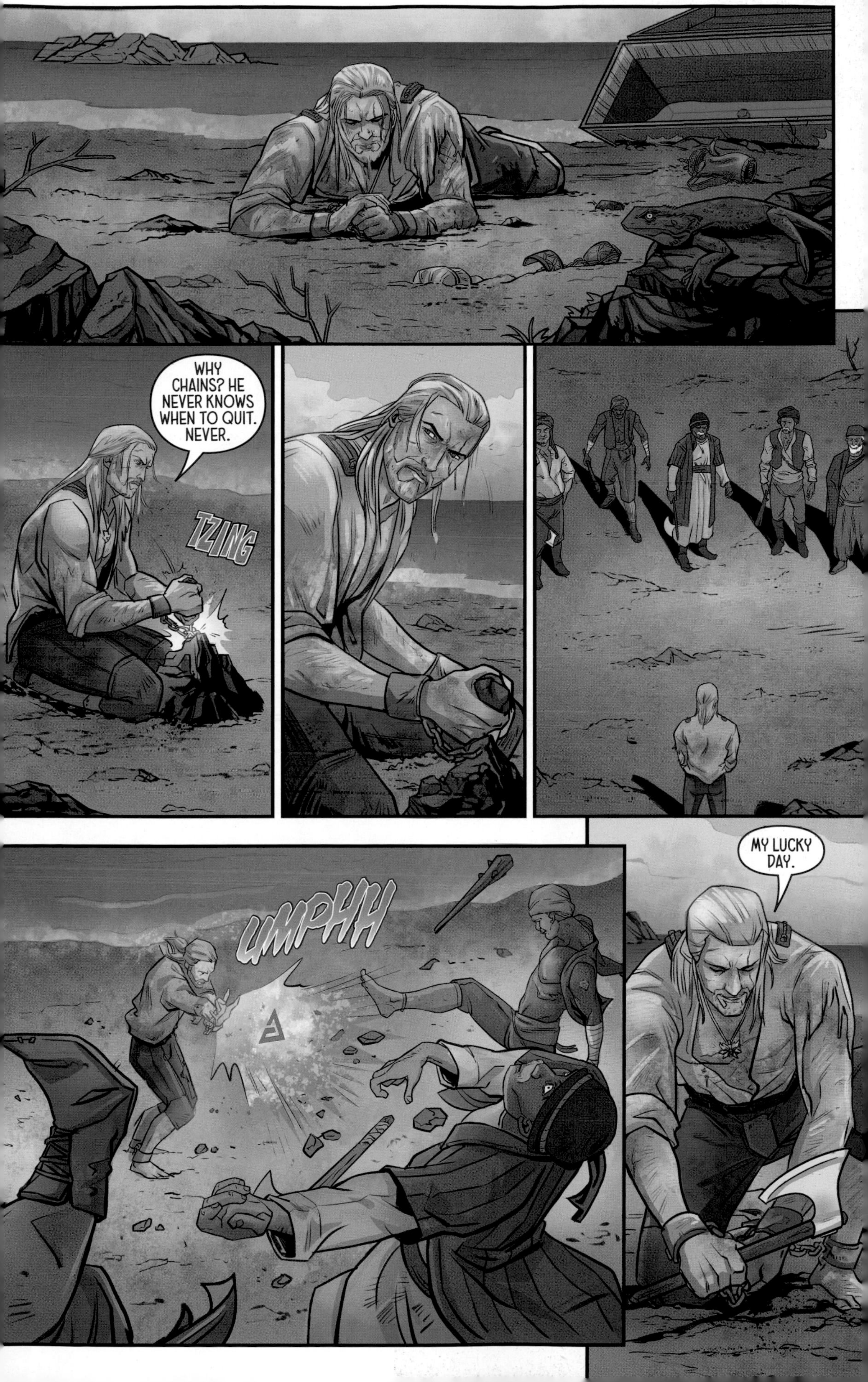
WHY CHAINS? HE NEVER KNOWS WHEN TO QUIT. NEVER.
TZING
UMPHH
MY LUCKY DAY.

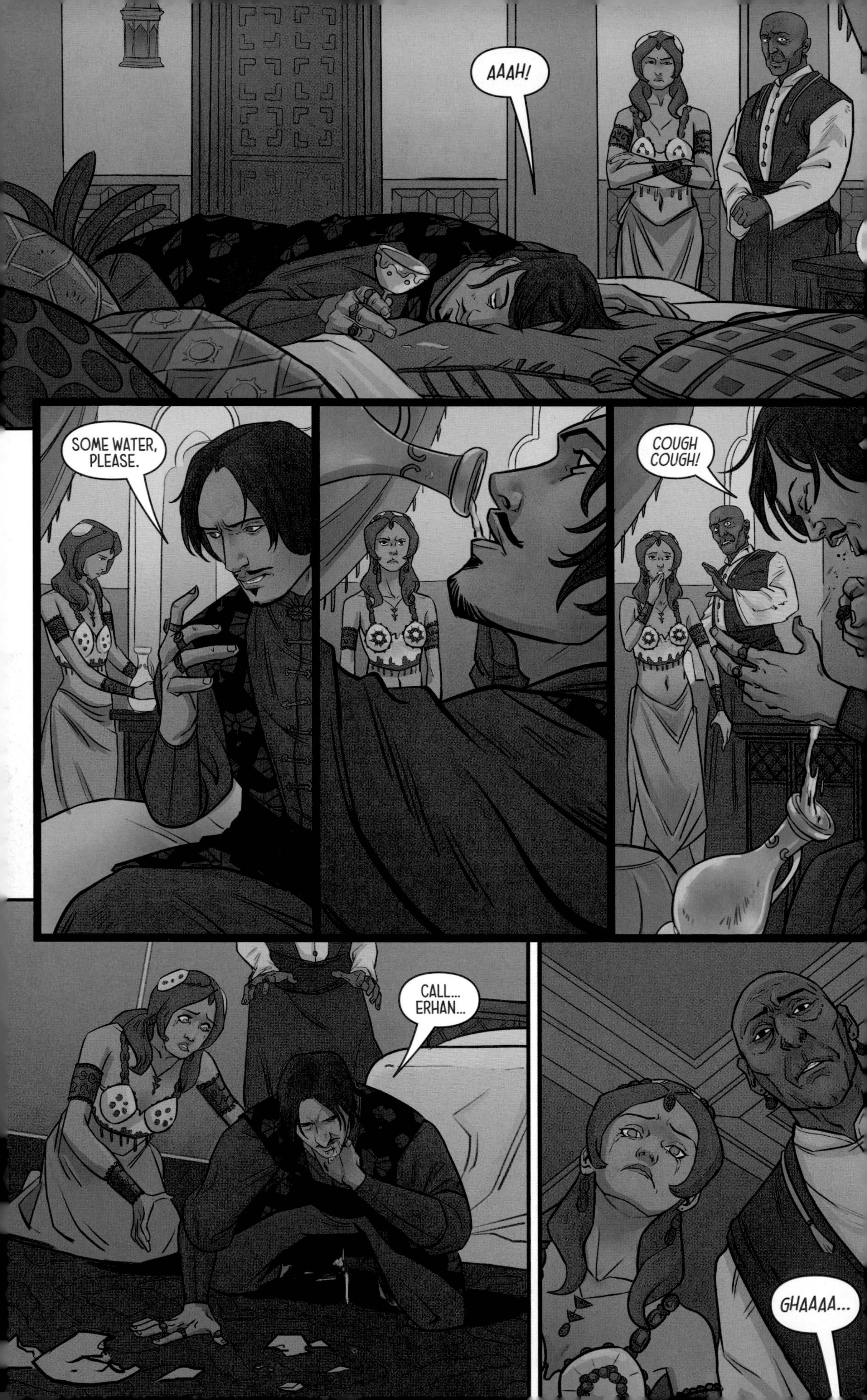
AAAH!
SOME WATER, PLEASE.
COUGH COUGH!
CALL... ERHAN...
GHAAAA...

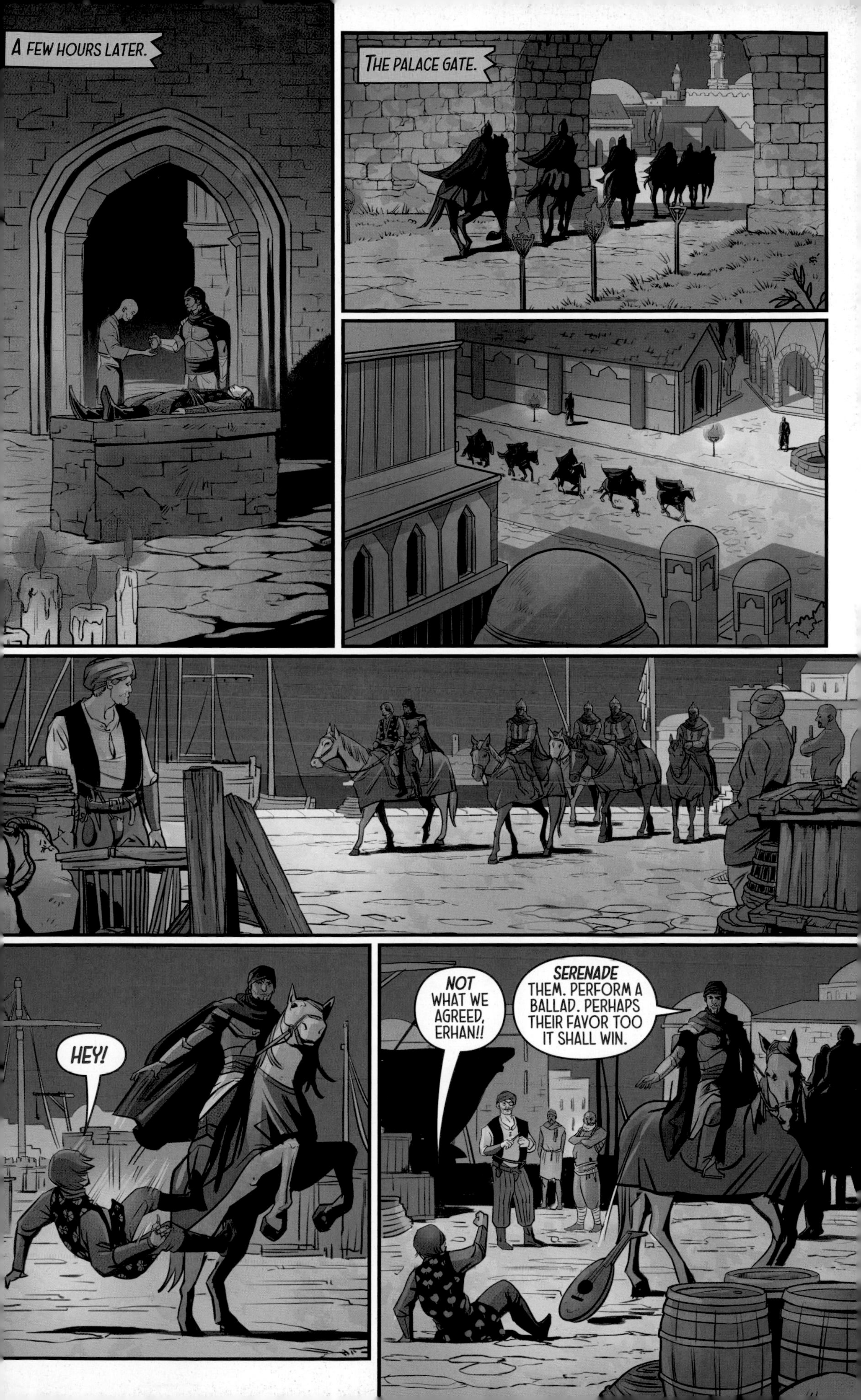
A FEW HOURS LATER.
THE PALACE GATE.
HEY!
NOT WHAT WE AGREED, ERHAN!!
SERENADE THEM. PERFORM A BALLAD. PERHAPS THEIR FAVOR TOO IT SHALL WIN.

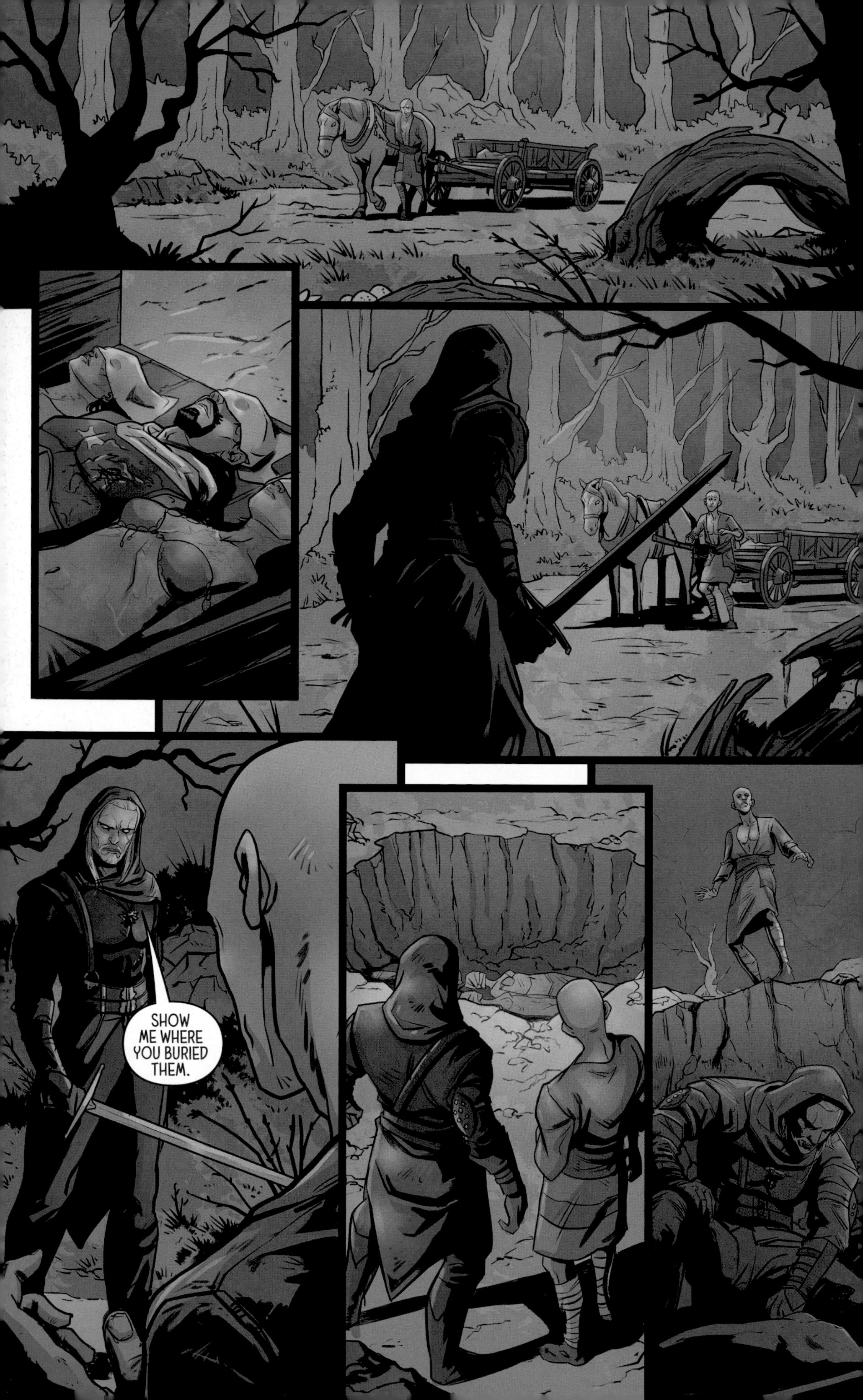
SHOW ME WHERE YOU BURIED THEM.

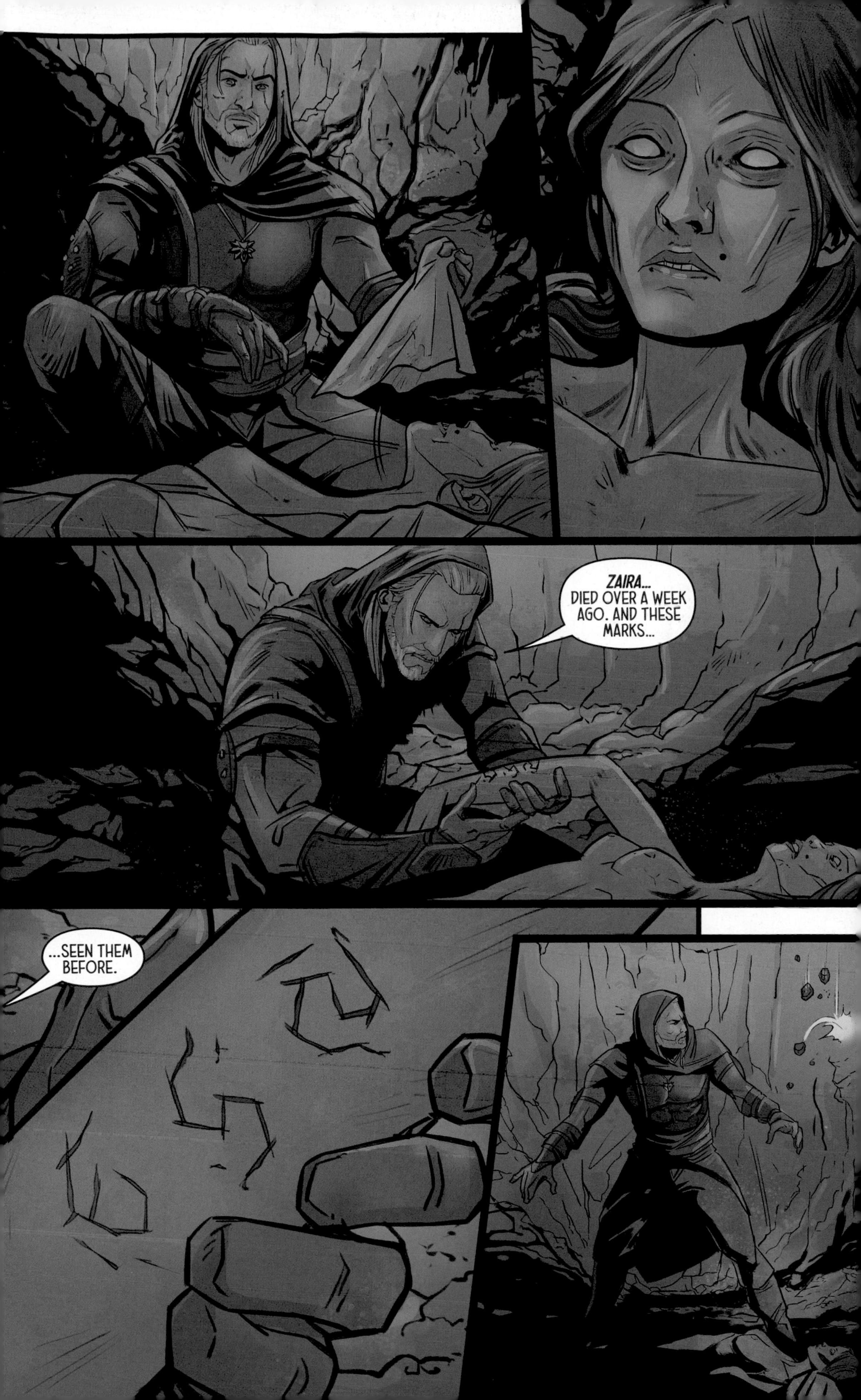
ZAIRA...
DIED OVER A WEEK AGO. AND THESE MARKS...
...SEEN THEM BEFORE.

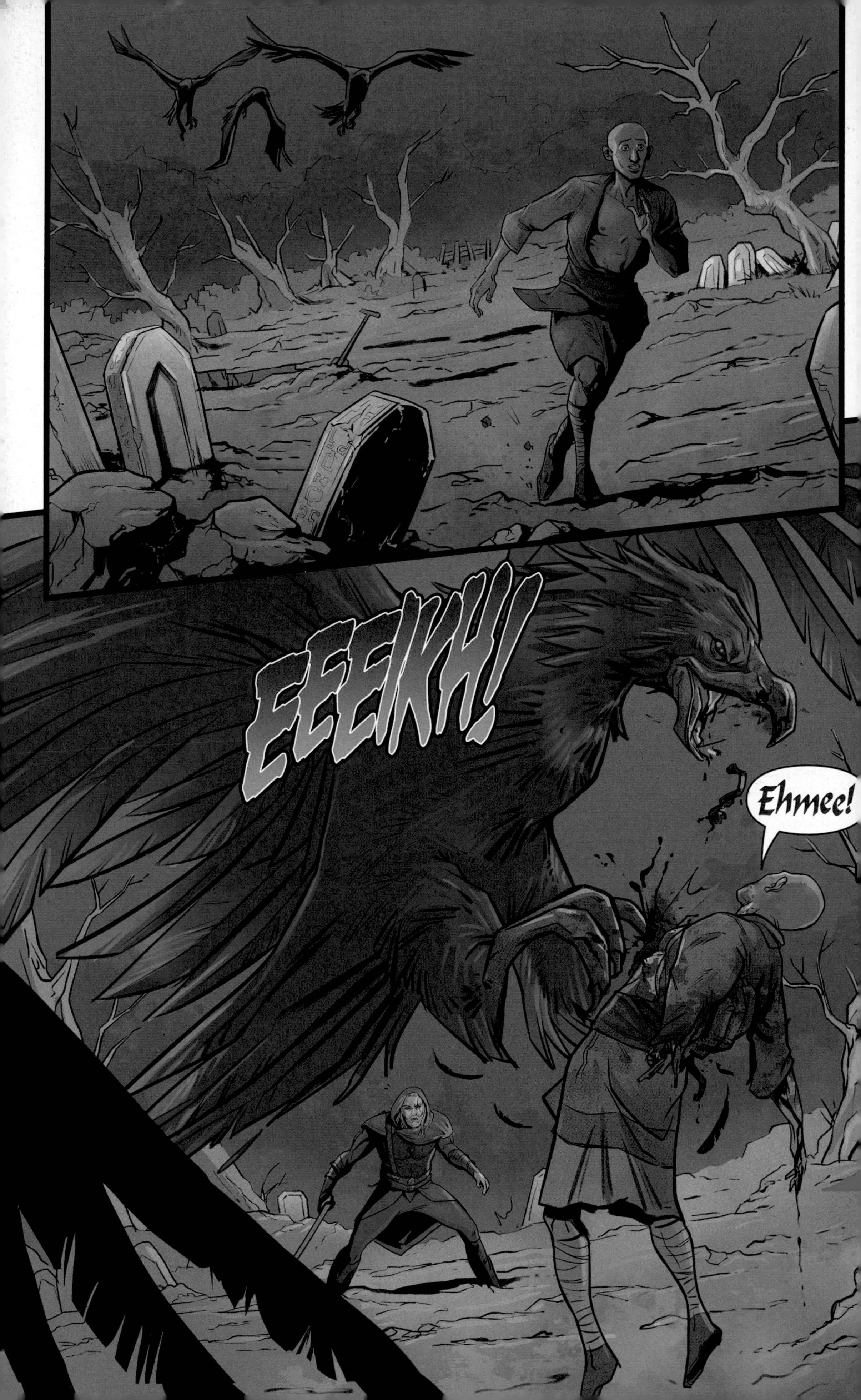
EEEKH!
Ehmee!

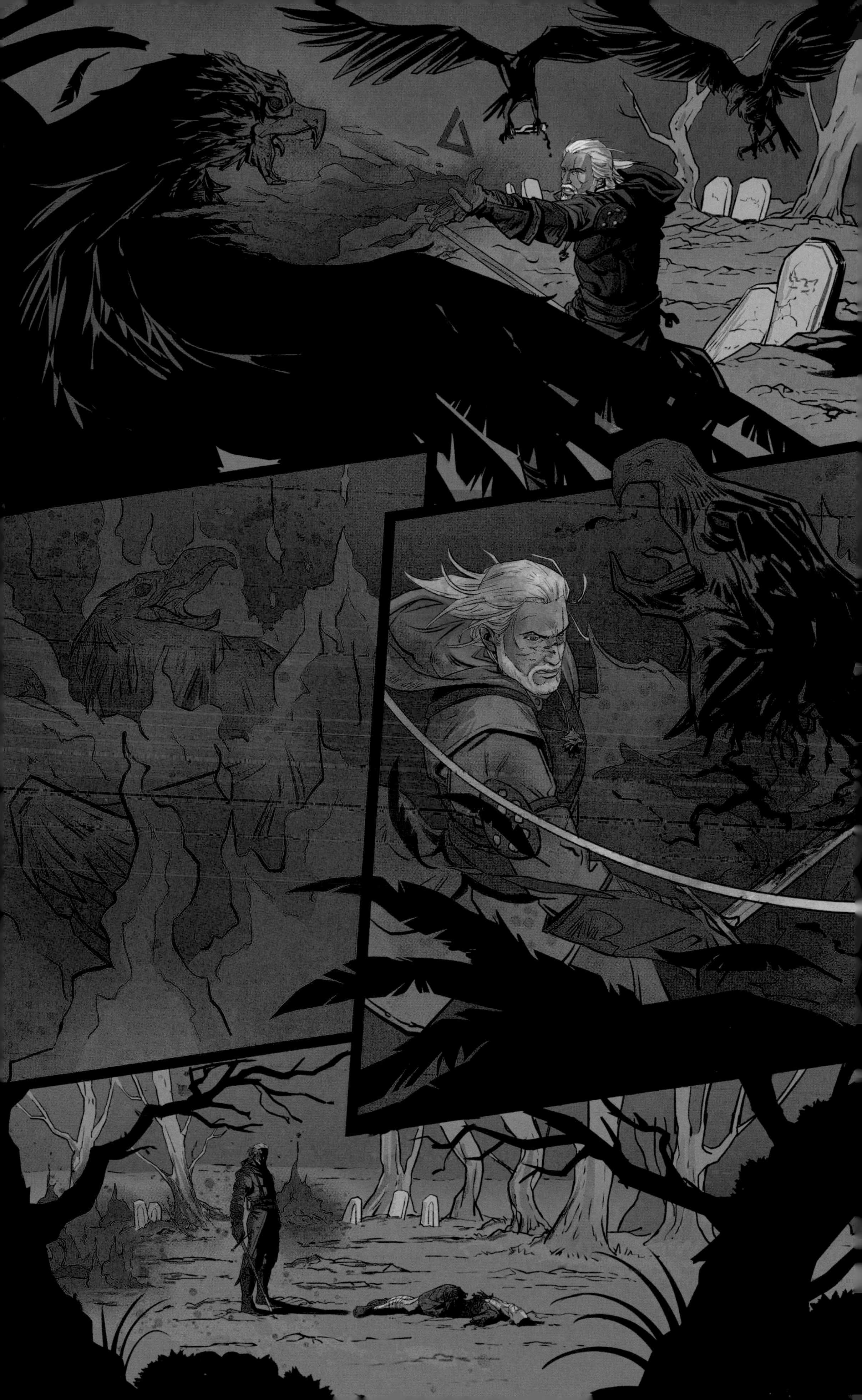

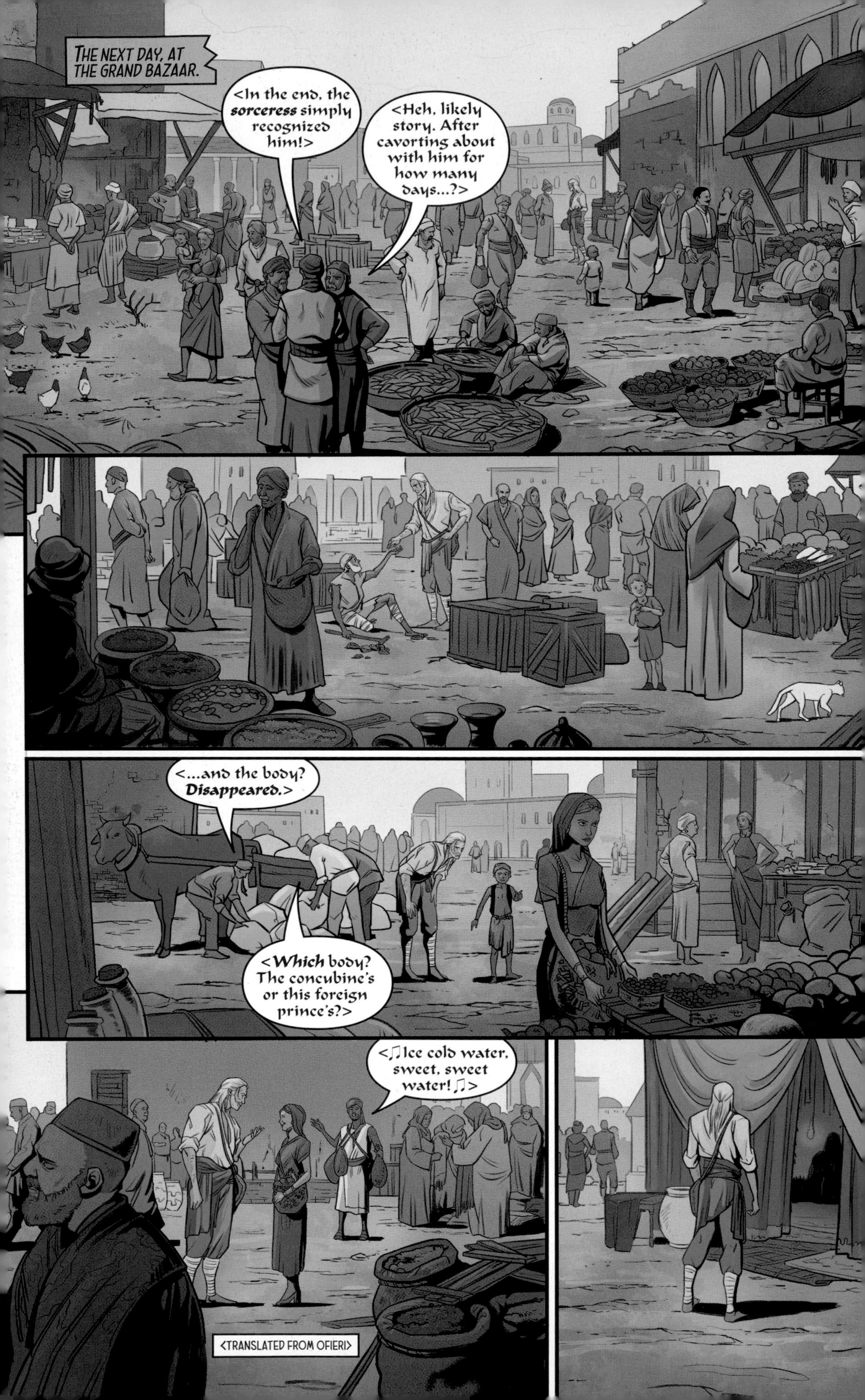
THE NEXT DAY, AT THE GRAND BAZAAR.
<In the end, the **sorceress** simply recognized him!>
<Heh, likely story. After cavorting about with him for how many days...?>
<...and the body? **Disappeared.**>
<**Which** body? The concubine's or this foreign prince's?>
<♫ Ice cold water, sweet, sweet water! ♫>
<TRANSLATED FROM OFIERI>

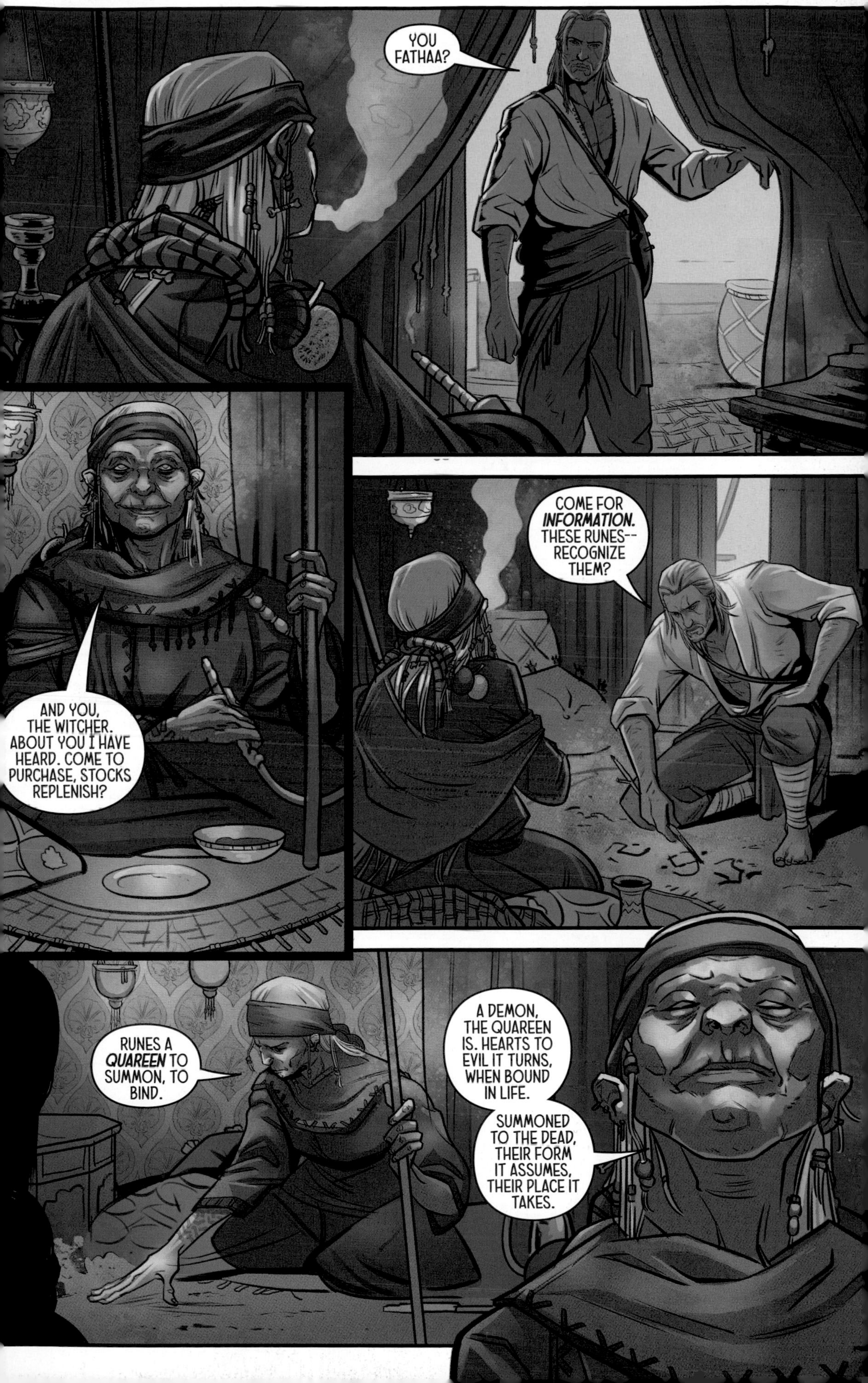
YOU FATHAA?
AND YOU, THE WITCHER. ABOUT YOU I HAVE HEARD. COME TO PURCHASE, STOCKS REPLENISH?
COME FOR *INFORMATION.* THESE RUNES-- RECOGNIZE THEM?
RUNES A *QUAREEN* TO SUMMON, TO BIND.
A DEMON, THE QUAREEN IS. HEARTS TO EVIL IT TURNS, WHEN BOUND IN LIFE.
SUMMONED TO THE DEAD, THEIR FORM IT ASSUMES, THEIR PLACE IT TAKES.

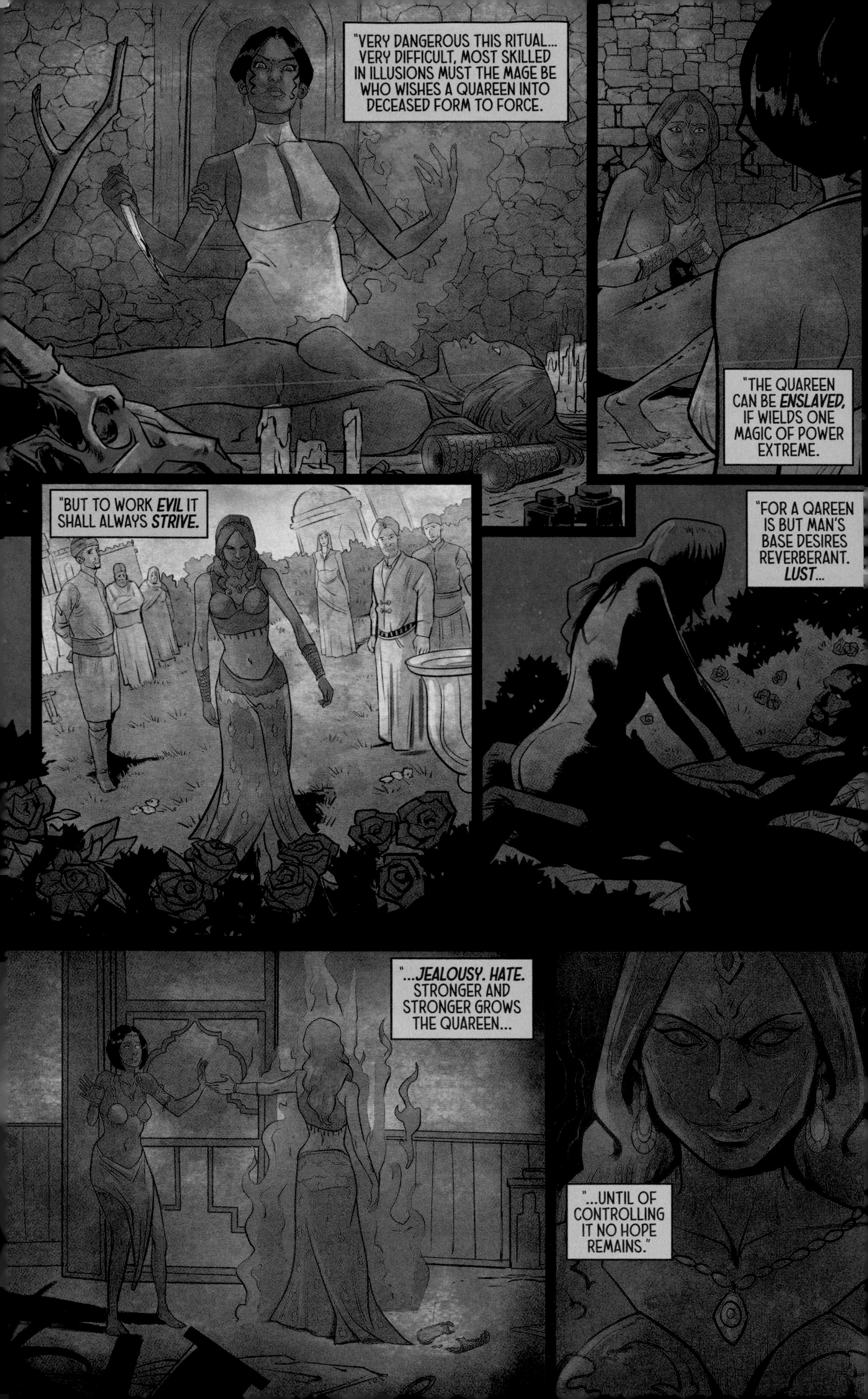
"VERY DANGEROUS THIS RITUAL... VERY DIFFICULT, MOST SKILLED IN ILLUSIONS MUST THE MAGE BE WHO WISHES A QUAREEN INTO DECEASED FORM TO FORCE.
"THE QUAREEN CAN BE *ENSLAVED,* IF WIELDS ONE MAGIC OF POWER EXTREME.
"BUT TO WORK *EVIL* IT SHALL ALWAYS *STRIVE.*
"FOR A QAREEN IS BUT MAN'S BASE DESIRES REVERBERANT. *LUST*...
"...*JEALOUSY. HATE.* STRONGER AND STRONGER GROWS THE QUAREEN...
"...UNTIL OF CONTROLLING IT NO HOPE REMAINS."

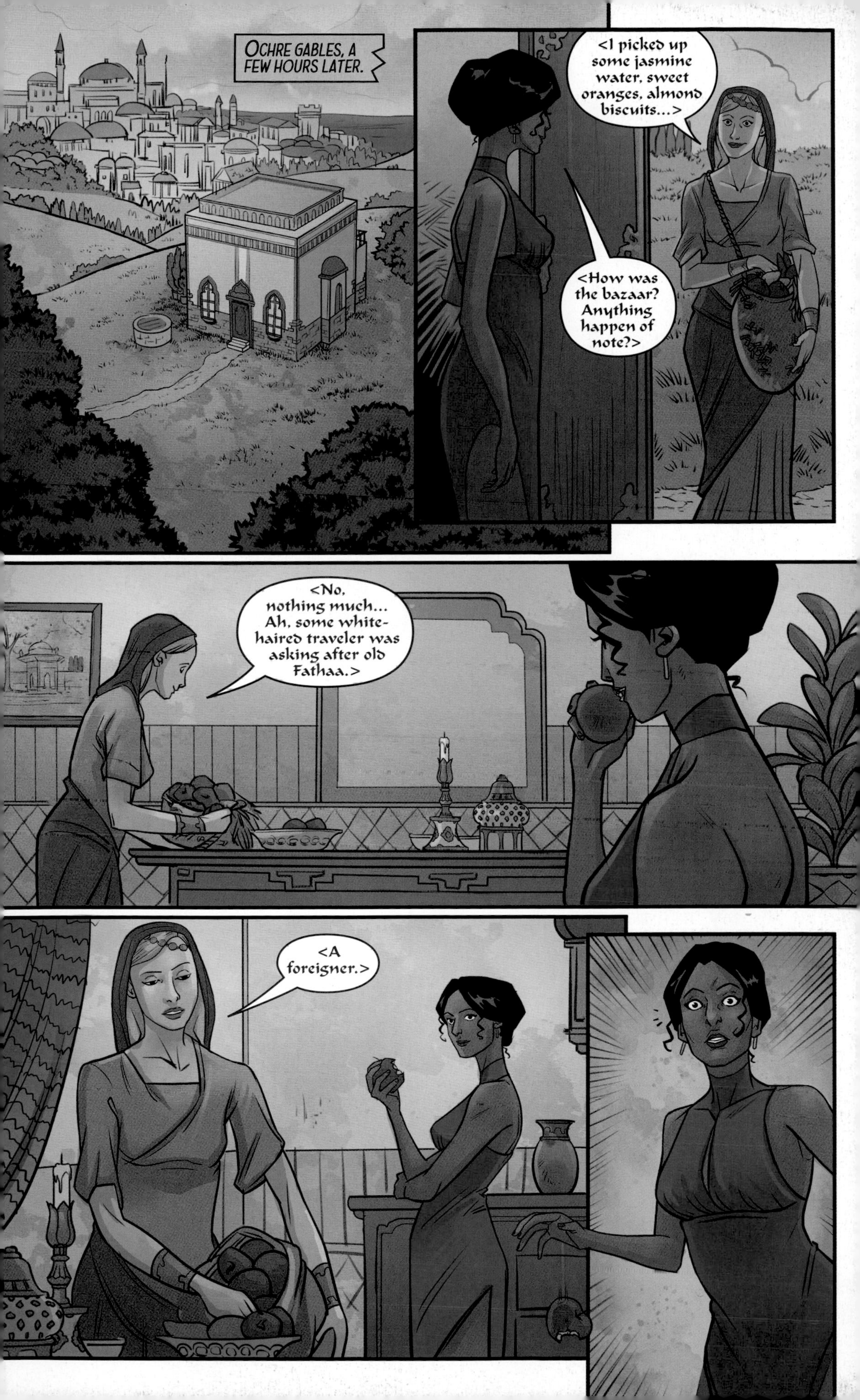

OCHRE GABLES, A FEW HOURS LATER.
<I picked up some jasmine water, sweet oranges, almond biscuits...>
<How was the bazaar? Anything happen of note?>
<No, nothing much... Ah, some white-haired traveler was asking after old Fathaa.>
<A foreigner.>

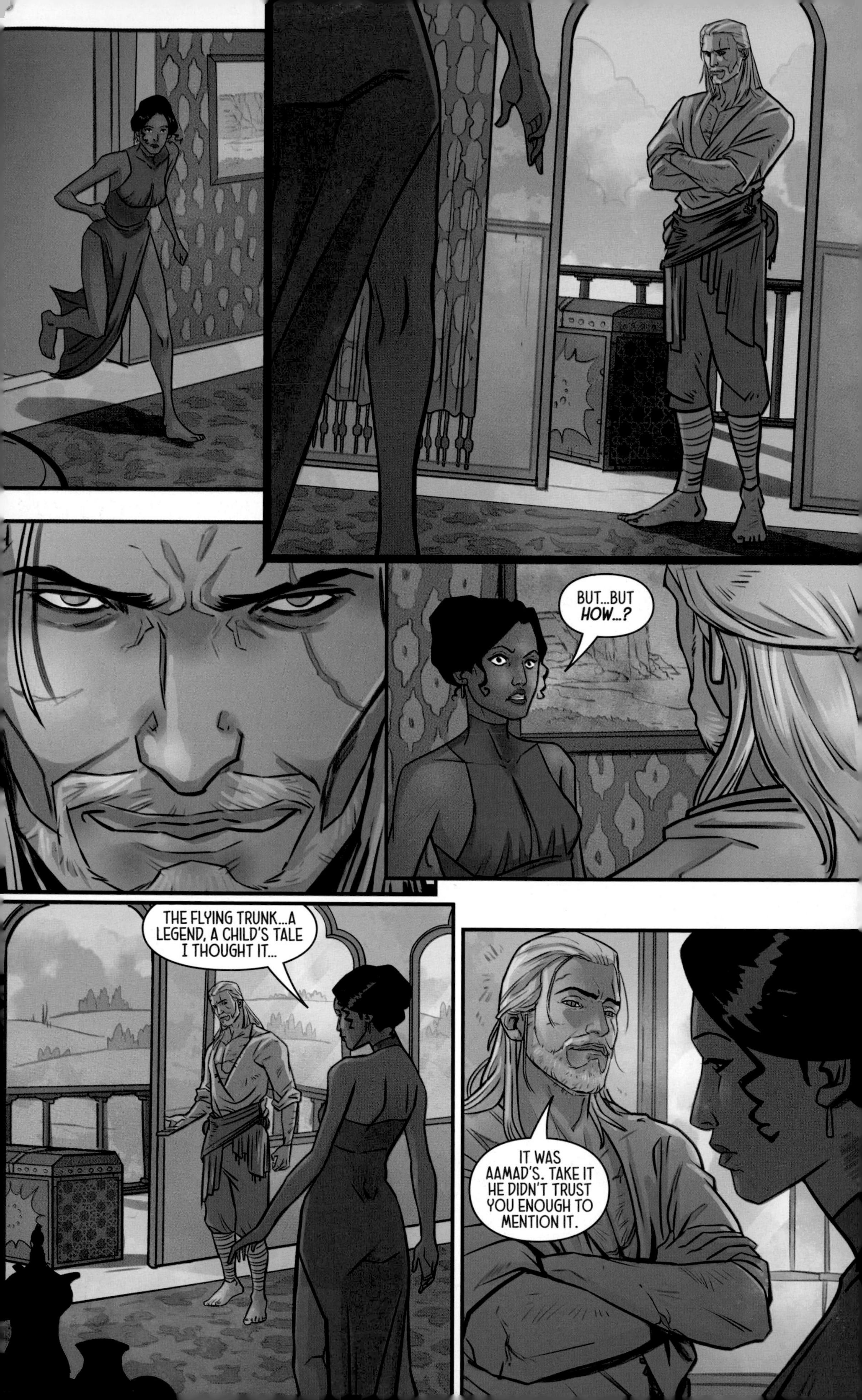
BUT...BUT HOW...?
THE FLYING TRUNK...A LEGEND, A CHILD'S TALE I THOUGHT IT...
IT WAS AAMAD'S. TAKE IT HE DIDN'T TRUST YOU ENOUGH TO MENTION IT.

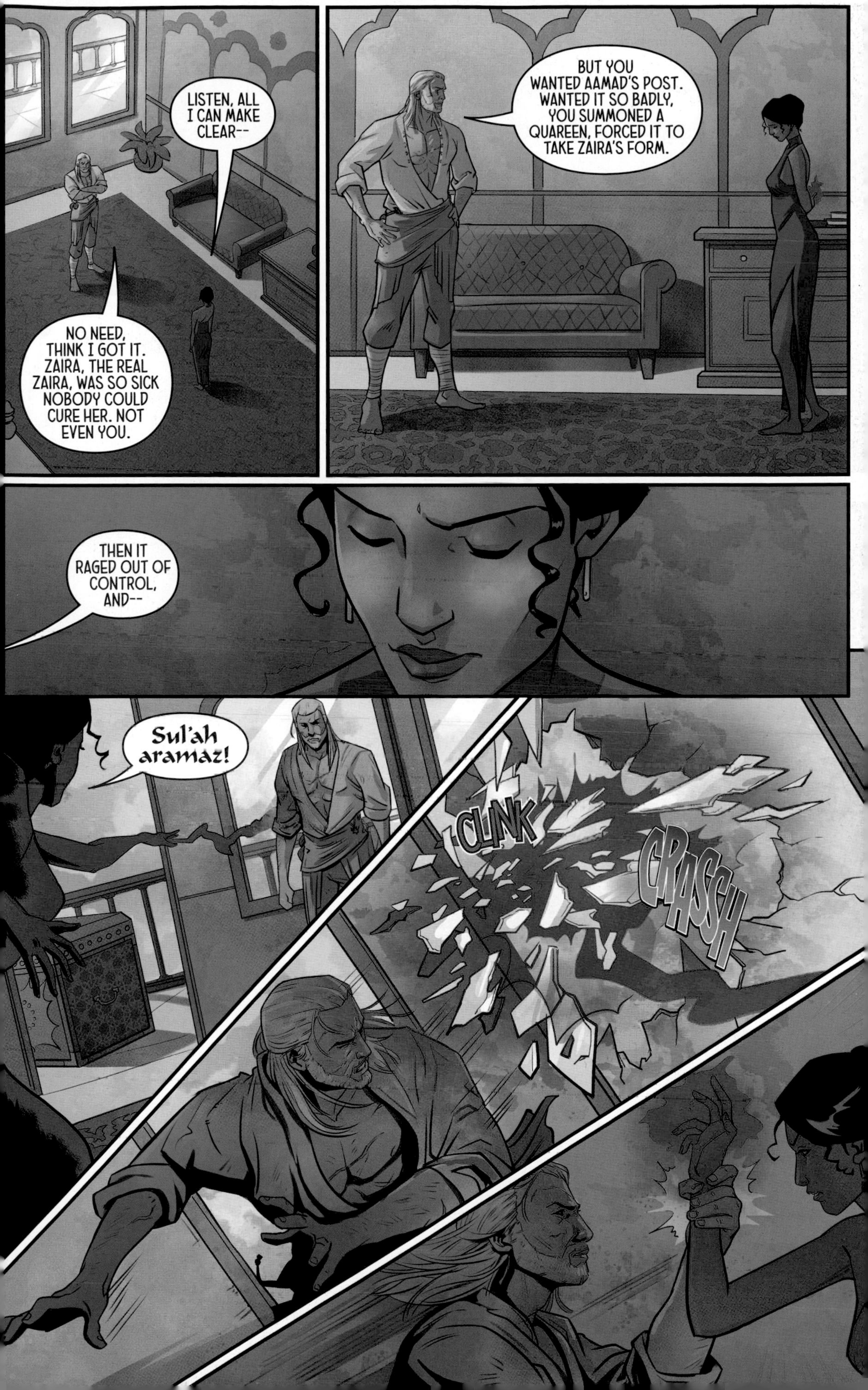

LISTEN, ALL I CAN MAKE CLEAR--
NO NEED, THINK I GOT IT. ZAIRA, THE REAL ZAIRA, WAS SO SICK NOBODY COULD CURE HER. NOT EVEN YOU.
BUT YOU WANTED AAMAD'S POST. WANTED IT SO BADLY, YOU SUMMONED A QUAREEN, FORCED IT TO TAKE ZAIRA'S FORM.
THEN IT RAGED OUT OF CONTROL, AND--
Sul'ah aramaz!
CLINK
CRASSH

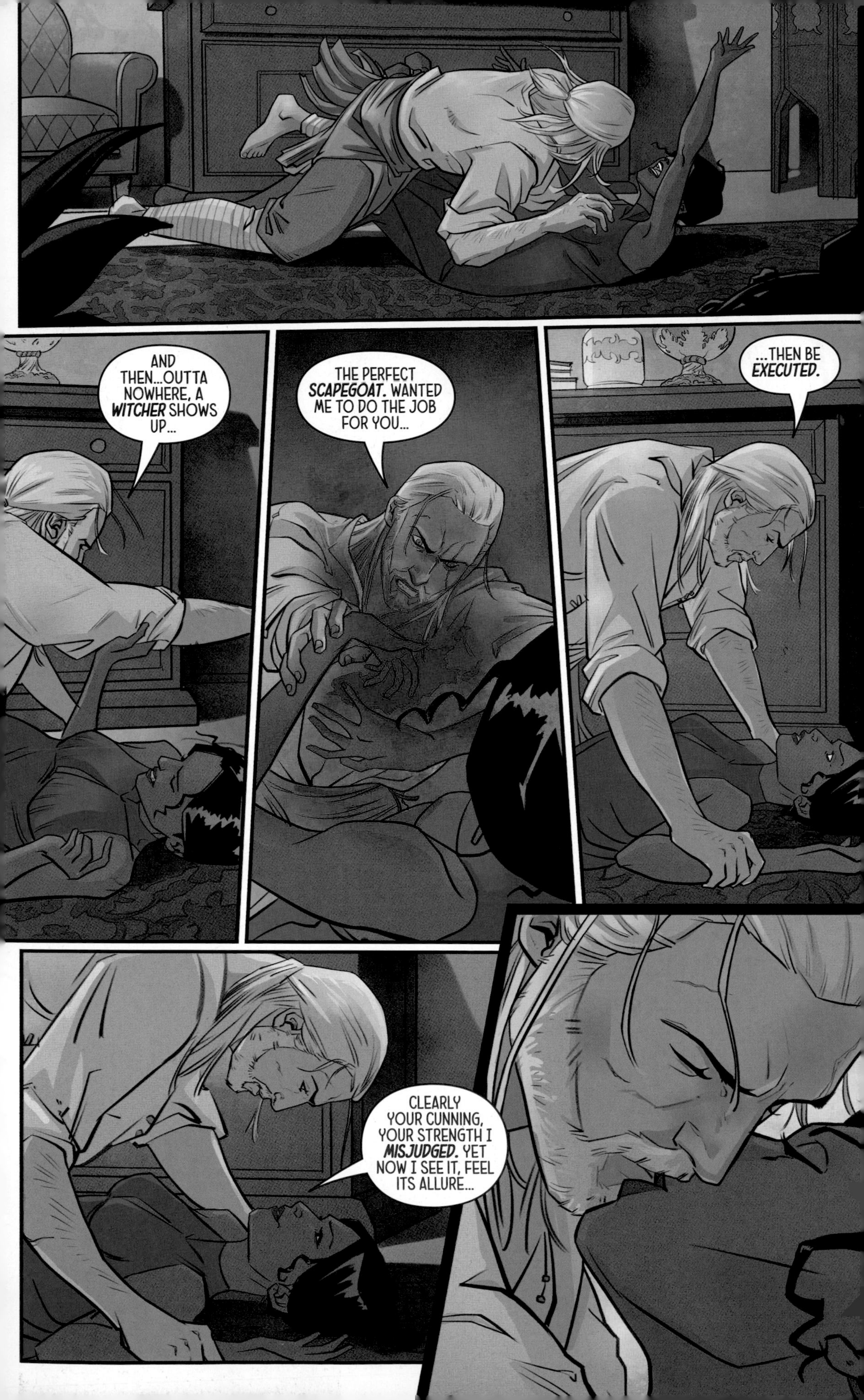
AND THEN...OUTTA NOWHERE, A WITCHER SHOWS UP...
THE PERFECT SCAPEGOAT. WANTED ME TO DO THE JOB FOR YOU...
...THEN BE EXECUTED.
CLEARLY YOUR CUNNING, YOUR STRENGTH I MISJUDGED. YET NOW I SEE IT, FEEL ITS ALLURE...

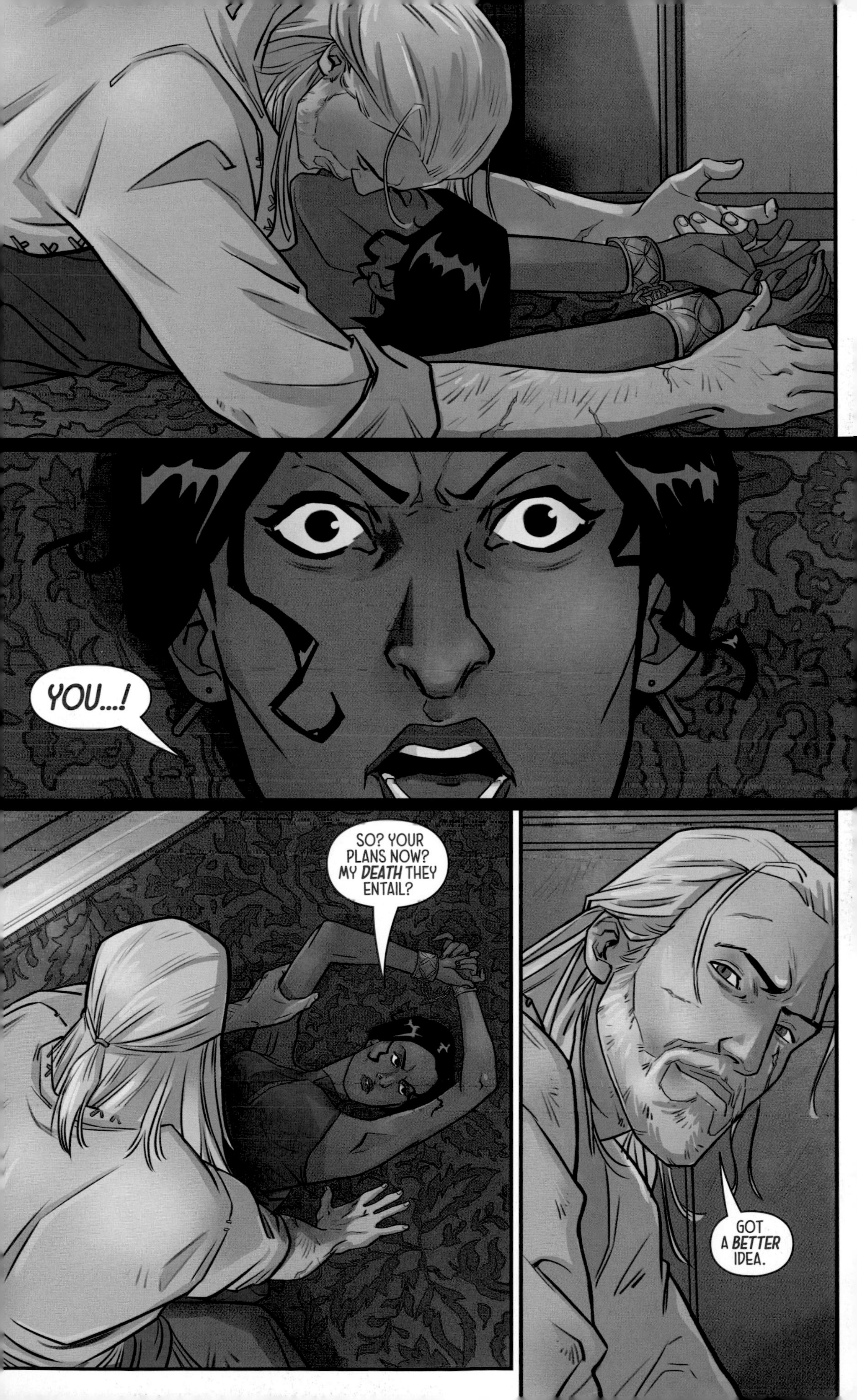
YOU...!
SO? YOUR PLANS NOW? MY DEATH THEY ENTAIL?
GOT A BETTER IDEA.

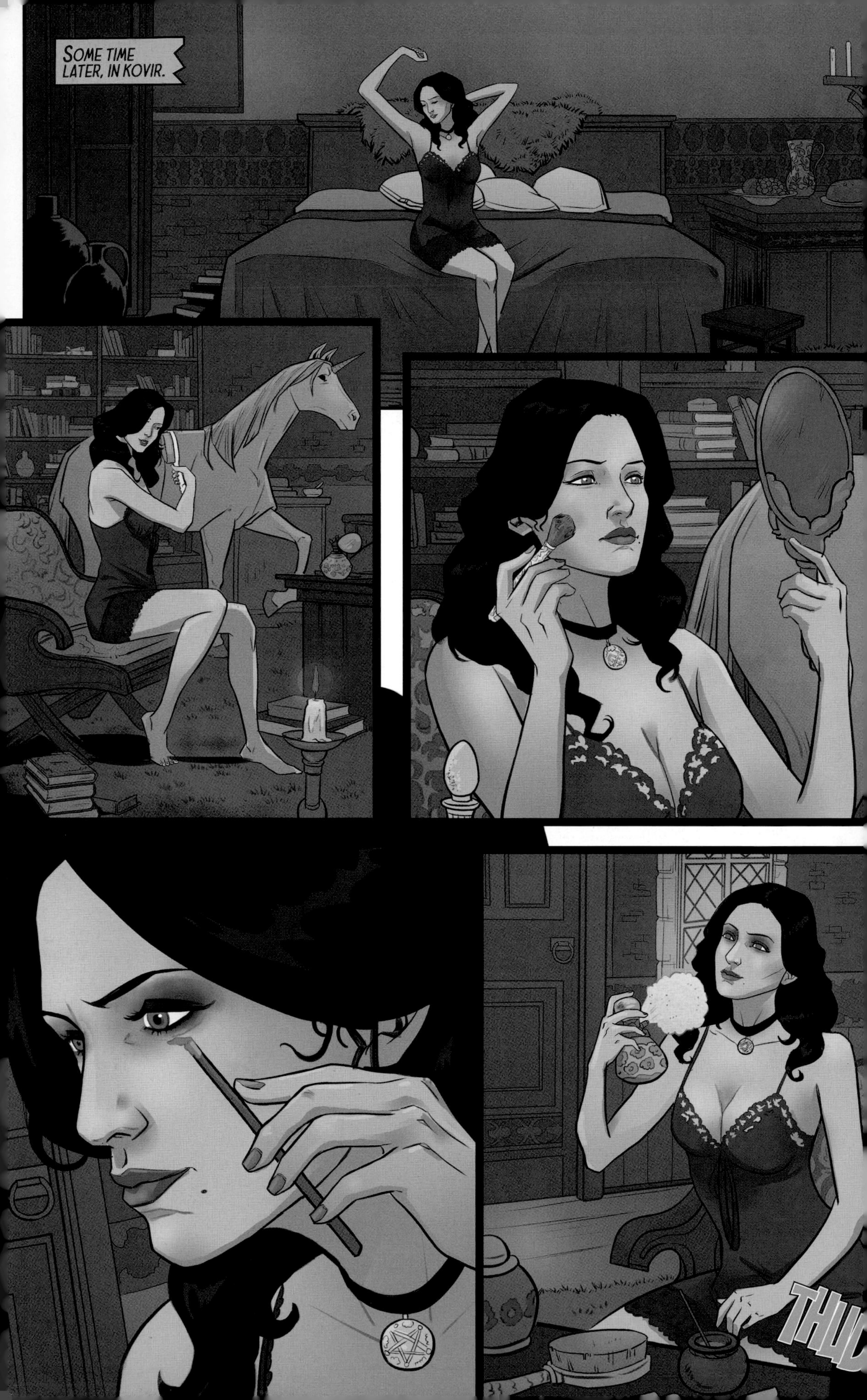
SOME TIME LATER, IN KOVIR.
THUD

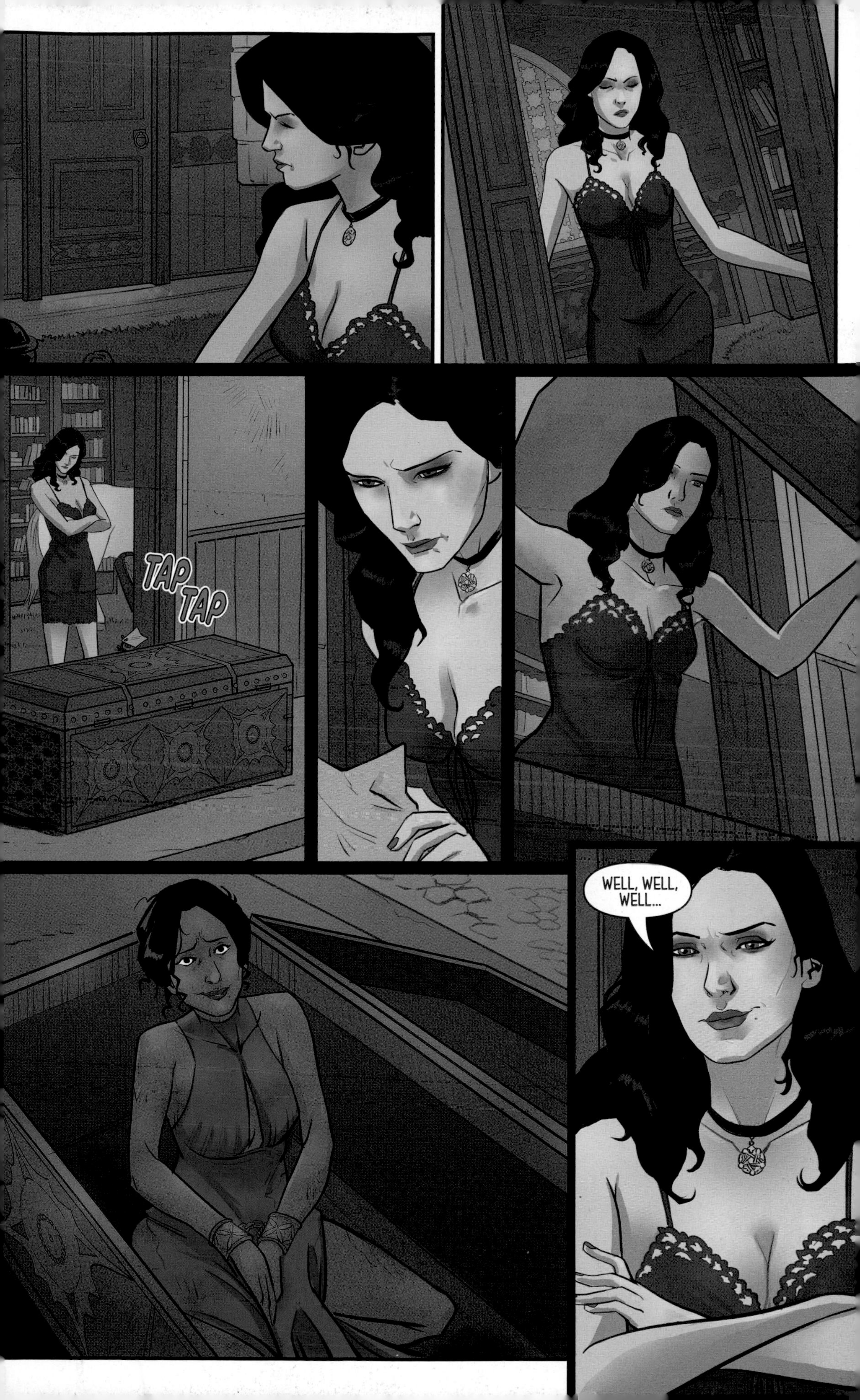
TAP
TAP
WELL, WELL, WELL...

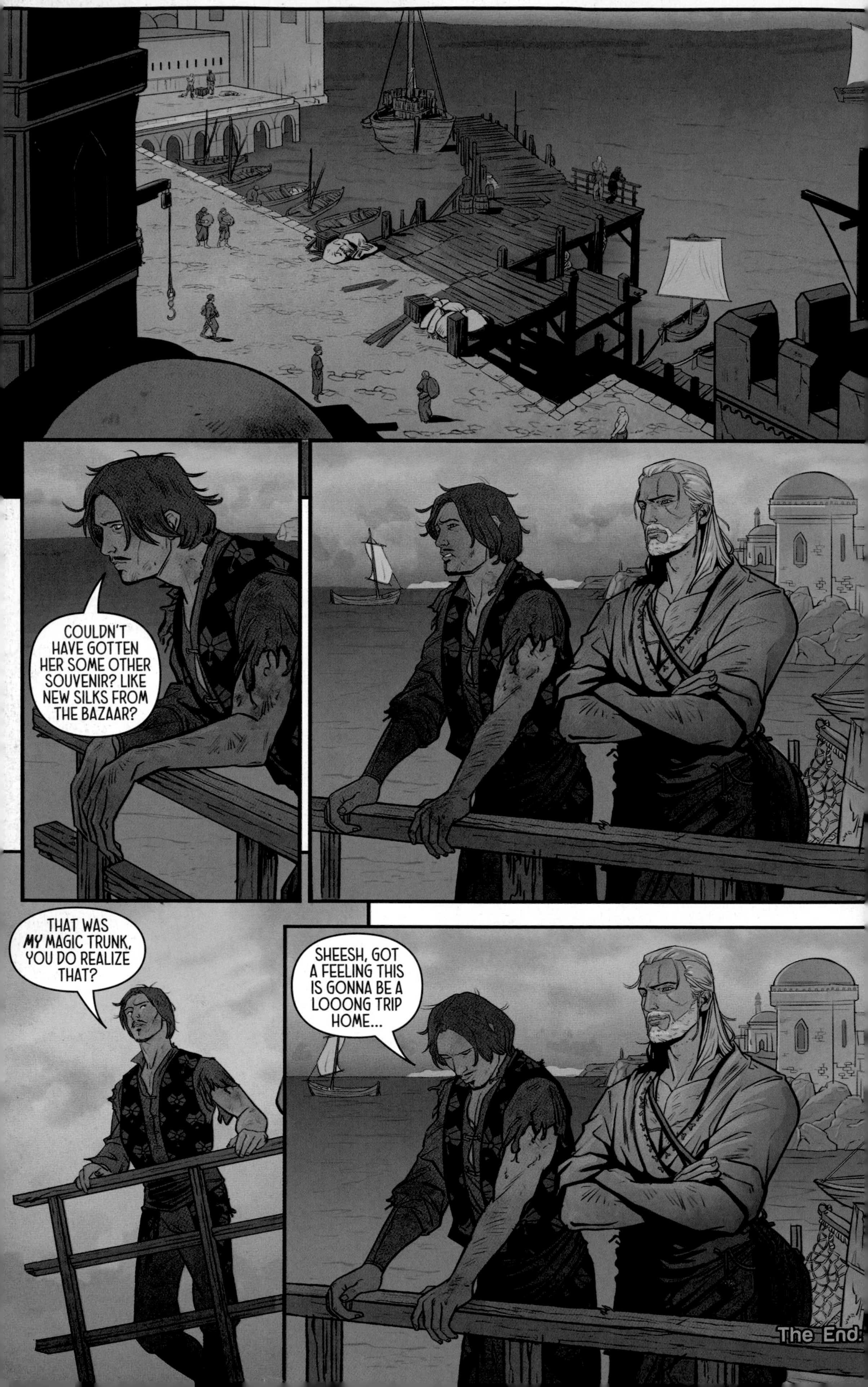
COULDN'T HAVE GOTTEN HER SOME OTHER SOUVENIR? LIKE NEW SILKS FROM THE BAZAAR?
THAT WAS *MY* MAGIC TRUNK, YOU DO REALIZE THAT?
SHEESH, GOT A FEELING THIS IS GONNA BE A LOOONG TRIP HOME...
The End.

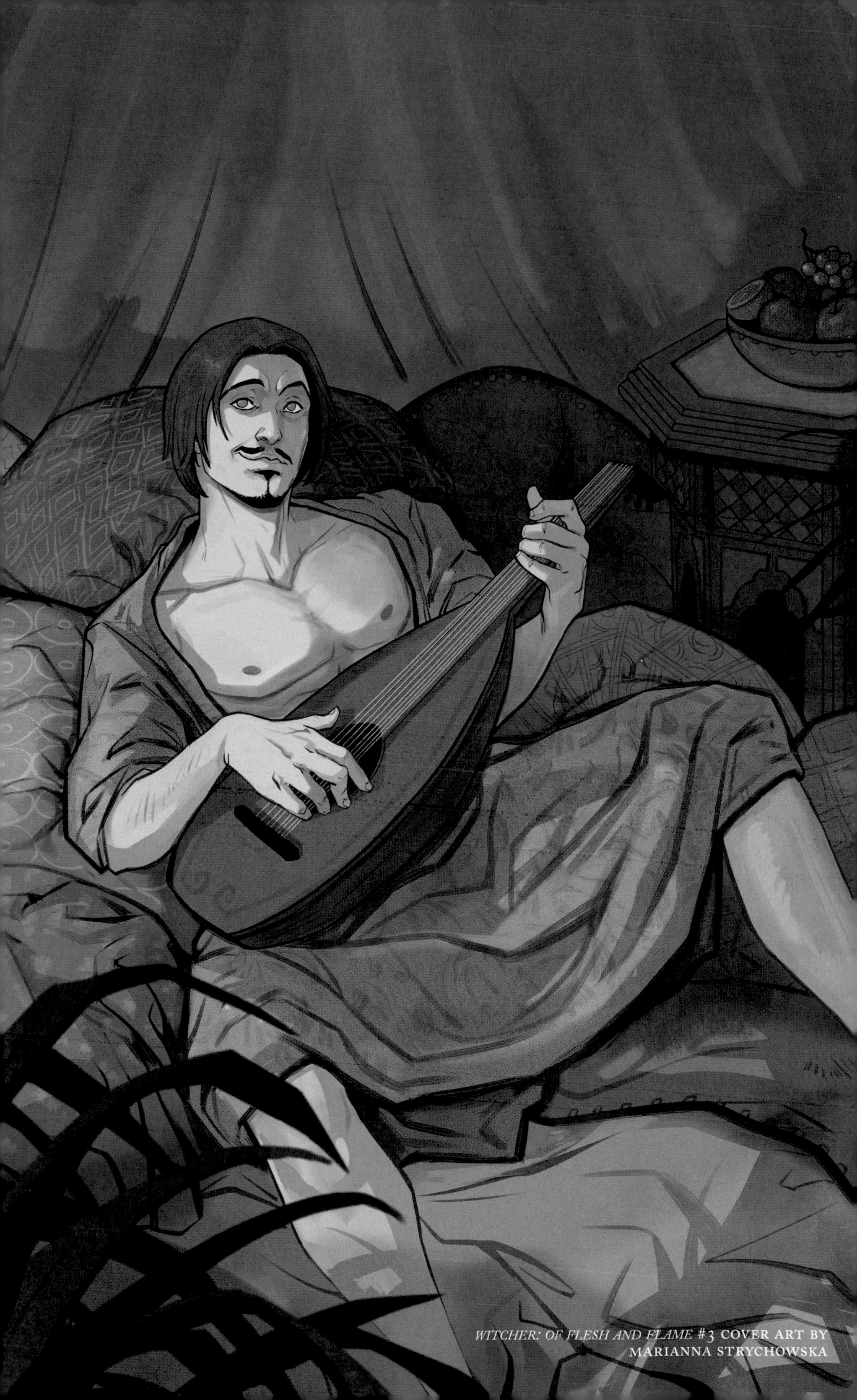

WITCHER: OF FLESH AND FLAME #3 COVER ART BY
MARIANNA STRYCHOWSKA

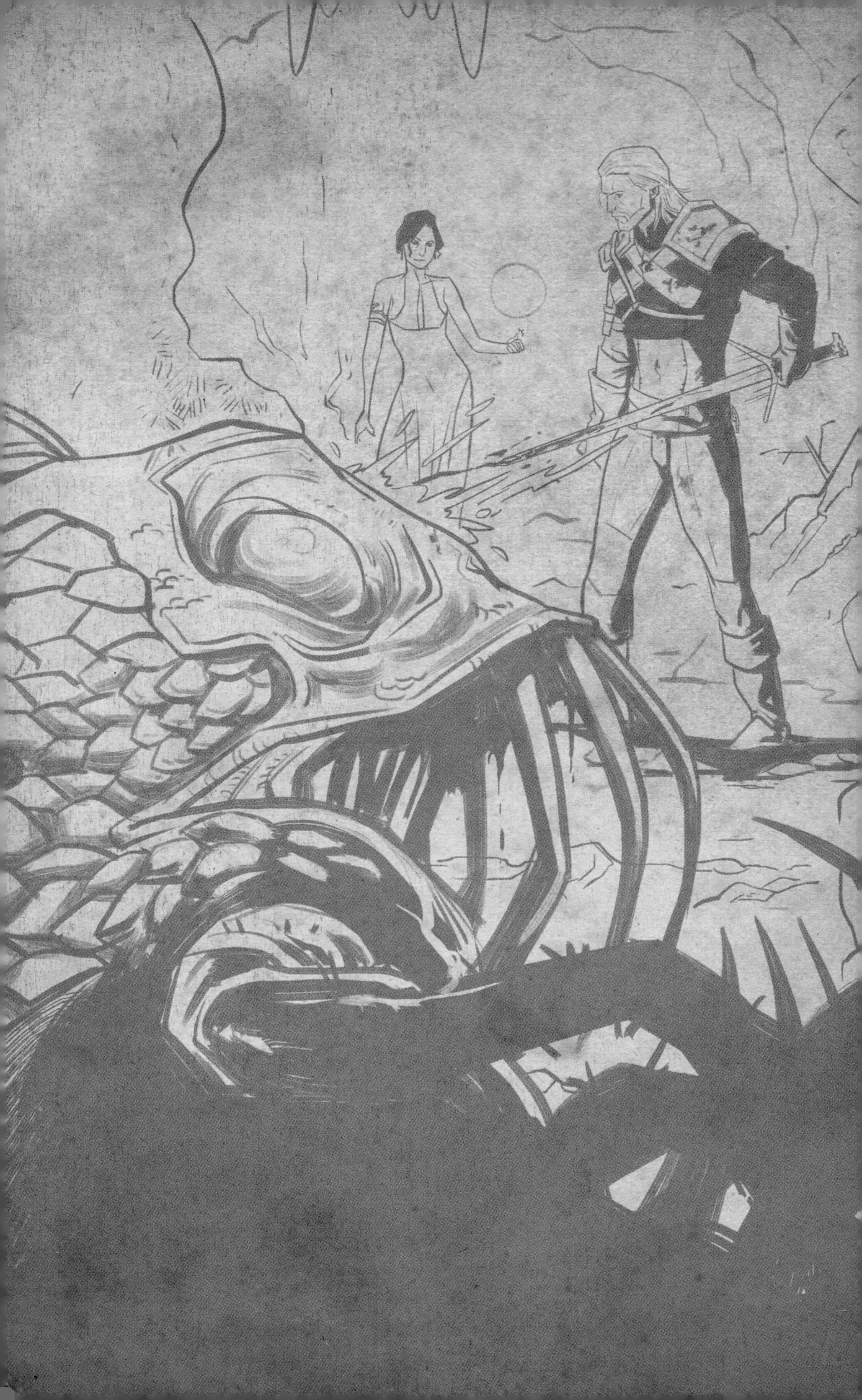